Michael Kidron and Ronald Segal are the authors of *The State of the World Atlas* (1981) and *The New State of the World Atlas* (1984).

Michael Kidron is a political economist who has written, among other books, *Western Capitalism since the War* and *Foreign Investments in India*. He is author, with Dan Smith, of *The War Atlas*. He is general editor of Pluto Projects.

Ronald Segal has written many other books, including a dictionary of African politics, *Political Africa;* a study of racial conflict in history, *The Race War;* books on the USA, on India and on the Middle East; and a major biography of Trotsky.

THE BOOK OF

BUSINESS

MONEY

AND

POWER

Michael Kidron
and
Ronald Segal

A Pluto Project

PAN BOOKS London and Sydney

First published 1987 by Pan Books Ltd,
Cavaye Place, London SW10 9PG
and simultaneously in hardback by Pluto Projects,
105A Torriano Avenue, London NW5 2RX

ISBN 0 330 28578 5

Text copyright © 1987 by Michael Kidron and Ronald Segal
Graphics and illustrations copyright © Visionslide Limited,
105A Torriano Avenue, London NW5 2RX

Designed by Trickett & Webb Limited,
The Factory, 84 Marchmont Street, London WC1N 1HE

Illustrations by Peter Bailey (pages 174-75);
Jeff Fisher (pages 104-05, 154-55, 187);
Carolyn Gowdy (pages 76-77, 118-20, 167);
Sally Kindberg (page 110);
Jonathan Mercer (pages 26, 43, 69, 140, 142)

Typesetting and artwork by Rapidset & Design Limited,
27 Swinton Street, London WC1X 9NW

Coordinated by Anne Benewick

Colour origination by Imago Publishing Limited
Printed and bound in Hong Kong by
Mandarin Offset Marketing (HK) Limited

10 9 8 7 6 5 4 3 2 1

CONTENTS

PREFACE

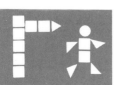 We came to this book through our work together on *The State of the World Atlas* (1981) and *The New State of the World Atlas* (1984), when we recognized that in opening some shutters, we were throwing light on many that were still closed.

We accordingly decided to examine the world business system, the dominant source of power and the most pervasive of influences in our world. And we were encouraged in our decision by the discovery of how even more richly graphic representation could here be used to communicate information.

We realized from the outset that comprehensiveness would be impossible. We had no large – or indeed any – team of researchers to assist us. But in any event, the system is so complex that the most resourceful exploration can provide only selective insights; and so wild in so many of its manifestations that only a small, if significant, part of it can be tamed by analytical treatment. Those who come to this book expecting to learn everything that there is to know about business are bound to be disappointed. Those who come in the hope of discovering something of which they were previously unaware will, we hope, emerge exultant, if also perhaps more than a little alarmed.

Readers will find that we have sometimes placed facts in fictional settings. Where we have done so – mainly in interludes between chapters – there should be no confusion. We have adopted the technique only where the dearth of comparative information, or its very abundance, favours an impressionist treatment. And indeed, the world of business is such an intermingling of the real and the unreal that it is sometimes difficult, if not impossible, to know where one begins and the other ends. The accepted demarcations have been observed, but with less than total faith in their validity.

One further new technique we have employed is that of playable games. And here too, we believe that the technique itself says something about the essential nature of the business system. For much of business is conducted as a game with rules – if only there to be broken – and where winning is all that matters. That the counters may well be people is of little consequence. Cruelty is as irrelevant as compassion. The game is its own morality.

The business system has always been in a state of movement and change. And at no time have such movement and change been more rapid than at present. We have tried to provide the most recent information and we were amending the text, to take account of relevant events, even as the book was being prepared for press. Such last-minute updating proved to be less difficult for the US than for anywhere else.

We have been necessarily dependent, for the most part, on such conventional sources as the business press, reference books and special studies. The business press has, unquestionably, been the richest source of up-to-date information and background analysis. We have trawled widely but nowhere to more profitable effect than in the *Financial Times* of London and the US business periodical *Fortune*. To both of these, we owe especial thanks and gladly acknowledge our debt. There is one further technical matter. With the occasional exception of sterling, we have, as far as was feasible, translated all financial figures into US dollars, at the rate then prevailing. At the time of going to press, the exchange rate for sterling was around £1 = $1.50.

In many instances, we have presented companies and national economies in the format of a company profile. We have generally used the ranking in the relevant *Fortune* directories and, exceptionally (for the top 500 European companies) the ranking given by the *Financial Times*.

We have many people to thank for their help and in general do so in a special section of acknowledgements. A few people, though, we must single out for particular thanks: Anne Benewick of Pluto, for her unwavering commitment to the book; David Kewley, for his editorial advice and resolution; Ian Cockburn and Brian Webb, of Trickett and Webb, for inspired design; and Susan Segal, for the life-support system she so gladly supplied. We have also, of course, to thank each other, without whom we might separately have written any number of books in the time we have spent so agonizingly but, we hope, productively together.

For in the end, we trust, we have presented a view of the business system dominating our lives that provides both understanding and criticism. If nothing else, we will be glad to have encouraged a healthy scepticism.

It is said that an uncertain Kuzma Prutkov once wrote: 'If you see a giraffe in a cage, and the label says "Buffalo", don't believe your eyes.' The reader should take the business system, and even this book, with such advice in mind.

Michael Kidron and Ronald Segal,
August, 1986

A NOTE ON THE GAMES

Readers who wish to play the games will need to equip themselves with dice and counters, borrowed or taken — as so often happens in the business system — from rivals.

Where cards are needed, these appear with the game and may be photocopied. Where money is needed, readers should either borrow from other games, or photocopy the BMP Money provided on page 192.

1

THE BUSINESS OF BUSINESS

We all live in the world of business. And the world of business, in its structure, functioning and values, affects all our lives.

It is a world which has much in common with the playing of games. The overwhelming objective is to win, and it is an objective that dominates all other considerations. While some people may be players, most are merely counters, to be shifted or discarded altogether as the progress of the game requires.

But where particular games may come and go in popularity, business continually increases its hold. For it is based on the satisfaction, real or contrived, of human needs and desires.

The variety of human wants is reflected in the variety of business. Each business is unique, as defined by its market and governed by its management.

It can operate on a tiny or on a gargantuan scale.

It can reach no further than a suitcase on a street or it can cover the globe.

It can sell the very cheap, such as pins, or the very expensive, such as airports.

It can deal in one product or in tens of thousands.

It operates at the furthest limits of human imagination and ingenuity, or at the level of the crudely mundane.

It may be on the government's list of top priorities, or on no government list at all.

It can account for its conduct to the public, or it can be pathologically secretive about its affairs.

It may be a way of reaching a ripe old age, or it may be a risky business.

It feeds the public, and, above all, it feeds itself.

TIDDLERS AND TITANS

'Just me and my wife work here. In effect, one and a half people. We're on twenty-four hours a day: when she's asleep, I'm up, and vice versa.'
Outworker in Cumbria, Italy

Most businesses in the world are small, though not all as small as this. Small businesses are important collectively, and in their own right.

Some 99 per cent of all businesses in Italy, Japan and Switzerland are small: in Italy, with an average of 8 employees; in Japan and Switzerland, with an average of 15 employees.

Some businesses are very big, with most of the biggest having their headquarters in a few rich countries.

Headquarters of the world's 50 biggest industrial companies, 1984

USA	22
West Germany	6
Japan	6
Italy	3
Britain	3
Britain/Netherlands	2
France	2
Netherlands	1
Brazil	1
Kuwait	1
Mexico	1
Switzerland	1
Venezuela	1

In any one year, the income of the world's 50 biggest industrial companies represents more than four times the output of Africa, more than three times the output of South America, more than the total output of the USSR or Japan, and half that of the US.

Exxon, biggest industrial company in the world, 1980-84

More than 80 per cent of Exxon's profits come from oil and gas, and 45 per cent of its profits come from the US. An early 1980s survey showed that it

- was producing some 450 million barrels of petroleum products a year; and had
- some 6.5 billion barrels of proved oil reserves
- 50,000 petrol stations

- a fleet of 400 ships travelling from over 100 ports to 270 destinations
- one of the world's largest chemical companies (5.9 per cent of its sales and 2.2 per cent of its profits)
- more than 880,000 stockholders and more than 880 million shares (since 1983, it has bought back almost 10 per cent of its shares, at a cost of over $4 billion)
- more than $3.2 billion in cash and marketable securities
- more than 400 lawyers.

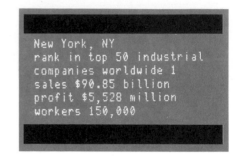

```
New York, NY
rank in top 50 industrial
companies worldwide 1
sales $90.85 billion
profit $5,528 million
workers 150,000
```

There is no invulnerability, even at the very top of business. At the end of 1985, Exxon, with annual sales of $93.2 billion, lost its top place to the one-time champion, General Motors, with annual sales of $96.4 billion. But its annual net income, or profit, was still larger, at $4.87 billion, compared to $4 billion for General Motors.

PRICE AND PRODUCT

Some businesses operate by making and selling a relatively few hugely expensive products; others, no less successful in their own way, by making and selling huge quantities of cheap throwaways.

Boeing's 747 jumbo jet is the world's biggest commercial passenger aircraft. But costly as such products are, the market for commercial aircraft is still vast enough to purchase them in quantities. Between 1985-94, Boeing is planning for business worth $178 billion.

BICS and Boeings

One Boeing jumbo jet costs $100 million, the same as one billion BIC disposable pens.

In 1982, Boeing delivered 176 aircraft, of which 25 were jumbos; in 1983, it delivered 204 aircraft, of which 23 were jumbos.

Whereas in 1981, BIC delivered an average per day of 11.6 million pens and 2.37 million lighters; and in 1982, 10.8 million pens and 2.44 million lighters.

```
Boeing

Seattle, Washington
rank in top 500 US
industrial companies 21
sales $13.64 billion
profit $566 million
workers 104,000

(1985)
```

```
3M

St Paul, Minnesota
rank in top 500 US
industrial companies 47
sales $7.85 billion
profit $664 million
workers 85,466

(1985)
```

```
Société Bic

Clichy, France
rank in Europe's top 500
companies 335
sales $592 million
profit $51.4 million
workers 12,600

(1982-83)
```

THERE OR EVERYWHERE

Size in business is often synonymous with spread.
The bigger the business, the more it can afford –
indeed, the more it may need – to spread itself.
Single-location businesses, however, though they
may not be so big, can still be very profitable.
Some businesses – by their very nature – are
easier to expand than others.

ONE OR MANY

Likewise, the importance of a business need not
reflect the product range it offers. Some companies do very well on the basis of one major product; others prosper because they produce many.

SKF (Sweden) is the world's leading producer of
ball and roller bearings, which account for 80 per
cent of its profits. It operates 16 manufacturing
plants in 9 countries. In 1982, it provided 20 per
cent of all bearings used in the West and was twice
the size of its closest competitor.

Minnesota Mining and Manufacturing (3M) has
already introduced 50,000 products and adds over
a hundred major new products a year. Its target :
that 25 per cent of its sales should come from products less than five years old.

Its largest single division, accounting for 17 per
cent of its sales, is tape and allied products. It also
manufactures graphic systems, abrasives, adhesives, building materials, chemicals, protective
products, recording materials, electrical products
and health care products.

Fine food

What do you do if you have a stately home on the
west coast of Brittany and no personal fortune to
keep it up? Mme Alyette de la Sablière wasn't
short of ideas. She took a management course, acquired a bank loan and transformed the Chateau
de Locguénolé into a four-star hotel with a top
chef. In 1968, when she started, many people
thought she was mad. By 1984, she had a turnover
of FF8 million and the restaurant was highly
acclaimed in the leading French food guides.

The chateau employed 49 people (if she employed 50, she would, under French labour laws,
have had to introduce a works council, which Mme
de la Sablière regarded as unsuitable for her type
of business). The restaurant accounted for about
two thirds of the hotel's turnover, but for a smaller
proportion of profit than that provided by the letting of rooms.

It was not all gladness and light. Some customers walked off with objects that were not on the
menu. One million francs' worth of objects had
been stolen over the previous 10 years. 'Someone
even walked away with a Persian carpet' Mme de
la Sablière said. 'Now we keep the books locked in
the library'.

Fast food

The first McDonald's restaurant was opened in
1955. By the end of 1983 the chain stood at 7,778
restaurants and served 17 million customers a
day. McDonald's is the world's largest single commercial user of beef and the second largest of
chicken.

```
SKF

Sweden
rank in top 500 non-US
industrial companies 229
sales $2.18 billion
profit $120.8 million

(1984)
```

McDonald's restaurants by country, 1983

Australia	147
Austria	12
Bahamas	2
Belgium	9
Brazil	21
Canada	442
Costa Rica	3
Denmark	7
El Salvador	3
England	133
France	15
West Germany	190
Guam	2
Guatemala	3
Hong Kong	24
Ireland	5
Japan	395
Malaysia	5
Netherlands	27
Netherlands Antilles	2
New Zealand	17
Nicaragua	1
Norway	1
Panama	6
Philippines	5
Puerto Rico	5
Singapore	9
Spain	10
Sweden	15
Switzerland	8
USA	6251
Virgin Islands	3
Total	7778

(75 per cent franchises and affiliates)

The hamburger universities

'This is where you come to get your veins filled with ketchup. It's almost a religious experience.'

Ed Rensi, chief operating officer of McDonald's on the virtues of Hamburger University, Oak Brook

Oak Brook, Illinois, USA
London, UK
Munich, West Germany
Tokyo, Japan
Sydney, Australia

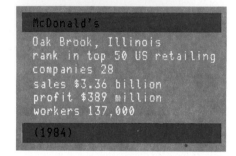

McDonald's

Oak Brook, Illinois
rank in top 50 US retailing
companies 28
sales $3.36 billion
profit $389 million
workers 137,000

(1984)

ESSENCE AND FANTASY

Some of the needs served by business are essential. Others are partly or wholly created by business itself, just so that it can satisfy them. The inventiveness of business stretches the limits of manipulation and fantasy.

Among essential needs, food is paramount. More money is spent on food than on any other product. Huge businesses have grown up around the manufacture and processing of food, and they cater for, and help to foster, an increasingly global palate.

The world's grocers

Sales of the world's largest food companies, 1985 or 1984, $ billion

	total	food	non-food
Nestlé	13.2	12.5	0.7
Unilever	21.6	11.7	9.9
General Foods	9.0	7.9	1.1
Beatrice Foods	9.3	7.0	2.3
Dart & Kraft	9.8	6.9	2.9
Procter & Gamble	13.5	2.8	10.7

In 1985, General Foods was taken over by Philip Morris for $5.6 billion, to form the biggest such consumer products company in the world.

Nestlé

Nestlé (Switzerland) is a major contender for the title of the world's largest manufacturing food company. In 1982, it had 295 factories in 55 countries. In 1984, as if not large enough already, Nestlé took over Carnation (milk products; pet foods; and ranked 116 in the top US industrial companies), for $3 billion. Within a year, it repaid the money it had borrowed for this purpose.

Nestlé was getting so big that apparently it could not see its own feet. A senior Nestlé executive was touring Italy when his eye was caught by a promising pasta business. He decided to buy it, only to discover that Nestlé owned it already.

```
Nestlé

Vevey, Switzerland
rank in top 50 industrial
companies worldwide 49
sales $13.2 billion
profit $632 million
workers 137,950

(1984)
```

The food alchemists

Many food products are not what they seem or are claimed to be. Television commercials may continue to promote food with romantic images of farmland and the cruel sea, but the truth if very different. Food is increasingly produced in industrial plants and chemical laboratories.

Up to 2,000 permitted additives have been developed and are now widely used: flavourings, preservatives, antioxidants, emulsifiers, dyes, colours, bleaches, humectants, anti-caking agents, surfactants, stabilizers, sequestrants, moisteners, non-nutritive sweeteners, thickeners and thinners, among much else.

At least 75 per cent of the products on supermarket shelves contain either artificial flavours or artificial scents.

If food is no longer what it appears to be, neither is its preparation in the kitchen. Clorox Corporation of Oakland, California, has come up with a 'food cosmetic', Kitchen Bouquet Microwave Browning Spray, to turn meat or fish cooked in microwave ovens from insipid grey to appetizing brown. (This follows on the fragrant heels of the company's Fresh Step, the catbox filler that releases mint herbal scent every time a cat steps on it.)

Smells and tastes

The UN International Children's Emergency Fund was perplexed by the persistent refusal of Algerian babies to be weaned on a protein drink it had developed. Nothing would persuade them to give up their mother's milk until the missing ingredient was isolated and added: a hint of onion. The company that created the additive is the biggest in the business: International Flavors and Fragrances.

IFF's 30 skilled technicians produce over 5,000 scents and 2,000 flavours a year, augmenting the 80,000 or so already developed. Among IFF's biggest customers are: Avon, Colgate, General Foods, Pepsi Co, Procter & Gamble and Unilever.

It has produced:

the smell of new car
(with hints of new leather)

the odour of cave

the essence of slum
(with a touch of garbage and urine)

the savour of sex
(synthesized gypsy moth sex attractants)

'Our business is basically sex and hunger'
IFF chairman Henry G Walter

' *"There's a Third World to be perfumed and to be sold flavours, especially tastes that will make low cost, high protein foods like soybeans palatable to everyone from Afghans to Zambians." Closer to home, he (Henry G Walter) imagines a society in which objects from telephones to tie clasps will breathe fragrances, some reassuring, others arousing.'*
Fortune

IFF control 10 per cent of the world business in 'smellies'; another 12 companies control 40 per cent; and a further 60 companies the remainder.

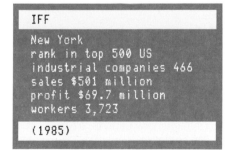

```
IFF

New York
rank in top 500 US
industrial companies 466
sales $501 million
profit $69.7 million
workers 3,723

(1985)
```

Meanwhile, back on the farm . . .

'SCS Biotechnology of Chipping Norton, Oxfordshire, is marketing a deodorant for farms which farmers and nature lovers will find preferable to the odours normally associated with agriculture.'
Financial Times

BUGS AND BUBBLES

The business of biotechnology, or the factory farming of microbes, pushes at the frontier of scientific knowledge and skills. The natural abilities of micro-organisms have been exploited in some form or other, as turning sugar into alcohol, since ancient times. Now it is possible, through genetic engineering, to give such micro-organisms un-natural abilities and breed them to carry out chemical tasks outside their normal capacity.

The possibilities seem infinite. New and established companies, especially in the pharmaceutical business, are pursuing a variety of applications.

Shell has developed new microbes, one of which has a voracious appetite for metal and might be encouraged to munch away at a metal deposit that is poisoning a petrochemical catalyst.

In the USSR, by the early 1980s, at least 86 plants had been built to exploit single-cell protein. They produce more than a million tonnes of such protein per year.

Number of US companies using biotechnology, 1983

pharmaceuticals	136
animal agriculture	61
plant agriculture	53
specialty chemicals and food	44
commodity chemicals and energy	33
environment	24
electronics	1

Novo

Novo Industri (Denmark), is a leading company in biotechnology, with a range of pharmaceutical products and particular success in the manufacture of human insulin. The company is also concerned in the production of enzymes, with most rapid growth coming from serving the detergent and starch industries. The Novo Group has 32 subsidiary companies in 21 countries.

The immense sums of money to be made out of exploiting biotechnology depend on the measure of legal recognition given to the proprietorship of new developments.

Genetic engineering is one such development: so new that operating rules for granting patents in the technology are yet to be decided, mainly in the courts. Companies are waiting on the outcome.

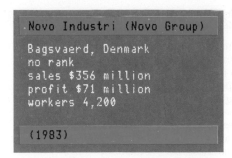

```
Novo Industri (Novo Group)

Bagsvaerd, Denmark
no rank
sales $356 million
profit $71 million
workers 4,200

(1983)
```

Genentech v Biogen

Genentech, a leading US genetic engineering company, has already engaged in battle with Biogen, a European biotechnology company, over the patent for alpha interferon. Interferon acts chiefly by enhancing the body's own defences against disease and may be effective in the treatment of cancer. Since the cancer chemotherapy market in the US and Europe alone is worth some $10 billion a year, there is much at stake.

'The strength of . . . patents in the technology will help us decide how much to invest in biotechnology in the future.'
High executive of Sandoz (Switzerland)

Spring fever

At the other end of the scale of human imagination, the mineral water business is concerned with one of the least sophisticated of products. It involves little more than what freely falls from the sky and flows out of the ground.

But increasing health awareness, promoted by huge expenditures on advertising, is augmenting the commercial importance of the market.

Vichy advertises its high mineral content. Spa claims that its water is so pure that it can safely be poured into a car battery. Perrier traps the bubbles separately from the natural water and puts the two together at a later stage to guarantee uniformity of fizz.

Evian

Purveyor of the world's leading bottled still water, Evian is wholly owned by the BSN group. In 1982, 5 per cent of BSN's sales came from Evian water.

```
BSN

Paris
rank in top 500 non-US
industrial companies 165
sales $3.1 billion
profit $86.3 million
workers 37,340

(1984)
```

FISSION AND FASHION

The nuclear power industry is one business that is of central concern to the state. Besides being of immense strategic and military importance, nuclear power is seen as a potentially major source of energy for the future. In spite of public opposition in the US and most of Western Europe, where nuclear power is expanding slowly or not at all, it is a fast growing industry worldwide, above all in the Far East, the USSR and France.

The nuclear business

In 1985, there were 375 nuclear plants producing 1395.6 TWh of electricity. More than 143 of them were in Western Europe, 93 in the US, about 50 in the USSR, 17 in Eastern Europe, and about 46 in Asia (33 of them in Japan alone).

Cogema

The French nuclear business is the most expansive in the West, and Cogema is at its core. In 1984, Cogema supplied materials and services for 112 operational nuclear reactors, in France and abroad, which accounted for 45 per cent of installed capacity worldwide.

Cogema's share of world sales, 1984, percentages

natural uranium production	20
enriched uranium output	33
reprocessed oxide fuels annual average 1974-84	80

Nuclear power's share of electricity consumption 1985, percentages

Argentina	10.1	Japan	22.4
Belgium	59.8	South Korea	25.9
Brazil	1.7	Netherlands	6.1
Bulgaria	31.6	Pakistan	0.9
Canada	12.7	Spain	24.0
Czechoslovakia	14.6	Sweden	42.3
Finland	38.2	Switzerland	39.8
France	64.8	Taiwan	53.1
West Germany	31.2	UK	19.3
Hungary	23.6	USA	15.5
India	2.4	USSR	10.3
Italy	3.8	World total	18.3

Companies in the nuclear business

AECL
Atomic Energy of Canada. Crown (state) corporation. Manufacturer of Candu 600 reactors in service in various countries.

ANDRA
Agence Nationale pour la Gestion des Déchets Radioactifs (France). Agency of the Commissariat à l'energie atomique (CEA).

Asea Atom
Reactor and servicing subsidiary of ASEA, Swedish heavy engineering company. 1984: sales of parent company, $4.4 billion; pre-tax profits, $44.7 million.

BNFL
British Nuclear Fuels. State corporation. 1983-84: sales, £460 million; pre-tax profits, £71 million.

CEA
Commissariat a l'energie atomique (France).

Cogema
Compagnie Générale des Matières Nucléaires, wholly owned by CEA.

Comurhex
Joint subsidiary of Uranium Pechiney Ugine Kuhlmann (51%), Cogema (39%), and Compagnie Française de Mokta (10%), all state controlled.

DBE
Deutsche Gesellschaft für Bau und Betrieb von Entlagern für Abfallstoffe, owned by the West German federal government, public institutions and private interests.

DWK
Deutsche Gesellschaft für Wiederaufarbeitung von Kernbrennstoffen, owned by a group of utilities.

ENUSA
Empresa Nacional del Uranio, public company owned 60/40 by two state agencies, Instituto Nacional de Industria and Junta de Energia Nuclear (Spain).

Eurodif
International consortium shared by France (61.53%); Italy (16.25%); Belgium (11.11%); Spain (11.11%).

Framatome
Principal contractor in a quarter of all French reactor export deals, with 59 pressurized water reactors (PWRs) in service or under construction worldwide. Owned equally by CEA and Creusot-Loire.

General Electric (US)
1985 sales $28.3 billion; profit $2.3 billion.

NAGRA
Nationale Genossenschaft für die Lagerung Radioaktiver Abfälle, cooperative of six Swiss utilities and the Swiss federal government.

NFI
Japan's Nuclear Fuel Industries, a full and equal merger of Furukawa Electric Company and Sumitomo Electric Industries.

NIREX
Britain's Nuclear Industry Radioactive Waste Executive, a joint agency of BNFL, Central Electricity Generating Board, South of Scotland Electricity Board, UK Atomic Energy Authority.

NNC
Britain's National Nuclear Corporation, jointly owned by the Atomic Energy Authority (35%), GEC (30%), and a consortium, British Nuclear Associates (35%).

RBU
Reaktor Brennelement Union, West Germany, owned 60 per cent by Kraftwerk Union. Makers of fuel assemblies for light water reactors (LWRs).

RTZ
Rio Tinto-Zinc. One of the world's largest mining finance houses, with a controlling share (46.5%) in Rossing Uranium, Namibia. RTZ produces 17.5% of known uranium ore. 1984 sales $7.9 billion; profit $219 million.

SKBF
Swedish National Fuel Supply Company. Jointly owned subsidiary of one state-run and three mixed state/private sector utilities.

SMDC
Saskatchewan Mining Development Corporation. Canadian crown (state) corporation with 50% stake in Key Lake, world's largest uranium mine and source for one tenth of uranium ore (outside Soviet bloc).

South African gold mining houses
Producers of uranium ore as a by-product of gold mining. Important source in aggregate rather than individually, except for Anglo American, the giant mining finance house, an important source in its own right.

Synatom
Consortium, owned 50/50 by private sector utilities and government holding company, to operate from prospecting and mining to processing and reprocessing.

Urenco
Owned by BNFL, Ultra-Centrifuge Nederland NV, a joint state/private-sector Dutch company, and Uran-Isotopentrennungs Gesellschaft (Uranit) of West Germany, in which private sector companies participate.

Westinghouse Electric (US)
Controls 40% of the world market in reactors. 1985 sales $10.7 billion; profit $605 million.

MINING

RTZ, Britain
Cogema, France
SMDC, Canada
gold mining companies, South Africa
utilities

uranium ore: 220 million tonnes

MILLING

RTZ, Britain
Cogema, France
SMDC, Canada
gold mining companies, South Africa
utilities

'Yellowcake': 260,000 tonnes

CONVERSION

BNFL, Britain
Department of Energy, USA
Comurhex, France

uranium hexafluoride gas

ENRICHMENT

Urenco, Britain
West Germany
Holland
Eurodif, France with Italy
Spain
Belgium
Department of Energy, USA
Techsnabexport, USSR

UF 8: 42,000 tonnes

FUEL FABRICATION

BNFL, Britain
Cogema, France
RBU, West Germany
NFI, Japan

U235: 28,000 tonnes
steel cladding: 28,000 tonnes

In the saddle of the nuclear fuel cycle

The nuclear fuel cycle is highly complex. It involves huge companies and agencies and small specialist firms: state owned, privately owned, and mixed. Although not shown here, the USSR and China are represented at every stage of the nuclear fuel cycle.

WASTE DISPOSAL

NIREX/BNFL, Britain
Synatom, Belgium
AECL, Canada
Cogema/ANDRA, France
DWK/DBE, West Germany
ENUSA, Spain
SKBF, Sweden
NAGRA, Switzerland

WEAPONS MANUFACTURE

REPROCESSING

BNFL, Britain
Cogema, France

spent fuel: 70,000 tonnes

ELECTRICITY PRODUCTION IN NUCLEAR REACTORS

Westinghouse, USA
General Electric, USA
Framatome, France
Atomic Energy of Canada
National Nuclear Corporation, Britain
Asea Atom, Sweden

ELECTRICITY PRODUCTION
806,000 TWh

Safer, more conventional toys

Unlike the nuclear industry, no public controversy surrounds the business of toymaking, to which – not surprisingly – the state seems quite indifferent. In Britain, for instance, the government has stood idly by while the toy industry has virtually disappeared. But toymaking can still be a profitable business. And despite the image of its product, it can also involve stress and danger.

Barbie

The great success of Mattel was based on its Barbie doll, which had already sold well over 100 million by the end of the 1970s, propelled in the market by its developed breasts, its lavish wardrobe for virtually all occasions, its boyfriend Ken, sister Skippers, black friend Francis and numerous other friends and relatives; as well as by the Barbie Bulletin and the International Barbie Doll Collectors' Gazette.

Barbie grew up fast. In her late twenties, she now has her own work-out centre, computer-equipped work station and attaché case, complete with calculator, business cards and news magazine.

```
Mattel

Hawthorne, California
rank in top 500 US
companies 300
sales $1.05 billion
profit $78.7 million
workers 20,000

(1985)
```

At Marvin Glass & Associates of Chicago, a toy and games think tank, with its secrecy symbolized by its windowless building, several employees died when a toy engineer went berserk with a real gun.

OPEN AND CLOSED

Some businesses disclose a great deal about themselves: the pattern of share ownership, including details of directors' personal and family trust holdings; the spread of operations, at home and abroad; health and safety provisions; labour relations and relations with major suppliers and customers; environmental impact (more unusually); charitable and political contributions; and other matters that allow for some social audit as well as the financial one in the published balance sheet (sales, net income, outstanding debt, cash reserves, and so on).

Others hold their cards close to their chests. Among secretive businesses, none are more so (with the possible exception of the USSR and its lookalikes) than the private companies that control most of the world's trade in grain:

- André, Lausanne (André family)
- Bunge Corporation (Hirsch and Born families)
- Cargill Inc., Minneapolis (Cargill and Macmillan families)
- Continental Grain Company, New York City (Fribourg family)
- Louis-Dreyfus Company, Paris (Louis-Dreyfus family)

André

Virtually nothing is known.

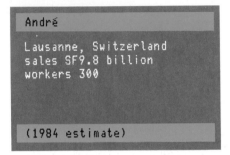

```
André

Lausanne, Switzerland
sales SF9.8 billion
workers 300

(1984 estimate)
```

Cargill

'Some of our best customers have never heard of us.'
　　Cargill brochure

Cargill is perhaps the largest of the five companies and the largest grain trader in the US.

Cargill's share of US grain exports, mid 1970s estimate, percentages

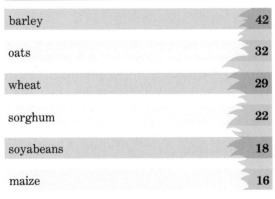

barley	42
oats	32
wheat	29
sorghum	22
soyabeans	18
maize	16

But only 40 per cent of Cargill's business is in grain. Its conglomerate expansion has propelled it into cotton and metal trading, flour processing, chemicals, steel manufacturing, poultry processing, salt mining, sunflower and other oilseed processing, meat, cocoa, sugar, molasses, barge construction, waste disposal, fire protection systems, scientific research installations. Its transnational empire comprises 140 subsidiaries in 36 countries. It has 14 ocean vessels, 3,000 rail cars, 400 river barges and 40 port elevators in the US.

```
Cargill

Minneapolis
who really knows
outside the boardroom?
sales over $12 billion
profit $120 million
workers 14,500
```

Bunge

The Bunge Corporation is so secretive that it is not even certain where it really belongs. It grew up in Holland in the nineteenth century, migrated to Argentina, and during the last decade, its ruling families have lived in Brazil and Spain as well as in Argentina. It is so rich that when Jorge and Juan Born were kidnapped in Buenos Aires by urban guerrillas in September 1974, the largest private ransom demand ever made, for some $60 million, was paid without apparent difficulty. Jorge Born was reported to have given personal instructions on how to raise the funds from various subsidiaries in Europe.

The corporation is so secretive that few of its subsidiaries even bear its name. In Argentina, its reach is enormous. As well as dominating Argentina's grain trade, the Bunge Corporation controls 40 per cent of its paint business, 33 per cent of its tin cans and 20 per cent of its textiles.

It also has interests in vegetable and fruit farming, cotton trading, milling, soybean and tomato processing, pharmaceuticals, chemicals, banking, timber, mining, and resort properties.

SAFE AND SORRY

Business involves risk. The degree of risk, and the kind of risk, may differ from business to business, or from company to company. But risk is always present. Besides dangers of financial reverse or, perhaps, ruin, there are the attendant physical and mental stresses suffered by those affected, as well as the more obvious physical dangers faced by those whose occupations require them to risk limb and even life.

One business - the insurance business, which is itself not without risks - thrives on the risks borne in other businesses.

The Danger League

One giant British insurance company charges different rates according to the degree of danger involved in particular occupations. Class 1 represents the safest work; Class 5, the most dangerous for which insurance is available.

Class 1
accountants
architects
clerks
doctors
opticians
solicitors
teachers

Class 2
builders (superintending only)
cafe proprietors (excluding deep-fat frying)
commercial travellers
florists (retail)
hairdressers
surveyors (site work)
wine merchants

Class 3
carpenters (self-employed)
compositors
garage proprietors
interior decorators (self-employed)
licensed victuallers
lithographers
market gardeners
veterinary surgeons

Class 4
builders (self-employed) *
carpenters (employees)
electricians (domestic and commercial)
farmers
florists (delivery)
garage mechanics
interior decorators (employees)
painters and decorators (self-employed)
panel beaters
plumbers (self-employed)
toolmakers

Class 5
builders (employees) *
carpenters (shuttering)
electricians (industrial)
milk deliverers
painters and decorators (employees)
plumbers (employees)

* excluding demolition, roofing, scaffolding, steeplejacks and structural steel erectors.

Categories of risk

Some guidelines for whole life and endowment policies issued by a managed funds company

aircraft worker
'extra if flying in an aircraft under test or more than 50 hours per year'

asbestos worker
'although no fixed charge is specified for asbestos workers, it is our practice to have careful regard to any occupation within this classification in normal underwriting. Full particulars of duties, with dates and durations, will be needed.'

atomic energy worker
'no extra unless duties involve working in the Hot Zone of a nuclear reactor, with explosives or research work.'

bomb disposal worker
'refer to underwriters'

professional boxer
'refer to underwriters'

construction worker
'refer to underwriters'

chemical worker
generally no extra but 'information required on exact nature of duties and chemicals handled'

crop sprayer (flying)
'refer to underwriters'

demolition worker, handling explosives
'extra premium, and information required on exact nature of duties'

diver (occupational)
'refer to underwriters'

electrical worker (power linesman)
'extra premium, and information required on exact nature of duties, including height worked at'

explosives handler
'extra premium and information required'

fisherman
'extra premium in case of those away from port for more than seven days and involved in deck duties'

jockey
'extra premium and information required on whether professional or amateur and flat racing, steeplechasing or National Hunt'

lift (elevator) installation worker
extra premium

mining, using explosives
extra premium

missionary
generally no extra but information required on 'territory in which proposer is working'

motor car and cycle circuit racer (professional)
'probably decline'

off-shore oil rig worker
'refer to underwriters'

oil worker
'refer to underwriters'

photographer (aerial/stunt)
'refer to underwriters'

quarry worker, handling explosives
extra premium

steeplejack
extra premium

wrestler
'refer to underwriters'

The Stress League

The Stress League rates occupations from 10 to zero: the higher the rate, the greater the pressure

miner	8.3
police officer	7.7
construction worker	7.5
journalist	7.5
pilot (civil)	7.5
prison officer	7.5
advertising	7.3
dentist	7.3
actor	7.2
politician	7.0
doctor	6.8
tax officer	6.8
film producer	6.5
nurse, midwife	6.5
fire fighter	6.3
musician	6.3
teacher	6.2
personnel	6.0
social worker	6.0
manager (commerce)	5.8

marketing/export	5.8
press officer	5.8
professional footballer	5.8
sales representative, shop assistant	5.7
stockbroker	5.5
bus driver	5.4
psychologist	5.2
publishing	5.0
diplomat	4.8
farmer	4.8
armed forces	4.7
vet	4.5
civil servant	4.4
accountant	4.3
engineer	4.3
estate agent	4.3
hairdresser	4.3
local government officer	4.3
secretary	4.3
solicitor	4.3
artist, designer	4.2
architect	4.0
chiropodist	4.0
optician	4.0
planner	4.0
post deliverer	4.0
statistician	4.0
lab technician	3.8
banker	3.7
computing	3.7
occupational therapist	3.7
linguist	3.7
beauty therapist	3.5
vicar	3.5
astronomer	3.4
nursery nurse	3.3
museum worker	2.8
librarian	2.0

BUSINESS FOR BUSINESS

Within the enormous variety of businesses, there are many specifically designed to cater for business needs or misfortunes. They include a multitude of intermediaries: accountants; advertising firms; brokers in barter, commodities, insurance, money, stocks; rating agencies; the financial press; financial information services; insurance companies; official receivers as well as other specialists in bankruptcy; security services; product quality surveillance agencies; tax specialists; as well as, of course, the whole field of banking.

Business for business is an enormous and rapidly growing business sector.

Annual compound growth of US business 1977-84, percentages

business for business	20
manufacturing industry	7

Growth of management consultancy companies 1983-84, percentages

Britain	20
USA	22

Growth of marketing companies (mainly advertising services) 1983-84, percentages

Britain	18
USA	13

Growth of market research companies 1983-84, percentages

Britain	19
USA	15

Individually, some of the companies are spectacularly successful, especially in the communication of financial information. They play the game successfully.

SERVOPOLY

BUSINESS FOR BUSINESS

Servopoly is played with two dice by any number of players. The winner is the one who is the sole survivor or who has the most money when the players decide that they have had enough.

Each player starts with M25,000 and receives M2,500 each time on passing Go. One player also acts as Banker.

Money is made by buying businesses, initially from the bank, and collecting dues from players landing on them. The right to buy a particular business belongs to whichever player lands on it first.

Dues are payable for landing on a business owned by another player. Dues are 10 per cent of the face value of the business and rise steeply with the possession of other businesses in the same set. For example:

- The face value of Dentsu, Japan's largest advertising firm, is M2,200.
- Dues payable on landing on it are M220.
- If the owner has another advertising firm, dues rise to 25 per cent of face value or M550.
- If the owner has the whole set, dues rise to 50 per cent or M1,100.

For the four commodity markets, dues are 25 per cent of the face value for one; half the face value for two; the full face value for three; and twice the face value for the set.

A player landing on Government or Market draws a card from the top of the relevant stack and follows the instructions given.

A player sent to jail must buy release immediately by a payment of M500. If the player has one of the corrupt services, payment is M1,000; if both M2,000.

A player who lands on Public Holiday misses a turn.

Once a player has a set of businesses (excluding the commodity markets and corrupt services), any or all of the set may be expanded by takeovers. The cost of each takeover is half the face value of the business and when purchased, a token is placed on it. At any time, a business may make only one more takeover than those made by other businesses in the set. Five takeovers on one business may be exchanged for one maxi takeover.

With each takeover, the dues payable rise as follows:

- one takeover: to the face value of the business
- two takeovers: to twice the face value
- three takeovers: to three times
- four takeovers: to four times
- one maxi takeover: to six times.

For example, the payment for landing on Dentsu when it has made one maxi takeover, would be M13,200.

Businesses and their takeovers may be mortgaged to the bank: but only at half their value. They are redeemable only at full value.

A player unable to pay dues in full, to any other player or to the bank, is bankrupt and out of the game.

 takeover

 maxi takeover

BMP GAMES

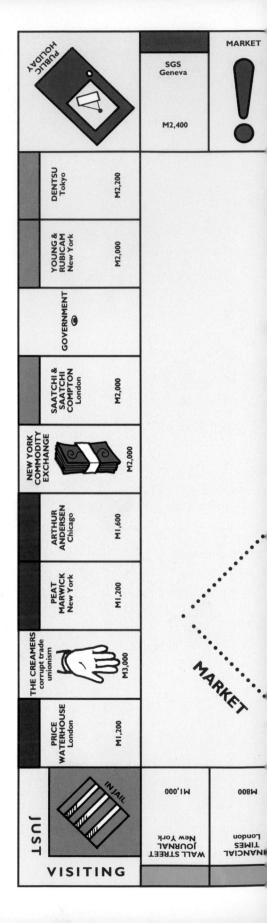

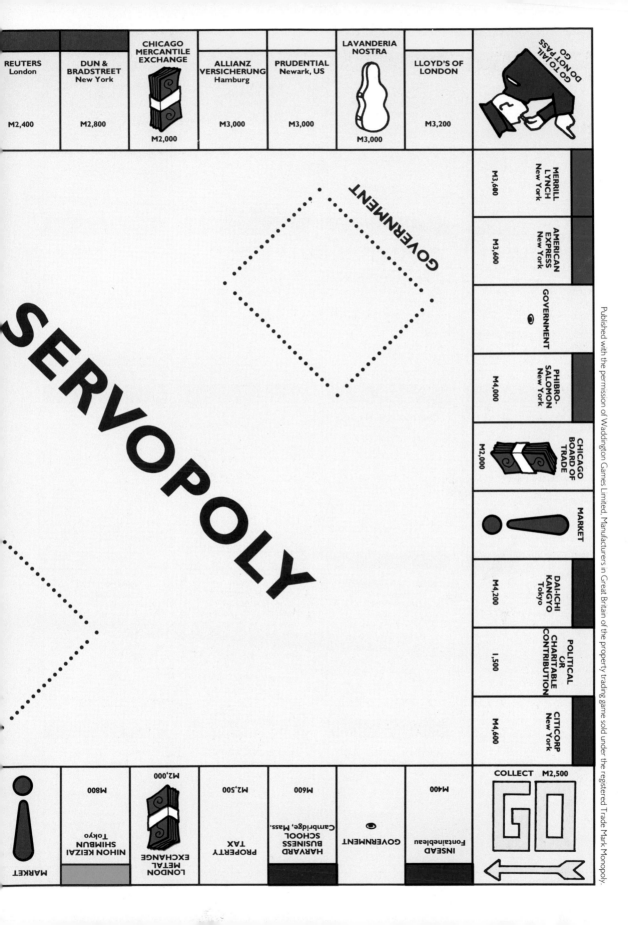

SERVOPOLY

REUTERS London — M2,400

DUN & BRADSTREET New York — M2,800

CHICAGO MERCANTILE EXCHANGE — M2,000

ALLIANZ VERSICHERUNG Hamburg — M3,000

PRUDENTIAL Newark, US — M3,000

LAVANDERIA NOSTRA — M3,000

LLOYD'S OF LONDON — M3,200

GO TO JAIL — DO NOT PASS GO

MERRILL LYNCH New York — M3,600

AMERICAN EXPRESS New York — M3,600

GOVERNMENT

PHIBRO-SALOMON New York — M4,000

CHICAGO BOARD OF TRADE — M2,000

MARKET

DAI-ICHI KANGYO Tokyo — M4,200

POLITICAL OR CHARITABLE CONTRIBUTION — 1,500

CITICORP New York — M4,600

COLLECT M2,500 GO

INSEAD Fontainebleau — M400

GOVERNMENT

HARVARD BUSINESS SCHOOL Cambridge, Mass. — M600

PROPERTY TAX — M2,500

LONDON METAL EXCHANGE — M2,000

NIHON KEIZAI SHIMBUN Tokyo — M800

MARKET

Published with the permission of Waddington Games Limited, Manufacturers in Great Britain of the property trading game sold under the registered Trade Mark Monopoly.

INSEAD
Fontainebleau
Institut européen d'administration d'affaires. Leading French and European seed-bed for multinational corporate management.

BUSINESS SCHOOLS

HARVARD BUSINESS SCHOOL
Cambridge, Mass.
Most prestigious US seed-bed for corporate management.

BUSINESS SCHOOLS

NIHON KEIZAI SHIMBUN
Tokyo
Owned by Nihon Keizai Shimbun Inc. which has more than twenty affiliated companies, including a Tokyo TV channel. Circulation, 2 million; sales 100 billion yen. (1984)

FINANCIAL PRESS

FINANCIAL TIMES
London
Mid-1984 circulation, 216,000. Owned by Pearson, London. Rank in top 500 non-US industrial companies, 415; sales, $1.1 billion. (1984)

FINANCIAL PRESS

THE WALL STREET JOURNAL
New York
Mid-1984: circulation, US 2,591,000, Europe 255,000. Owned by Dow Jones, New York. Rank in top 500 US industrial companies, 303; sales, $1.04 billion; net income, $139 million. (1985)

FINANCIAL PRESS

PRICE WATERHOUSE
London
Largest international accountancy firm with head-quarters currently outside the US. Revenues, $1.2 billion; 2,116 partners. (1984-85)

ACCOUNTANCY FIRMS

PEAT MARWICK
New York
Rank among accountancy firms worldwide, 2; revenues, $1.3 billion; 2,340 partners. (1984)

ACCOUNTANCY FIRMS

ARTHUR ANDERSEN
Chicago
Rank among accountancy firms worldwide, 1; fee income, $1.4 billion; 1,528 partners. (1984)

ACCOUNTANCY FIRMS

SAATCHI & SAATCHI COMPTON
London
74 offices in 40 countries. Rank among advertising agencies worldwide, 6; in Europe, 1; billings, $2.3 billion. (1984)

ADVERTISING AGENCIES

YOUNG & RUBICAM
New York
Rank among advertising agencies worldwide, 2; in US, 1. Now in joint ventures with Dentsu. Billings, $3.2 billion. (1984)

ADVERTISING AGENCIES

DENTSU
Tokyo
Rank among advertising agencies worldwide, 1. 3,000 clients. Pre-books half of all Japan's commercial TV prime time. Billings, $3.5 billion. (1984)

ADVERTISING AGENCIES

SGS
Geneva
Société Général de Surveillance. World's number one control and inspection company. Checks on behalf of governments and central banks the content and quality of shipments. Revenues, $700 million. (1985)

FINANCIAL INFORMATION

REUTERS
London
World's leading transmitter of financial information. Rank in top 500 European companies, 76 (1984). Sales, $630 million. (1985)

FINANCIAL INFORMATION

DUN & BRADSTREET
New York
World's leading credit rating agency (owns Moody's Investor Services). Rank in top 100 US diversified service companies, 22; sales, $2.4 billion. (1984)

FINANCIAL INFORMATION

ALLIANZ VERSICHERUNG
Hamburg
West Germany's largest insurance concern. In 1984 bought control of Riunione Adriatica di Sicurta, Italy; and in 1986, Britain's Cornhill Insurance. Rank in top 500 European companies, 10; investments, DM11.1 billion.

INSURANCE

PRUDENTIAL
Newark, N.J.
World's largest life insurance company. Assets, $79 billion; premium income, $15 billion; and with a face value of life insurance policies, $533 billion. (1984)

INSURANCE

LLOYD'S OF LONDON
World's largest re-insurers with 20 per cent of world market in marine insurance. Assets massive but incalculable. Premium income, £2.9 billion; underwriting profit, £57 million. (1982)

INSURANCE

MERRILL LYNCH & CO
New York
World's largest stockbroking firm. Has one million customers in its cash management account. Revenues, $6 billion; assets, $31 billion. (1984)

FINANCIAL SERVICES

AMERICAN EXPRESS
New York
World's leading traveller's cheque company; also in banking, investment services, insurance and charge cards. Revenues, $12.9 billion; assets, $62 billion. (1984)

FINANCIAL SERVICES

PHIBRO-SALOMON
New York
World's largest diversified service company. Merged Philipp Brothers, world's largest commodity traders and Salomon Brothers, leading investment bankers. Sales, $28.9 billion; assets, $58 billion. (1984)

FINANCIAL SERVICES

DAI-ICHI KANGYO BANK
Tokyo

Rank among banks worldwide by assets, 2; assets, $125 billion; net income, $258 million. (1984)

COMMERCIAL BANKING

CITICORP
New York

Rank among banks worldwide by assets, 1; assets, $151 billion; net income, $890 million. (1984)

COMMERCIAL BANKING

THE CREAMERS
Corrupt Trade Unions

Revenues considerable but unrecorded.

CORRUPT SERVICES

LAVANDERIA NOSTRA
Organized Crime

Revenues vast but unrecorded.

CORRUPT SERVICES

LONDON METAL EXCHANGE

World's number one market for trading in base metals.

COMMODITY MARKETS

NEW YORK COMMODITY EXCHANGE

Third largest commodity market in the world. 14 per cent of all contracts traded in US. Leading market for gold futures.

COMMODITY MARKETS

CHICAGO MERCANTILE EXCHANGE

Second largest commodity market in the world, 27 per cent of all contracts traded in US.

COMMODITY MARKETS

CHICAGO BOARD OF TRADE

Largest commodity market in the world. 45 per cent of all contracts traded in US.

COMMODITY MARKETS

MARKET

Saudi royal family goes public. All players with business services of any kind (including commodity markets) increase the money they hold by 10 per cent. The player who picks the card has inside information and gets 25 per cent.

MARKET

Russian agriculture privatized. If you have a business school, increase the money you hold by 10 per cent. If you have a business paper, increase by 25 per cent. If you hold the Chicago Board of Trade, surrender half your money to the central bank.

MARKET

Latin American countries form debtors' cartel. If you hold a commercial bank, you've just lost it.

MARKET

Election time. If you hold an advertising agency, increase your money by 10 per cent. If you hold the advertising set, increase your money by 25 per cent.

MARKET

Computer operatives are on strike. If you hold a financial information service, surrender 10 per cent of your money. If you hold the set, surrender 25 per cent.

MARKET

Widespread famine in Africa. Give a nominal sum to charity, care of the central bank.

GOVERNMENT

Sales tax doubles. If you hold either Lavanderia Nostra or The Creamers, take M2,000 from the central bank. If you hold both, take M5,000.

GOVERNMENT

All tax concessions on insurance cancelled. If you own an insurance service, surrender half your money. If you own all three, surrender 80 per cent of your money.

GOVERNMENT

New legislation to tighten accounting practices. If you own an accountancy firm, get M1,500 from the central bank. If you own the set, get M4,000. If you are out of the business, surrender 10 per cent of your money.

GOVERNMENT

Your books are called in for scrutiny. Go straight to Jail without passing Go.

GOVERNMENT

The US Federal Reserve sharply lowers discount rate to boost the economy. Whatever you own, increase your money by 10 per cent.

GOVERNMENT

Your business is nationalized. Accept twice whatever it is worth, under vehement protest; and start again.

Comrade Shareholders

It is with much pride and pleasure that I rise to deliver the annual report of the Union of Soviet Socialist Republics, Inc. As far back as 1981, we reached an annual value in production and sales of some $1111 billion, over ten times the annual sales of what was then the next largest company in the world, Exxon of New York.

Overall, our business grew by 3.2 per cent in 1985, an encouraging increase from the 2.6 per cent in the year before. But we will have to do much better and grow by some 4.7 per cent a year, if we are to reach our goal of doubling our business by the end of the century.

Ours, of course, is a fully integrated state company, whose operations take in the whole range of business activities, from the manufacture of missiles and the export of furs to various services like street-cleaning or mental rehabilitation.

Our oil industry has been somewhat disappointing, with prices declining and with oil output slipping to 613 million tonnes, the first fall since the Great Patriotic War. Our fields are now working at only 40-45 per cent of their capacity, and we plan that this level should urgently be raised to over 60 per cent. No less than 60 per cent of our foreign exchange earnings have been coming from the sale of oil, and the steep falls in the oil price are creating real difficulties. Every fall of $1 in the price is costing us US $550 million over a year.

Fortunately, the Siberian gas pipeline project is making remarkable progress, and we look forward to a profitable relationship with our Western trading partners. Attempts by the United States to deprive us of access to necessary technology have, I am glad to say, been frustrated by our own ingenuity as well as by the interests of those companies in the West which have construction and supply contracts with us.

We have, most regrettably, suffered a serious accident at one of our many nuclear power stations. But we have taken urgent steps to contain the damage; have compensated those injured or inconvenienced, within the bounds of our proper operations; and have demoted or dismissed those managers guilty of incompetence. Our faith in nuclear power remains undimmed, though we are aware that more caution must be exercised in the functioning and development of this sector.

Our subsidiary for the development of outer space is keeping ahead of our competitors, and we have confidence that this long-term investment will not prove to be misplaced, if only through the spin-off in advanced military technology.

Our manufacturing subsidiaries are still performing far below the level that we expect of them. In part we are to blame. At least 30 per cent of the machinery in our factories is more than 15 years old, and this is one reason why six million workers have to be employed in repair shops. Much of the machinery we produce is obsolete or faulty. Quality controls are woefully inadequate. This is particularly true in the area of consumer goods, where shoddy products pile up on the shelves of our retail outlets. And indeed our whole complex service sector leaves much to be desired.

THE SOVIET BUSINESS

CCCP

One result, as you know, is that much popular consumption is going to our domestic competitor, the so-called black economy. As I recently told an important political rally: Try to get your flat repaired - you will definitely have to find a moonlighter to do it for you. And he will steal the materials he needs from a construction site.

We are taking urgent steps to deal with all these problems. We must make our managers more accountable for the efficiency of their enterprises. Shortcomings will result in demotions or even dismissal. We must, and will, do something about a labour productivity that is a mere 55 per cent of the level prevalent among our Western competitors. There is too much feather-bedding and an irrational resistance to the relocation of labour. We will see to it that trade union officials exercise a greater sense of responsibility in representing the views of the management to which they belong. But we must also provide material incentives for both managers and workers, if we are to succeed in securing efficiency and the supply of better quality goods. Needless to say, the cost of such incentives must be met by charging higher prices for improved products.

In passing, I must refer to one industrial enterprise whose very success is a serious source of concern. The consumption of company vodka has reached dimensions which undermine the capabilities of our workforce. Measures have been introduced to control strictly the output and sale of this product. Nor will we allow competition in this sector from anti-social elements who have taken to making alcohol illicitly, instead.

Our agricultural subsidiaries too, I regret to report, are still presenting us with problems. You cannot ignore the effect of the unreliable weather, of course, but let us be frank and admit that our unsatisfactory performance is largely the result of incompetent organization, complacency and even irresponsibility. There must be a stop to the continuing investment of so much capital in this sector, and an examination of how efficiency can be secured, if necessary by structural changes that we have so far refused to contemplate.

I cannot end without a warning to our managers, however highly placed, who are inadequate to their duties. As you know, we have already replaced 14 of our district first secretaries, the regional supervisors of our company, as well as our central executive officers for oil, gas and electric power. Nor will we countenance corruption in our company. Any evidence will be ruthlessly investigated and any proof will be met with the greatest severity, including perpetual retirement.

We are committed not only to efficient and honest, but to open management. Our shareholders and workforce, even our customers, are entitled to know as much about our operations as is consistent with prudent business practice.

It only remains for me to record our sorrow at the loss of several on our board who have grown old in service to the company. We are fortunate in having still amongst us those who have so many years of experience with which to enrich our deliberations.

I must thank you for your patience in listening to me and direct you to the buffet where the usual caviar and champagne are ready to be served. I can assure you that Wassily Petrovich of the Forestry Commission, responsible for special assignments, has not put any of his new-fangled foodstuff in the sandwiches. We have every reason to take pride in our thriving biotechnology sector, but consuming its products is not part of our function.

Mikhail Yurevich Gordropov

2

GROWTH
OR
DECLINE

Although capable of infinite variety, business obeys common rules and shows a common pattern of behaviour.

Many businesses are started each year. If successful, they grow; if not, they sicken - and sometimes they die. They compete and from time to time collude, the better to compete. In principle, they use every means to succeed that is not denied them by the superior force of other businesses or the state.

STARTING UP

'A guy wakes up in the morning and says: "I'm going to be an entrepreneur." So he goes into work and walks up to the best technologist in the company where he is working, and whispers: "Would you like to join my company? Ten o'clock Saturday, my place. And bring some donuts."

Then he goes to the best finance guy he knows, and says: "Bring some coffee." Then you get a marketing guy. And if you are the right entrepreneur, you have three or four of the best minds in the business.

Ten o'clock Saturday rolls around. They say: "Hey, what is our company going to do?" You say: "Build left-hand widgets." Another hour and you've got a business plan roughed out. The finance guy says he knows where you can get some money.

So what have you done? You've not provided the coffee. You've not provided the donuts. You've not provided the ideas. You've been the entrepreneur. You made it all happen.'

Nolan Bushnell, founder of Atari

There is no magic formula to starting a business. Anyone can do it, though generally a little start-up capital is needed. In some cases this may be provided wholly or partly by the state; in others, by a bank, by friends or family.

New businesses everywhere tend to be small, and remain small. But the smaller a business is, and the newer it is, the more vulnerable it is. In Britain, between 1971 and 1981, the annual average share of business failures by companies with fewer than 20 workers was 50 per cent; and of companies employing 20-49 workers, still as high as 40 per cent.

FOCUS ON GROWTH

Businesses that succeed in growing usually offer something new: a new product or service; a new technique of production, management, distribution or marketing.

The rewards of successful innovation can be spectacular. In the photography industry, three innovations – the portable camera, the instant camera and the photocopier – generated a succession of three business giants, each a model for its generation: Kodak, Polaroid and Xerox.

Kodak

In the late 1870s, George Eastman, a young bank clerk in Rochester, New York, began experimenting with ways of making photography less cumbersome.

In 1880, having found a formula, he started producing dry plates commercially, and the Eastman Dry Plate and Film Company was born. In 1884, he introduced the first film in rolls. In 1888, came the Kodak camera (Eastman had a liking for the letter 'K' which he considered strong and incisive), light, portable and selling for $25. Purchasers returned the finished roll along with the camera and $10. The film was developed and printed, a new roll inserted in the camera, and the whole package returned.

In 1900, Eastman Kodak introduced the first Brownie camera, selling for only $1.00 and using 15-cent rolls of film.

Success followed success. Although other companies entered the field, innovation kept Eastman Kodak on top of the photography industry and growing at a faster pace.

In 1923, came a home movie camera, projector and film.

In 1935, the company began marketing Kodachrome, the first successful amateur colour film.

In 1951, the Brownie hand-held movie camera appeared.

In 1963, came the Instamatic camera, with film in a foolproof cartridge, making nearly all other amateur cameras obsolete. By 1976, the company had sold 60 million of these, dwarfing all the competition combined.

Average annual growth, 1889-1909, percentages

Eastman Kodak	17.5
US photographic industry	11.0
US manufacturing industry	4.7
US population	1.9

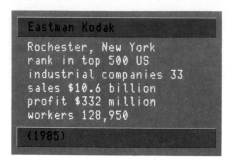

Eastman Kodak
Rochester, New York
rank in top 500 US
industrial companies 33
sales $10.6 billion
profit $332 million
workers 128,950
(1985)

But the company missed out on the major innovation of instant photography. The instant camera was to be developed by another company, which grew rich very quickly as a result.

Polaroid

In 1928, while an undergraduate at Harvard, Edwin Land discovered how to polarize light waves so as to reduce glare.

In 1937, he founded Polaroid and began manufacturing sunglasses. His company boomed during the Second World War, with the military demand for glare-free glasses, goggles and filters. By the end of the war, annual sales were $16 million.

In 1943, he started to experiment with the idea of developing and printing a photograph inside the camera.

In 1947, he successfully demonstrated instant photography, and the Polaroid Model 95 camera was born. Weighing just over 4lb and retailing for $90, it could produce a sepia-toned picture in 60 seconds. In 1949, its first year, its sales exceeded $5 million.

In 1950, black and white instant photography displaced the sepia original. In 1960, the company introduced 15-second pictures and automatic exposure.

In 1963, colour film and film cartridges joined the range, followed by the low-priced Swinger in 1965.

By 1970, Polaroid's annual sales had reached $500 million. Then in 1972, after some $500 million in development costs, came the SX-70 which produced pictures of brilliant colour that, unlike earlier versions, did not fade with prolonged exposure to light.

In 1978, annual profits topped $118 million, but then steeply declined.

Growth faltered, as the source of successful innovation ran dry and competitors homed in on Polaroid's market.

The tide turned again in January 1986, when Eastman Kodak was found guilty of infringing Polaroid patents in the US Federal Appeals Court and the US Supreme Court, and announced that it was abandoning the instant photography business.

Sales and profit of Polaroid, 1975-85, $ million

	sales	profit
1975	813	62.6
1976	950	79.7
1977	1,062	92.3
1978	1,377	118.4
1979	1,361	36.1
1980	1,451	85.4
1981	1,420	31.1
1982	1,294	23.5
1983	1,255	49.7
1984	1,270	25.7
1985	1,295	36.9

```
Polaroid
Cambridge, Mass.
rank in top 500 US
industrial companies 257
sales $1.3 billion
profit $36.9 million
workers 12,932
(1985)
```

It was Xerox that would profit from another major innovation in photography – the development of a copying machine – to grow further, faster, than any company before.

Xerox

Patent attorney and amateur physicist Chester Carlson experimented for several years in the use of static electricity to make instant copies on plain paper.

In 1937, he patented his initial process. Then, during the next seven years, he was turned down by more than 20 companies, including IBM and General Electric, which he approached to develop his invention commercially.

In 1944, the Battelle Memorial Institute signed a royalty-sharing contract and began developing the process.

In 1947, Battelle passed development rights to Haloid, a small photographic paper company in Rochester, New York. Carlson joined as consultant. In 1949, Haloid introduced the first copier, called Xerox (from xerography - the Greek words for 'dry' and 'writing').

But it was not until ten years later, in 1959, that Haloid Xerox produced the first reliable, easy-to-use copier: the 914, so-named because it could take sheets as large as 9 inches by 14 inches. The product was an immediate and phenomenal success and in 1961 the company changed its name to plain Xerox.

America's fastest

Growth of Xerox, 1959-74, $ million

	sales	profit
1959	33	2
1974	3,600	331

Success excited competition. By the start of the 1980s, more than 24 major companies – among them IBM, Kodak and Canon – were making copiers of their own.

Without a new major innovation, Xerox could not fight back, and diversified in 1982 – into insurance.

```
Xerox
Stamford, Conn.
rank in top 500 US
industrial companies 40
sales $8.95 billion
profit $475 million
workers 102,396
(1985)
```

FINDING THE MONEY

Innovation, though often a necessary condition for growth, is not enough by itself. Businesses that have new ideas must be able to finance their development.

This is normally done in one or more of several ways:

- retaining and reinvesting profits
- attracting outside investment (risk capital)
- borrowing
- receiving state subsidies.

Marks & Spencer, Britain's largest successful retailer, travelled all these routes except the last, which Volkswagen, the German car giant, travelled first.

The M & S story

Every week over 14 million customers shop at the 262 British outlets of Marks & Spencer. Its formula for success has been to provide goods of high and reliable quality at a relatively low price. Despite its predominance, M & S stocks a relatively small range of items: 5,000-6,000 compared with 20,000-30,000 for a typical retail chain.

Michael Marks, the immigrant founder of M & S, acquired his first stock by borrowing £5 worth of goods from a wholesale merchant.

In 1884, he opened a market stall in Leeds. By 1890, he was operating five penny bazaars at covered markets in the north of England. In 1894, he formed a partnership with Thomas Spencer, the wholesaler's cashier, who brought in £300 for his half share.

The partnership prospered. By 1898, each partner's capital had risen to £2,500. By 1900, there were 12 shops and 24 bazaars in market halls, with all expansion financed out of retained profits.

But Spencer wanted to retire. In 1903, the partnership was turned into Marks & Spencer Ltd with a registered capital of 30,000 £1 shares, and with all but a few of these subscribed equally by the two partners.

The new company continued its policy of re-investing profits; placing around 20 per cent annually in a general reserve for development.

After nibbling at less successful competitors, the company bought a chain of shops in the London area, for £15,000 cash.

High inflation during the First World War led to the first substantial borrowing for expansion; by 1924, the company had some £150,000 in bank loans and overdrafts.

In 1926, Marks & Spencer began selling shares to the public. By 1932, it had raised some £2 million in this way, with a further £2 million raised through debenture, or loan, stock taken up by a major insurance company, Prudential Assurance.

During the seven years of general economic depression, 1932-38, Marks & Spencer's sales grew at around seven times the rate of the retail trade in Britain, or an annual average 27 per cent as against 3.7 per cent.

From 1934 onwards, the company relied primarily on ploughed back profits for its massive expansion, with moderate borrowing, usually in debenture form, from the Prudential. In 1983, Prudential held debenture stocks with a nominal value of £45 million.

The company has avoided vertical integration to secure its supplies. Its relationship with suppliers is built on the assurance of enormous orders coupled with technical advice on product development.

In the mid-1980s, M & S was selling a third of all underwear and nightwear in Britain, a quarter of all men's socks and 14 per cent of all clothes. It was the giant in the clothing trade. But it was growing elsewhere: by 1984, 40 per cent of Marks & Spencer's sales came from the fast-growing food sector.

```
Marks & Spencer

London
rank in Europe's top 500
companies 12
sales £3.2 billion
profit £303 million
workers 41,026

(1985)
```

The people's car

In January 1934, Ferdinand Porsche, founder of the Porsche luxury car firm, submitted a proposal for the 'Construction of a German people's car (Volkswagen)' to the German Ministry of Transport. In June, he was contracted to complete a prototype within ten months.

Three years later, the government decided to back the result. It instructed the German Labour Front to invest 50 million reichsmarks in Volkswagen GmbH, to build the car, the factory and the associated new town (now Wolfsburg). The intention was to offer the car for 990 reichsmarks, payable in instalments of 5 marks a week, via the 'Strength through Joy' organization.

Work on the factory near Fallersleben, Lower Saxony, was interrupted by the war. Volkswagens were built, but for military use only. It was only in 1947 that the first cars were sold to the public. Control of the company passed to the Allied Military government in 1946 and then, in 1949, to the Federal government and the Land authorities.

Early wartime plans to privatize the company were realized in 1960. The company was restructured as an Aktiengesellschaft (joint stock corporation), and the public was invited to take up 60 per cent of the shares.

Subsequent infusions of funds came largely from new share issues: in 1966, 1970 and notably in 1978, when the increase in capital by DM300 million was the largest so far in the history of the Federal Republic.

In 1982, VW built its 20 millionth vehicle.

```
Volkswagen
Wolfsburg, West Germany
rank in top 50 companies
worldwide 32
sales $16 billion
profit $85.9 million
workers 238,353

(1984)
```

BIGGEST IS BEST

Business income grows faster than income in general, and big business income grows fastest of all. Sales of the top performers have increased dramatically over the last thirty years or so.

The 500 Club

Qualification for membership of the top 500 US industrial companies, sales, $ million

1954	49.7
1954 at 1983 prices	174.0
1983	418.0

For some companies, which started small, growth has been spectacular. Growth is not automatic nor ever assured. Both in the long and the short term, growth rates vary considerably, even between companies in the same industry.

Late but fast

Growth in sales of Occidental Petroleum, 1954-85

1954
Sales **$3,000**: too small for membership

1967
Sales **$826 million**: enters the top 500 US industrial companies at no 102

1968
Sales **$1 billion**: makes the $1 billion set

1979
Sales **$9.5 billion**: jostling the $10 billion set at no. 21

1983
Sales **$19.1 billion**: sitting at no.14

But even the fastest may slow down. In 1985, Occidental slipped to no. 19, with annual sales of $14.5 billion.

Whizzers and wozzers

Average annual growth of the best and worst performers in the 500 Club during 25 years, 1954-79

Sales growth, percentages	
Signal Companies (aerospace)	**19.4**
United Merchants & Manufacturers (textiles, flooring)	**3.4**

Earnings per share, percentages	
Crown Cork & Seal (metal products)	**21.0**
Allied Chemical (chemicals)	**-9.0**

Stocks/shares performance 1979 value of $100 invested in 1954	
Avon Products (soaps, cosmetics)	**$8,081**
Wheeling-Pittsburgh Steel (metal manufacturing)	**$68**

GOBBLING

In the period 1981-84, US gross national product rose 24 per cent: sales of the top 500 industrial companies fell 1 per cent and profits rose a mere 2-6 per cent.

As the production of wealth becomes more difficult and tedious than its profitable manipulation, so a new and more aggressive type of growth has become common – gobbling. Gobbling is the taking over of one business by another, with or without the morsel's consent.

Gobbling comes in many guises.

There is defensive gobbling and predatory gobbling, pre-emptive gobbling and idle, purposeless gobbling ostensibly pursued for its own sake. And there is premeditated, strategic gobbling.

GROWTH OR DECLINE

Gobbledegook

A gobbler's glossary

Arbs (Arbitrageurs)
Professional dealers who buy or sell shares in a gamble on the outcome of a takeover battle.

Bid, agreed
A bid which the management accepts and recommends to the shareholders.

Bid, contested
A bid which the management resists.

Black Knight
A corporate raider whose purchase of shares is directed at making a profit by forcing the threatened company into the hands of a White Knight (see below) buying out the raider.

Deadman's trigger
An irreversible move set in train before the outcome of an enemy's prior move is known.

Front-end loaded or two-tier deal
A transaction in two steps. First a cash tender for 51 per cent of the shares, then a less attractive offer (ie a bidding company's own shares) for the outstanding equity. The object is to stampede fast-footed professionals to sell out for cash, leaving other shareholders having to take up low-valued paper.

Golden parachute
Payment to top executives in the event of company control passing into other hands.

Greenmail
Takeover ploy in which a hungry investor buys a big chunk of a vulnerable company's stock, makes noises about taking control, and then sells out to a frightened management for a hefty profit. In 1984, there were some 50 recorded cases of 'greenmail', with total related payouts of $3.5 billion.

Grey Knight
Often appears dressed as a White Knight and comes softly into a bid battle but can turn rough. He is the last resort of a company seeking to escape from a Black Knight.

Junk bonds
A term used for the bonds of companies with low investment/credit ratings. Given new currency by the takeover frenzy in which high-interest, low-rated bonds are issued to finance buyouts, increasingly with the assets of the bought as security. In 1985 junk bonds accounted for $60 billion out of a total corporate bond sector of $425 billion.

Pacman ploy
A reverse takeover, where the company that is threatened turns and bids for the threatening company.

Poison pill
A prescription to kill off prospective bids with irrevocable financial commitments triggered by loss of control (eg the issue of preferred, or special, stock redeemable at high rates after a takeover).

Scorched earth
Selling off prize assets to make the threatened company less appealing to the unwelcome bidder.

Share buybacks
A device by which a target company buys its own shares in the market to put itself into debt, or otherwise reduce the market in its shares, and increase their value. In 1983, $7.6 billion were spent by US companies on their own shares; in 1984, $24.9 billion; in 1985, $11.2 billion.

Shark repellant
Any of various devices adopted to make a company less attractive to bidders. These include sinking deeply into debt; buying companies in heavily regulated businesses such as banking; providing for a 'staggered' board by which only a few directors can be elected in any one year.

Sweetheart deal
The sale of prize assets to a friendly suitor.

White Knight
Friendly counter-bidder, who carries the threatened company off to safety or at least more congenial possession.

Pacmania – or compulsive gobbling

For many years, there were 'Seven Sisters' dominating the world oil business: Exxon, Royal Dutch Shell, Mobil, British Petroleum, Texaco, Standard Oil of California, (Socal) and Gulf. Then in 1984, Gulf fell victim to sororicide, committed by Socal.

Engulf and devour: The Seven Sisters

Major oil company sales, 1983, $ billion

Exxon	88.6
Royal Dutch Shell	80.6
Mobil	54.6
British Petroleum (BP)	49.2
Texaco	40.1
Standard Oil of California (Socal, later Chevron)	27.3
Gulf	26.6

Fuelled by the profits bonanza that followed the oil price rise of 1974, Big Oil went on a takeover spree that took it into raw materials (coal and metals in particular) but also into apartment blocks, electrical goods, office equipment – and just about everything else. By 1979, the rush to diversify had largely subsided, although some activity continued: in that year, Sohio took over Kennecott, the copper producer, for $1.77 billion.

Diversification proved less profitable than expected. But when the stock market recession made it cheaper to buy oil on Wall Street at about $4 per barrel of proven reserves than to discover it in the ground at anything up to $11 per barrel, other business turned to gobble companies in Big Oil, while Big Oil turned on itself in a cannibalistic orgy of unprecedented proportions.

Slick attractions

Cost of oil company takeovers, 1981–85, $ billion

gobbler	gobbled	cost
1981		
Sohio	Kennecott (mining)	1.77
Elf Aquitaine	Texasgulf	2.74
Du Pont (chemicals)	Conoco	7.21
Kuwait Petroleum	Santa Fe International (transport, natural resources)	2.5
1982		
US Steel (metal manufacturing)	Marathon Oil	5.96
Occidental Petroleum	Cities Service	4.02
1983		
Phillips Petroleum	General American Oil	1.14
Diamond Shamrock	Natomas	1.52
1984		
Texaco	Getty Oil	10.1
Chevron (formerly Socal)	Gulf	13.3
Mobil	Superior	5.7
Phillips Petroleum	Aminoil and Geysers Geothermal	1.3
Texas Eastern	Petrolane	1.0
1985		
Royal Dutch Shell	Shell Oil	5.7
Olympia & York	Gulf Canada	2.1

Texaco's gobbling of Getty Oil in 1984 displaced an agreement in principle for Pennzoil to gobble 43 per cent of Getty Oil instead. Pennzoil sued and in late 1985 won from a Texas jury damages of $10.53 billion, plus interest, against Texaco. The verdict was disputed by Texaco in appeals to higher courts.

Winners and losers

From the gobbler's point of view, taking over other businesses is a rational step taken in accordance with changing market conditions and the shifting moods of management. In particular, there is a real incentive to gobble when assets are under-used, as they have been in recent years.

But what may be good for some businesses or some business buccaneers is not necessarily good for the economy as a whole. Takeover activity often sacrifices growth for repositioning. Between 1981 and 1984, when the biggest wave of takeovers flooded through America's boardrooms, GNP rose by 24 per cent, while sales of the top 500 US industrial companies fell by 1 per cent, and profits crept up by only 2.6 per cent.

In the words of the Great Gobblers:
'A lot of US managers fly around in their jet planes and go to their hunting lodges where they live like the nobility of old.'
Carl Icahn

'I wish people would stop calling me a "raider" when I put a billion or so dollars into a company and then make a few suggestions to make management more efficient. After all, shareholders are the owners of the company.'
T Boone Pickens

In other words:
'If the cash in corporate treasuries isn't invested to promote long-term growth but is spent instead to acquire the assets of other firms, a major potential source of investment has been dissipated.'
Peter Rodino, Chairman of the US House of Representatives Judiciary Committee

'We need to call a halt to these mergers.'
J Bennett Johnston, US Senator

Merger mania

Increasing value of Wall Street's 50 biggest mergers, $ billion

1981	49.9
1982	48.2
1983	38.4
1984	78.5
1985	94.6

In 1984, there were 18 megadeals of $1 billion and above, totalling $58.1 billion. In 1985, 36 megadeals totalled $92.7 billion.

Britain's manic moods

Acquisitions and mergers, 1963-85

	number	value, £ million at 1985 prices
1963	888	2,429
1964	940	3,371
1965	1,000	3,295
1966	807	3,077
1967	763	4,928
1968	946	11,145
1969	846	5,794
1970	793	5,730
1971	884	4,255
1972	1,210	11,023
1973	1,205	5,197
1974	504	1,749
1975	315	806
1976	353	1,064
1977	481	1,690
1978	567	2,159
1979	534	2,763
1980	469	2,087
1981	452	1,447
1982	463	2,569
1983	447	2,608
1984	568	5,806
1985	474	7,090

The passion for gobbling comes in waves. In terms of numbers acquired, Britain's highest tides occurred in 1972 and 1973. In terms of the aggregate values involved, at constant 1985 prices, 1968 remains the peak tide year. But 1985 was, in aggregate value terms, the third highest tide in 23 years. And early 1986 was marked by three takeover bids of £2 billion and more.

Rich pickings

The 50 biggest takeovers of 1983 put $260 million into the pockets of Wall Street investment advisory firms. In 1984, fees totalled $367 million; in 1985, $588 million, not counting further millions in commissions for securing the finance to clinch the deals.

■ Investment banks involved in the Texaco-Getty takeover received $50 million for their services.
■ Goldman Sachs received $18.5 million out of $50 million received by investment banks in the Texaco-Getty takeover.
■ Salomon Brothers received $28 million for their part in the takeover of Gulf Oil by Chevron (formerly Socal).

In 1985, Morgan Stanley pulled in at least $82 million in dealmakers' fees; First Boston, $72 million; and Goldman Sachs, $71 million.

Just as gobbling can be rational, so too can disgorging. All growing businesses, and gobblers in particular, will at some time feel the need to rid themselves of the bits that don't fit in with their developing structure.

Sometimes bits of the original core become redundant. Sometimes the bits that go have only recently been gobbled.

A gobbler, getting up from the table and gazing at itself in a mirror, may recognize an unmanageable blob.

To put itself in shape for success, it rationalizes - identifying the parts it doesn't need and the parts it needs to get...

It sells and buys, closes and opens, to suit its managerial capacity.

BAT spreads its wings

The big tobacco companies are major generators of cash, and the biggest of all, Britain's BAT Industries, is correspondingly flush.

With further growth in cigarette sales limited by health warnings and market saturation, and without the need to incur the risks of debt, BAT looked for expansion into other ranges of activity. A second range, or leg, was related: in the paper production essential to cigarette manufacturing. A third was remotely related, in the retail trade, with BAT taking over department stores and luxury product lines such as cosmetics. A fourth leg, financial services, seemed a natural expansion for such a heavy consumer of them.

BAT v Allianz

Autumn 1980
Allianz Versicherung, West Germany's largest insurer, decides to become a substantial minority shareholder in Eagle Star, one of Britain's top insurance companies.

1 June 1981
Allianz buys a 14.9 per cent stake for £58.2 million and tenders for a further 15 per cent at a maximum 290 pence a share. Eagle Star board urges resistance.

4 June
Eagle Star announces net assets exceed 450 pence a share and plans dividend increase.

9 June
Allianz's stake up to 28.1 per cent. Says it will not acquire further shares.

19 October 1983
Allianz raises stake to 29.99 per cent. Offers 500 pence in cash for remaining shares, to value company at £692 million. Eagle Star board rejects offer.

2 November
BAT offers 575 pence a share. Eagle Star board accepts.

28 November
Allianz raises bid to 650 pence a share; BAT counters with cash offer of 660 pence.

5 December
Allianz prepares to top BAT's £913 million after pursuing talks with the board of Eagle Star.

8 December
Talks break down.

12 December
Takeover Panel demands that Allianz outline terms by start of trading on the London Stock Exchange on 14 December.

14 December
Allianz bids 665 pence a share in cash (£920 million). BAT counters with 675 pence (£934 million).

21 December
Takeover Panel sets deadline of 4.30 p.m. on 30 December for final bids.

30 December
BAT bids £968 million or 700 pence per share. Allianz agrees to sell its stake of 30 per cent to BAT for 700 pence (£7) a share. Profit on the deal: £163 million.

Having bought Eagle Star, BAT snapped up Hambro Life, Britain's biggest unit trust-linked life insurance company, in 1984, for an agreed bid of £664 million. The name of the Hambro Life subsidiary was changed to Allied Dunbar.

BAT's new leg has grown at the expense of some older ones, with the company divesting itself of some of its earlier acquisitions:

Sold in 1984
International Stores (supermarkets) Britain, acquired 1972; and MacMarket (supermarkets), Britain, acquired 1979 - to Dee Corporation for £180 million.

Sold in 1984
British American Cosmetics: Lentheric, Britain, acquired 1965; Yardley, Britain, acquired 1967; Germaine Monteil, France, acquired 1968; Juvena, Switzerland, acquired 1977 - to Beecham Group for £104 million.

Sold in 1985
Mardon Packaging International, in a management buyout, for £200 million.

In 1986, BAT announced plans to sell for $600 million (£420 million) half its retailing business in the US - various relatively down-market stores - with the intention of retaining the broadly up-market department stores such as Saks of Fifth Avenue.

Four-legged BAT

Sales of BAT Industries, 1985

commercial activities	£ billion	%
tobacco	6.1	49
retailing (mainly US)	3.9	31
paper	1.5	11
other trading	1.2	9
total sales	12.7	100
financial services (turnover)	1.9	

```
BAT Industries

London
rank in world's top 50
industrial companies 47
sales $13.46 billion
profit $1.13 billion
workers 212,822

(1984)
```

Leveraged buyouts

Surplus bits of a company are often sold to their existing managements, in leveraged buyouts. Leveraged buyouts, through divesting a company of unmanageable weight, are increasingly popular. Everybody is supposed to win.

■ Assets are sold, below book value, usually to the existing management, which finances the purchase with money borrowed from banks, insurance companies and even government agencies.

■ The divesting companies get cash without the costs and possible perils of liquidating subsidiaries; sometimes retain an interest in the surrendered company; and increase the efficiency of their own operations.

■ The management retain their jobs.

■ The financial institutions open up new and relatively safe channels for investment. In Britain, for example, under 10 per cent of buyouts fail, compared with 30 per cent of all new businesses.

But as buyouts become more common, shareholders become more aware of their bargaining position, push prices higher and depress potential gains.

Multi-million dollar buyouts

Price and status of the biggest US buyouts, 1984-85, as reported December 1985, $

Beatrice	6.2b	pending
Macy	3.6b	pending
Storer Broadcasting	2.5b	completed
Revlon	1.8b	pending
Union Texas Petroleum	1.7b	completed
Jack Eckerd	1.6b	pending
Northwest Industries	1.4b	approved
City Investing (3 divisions)	1.4b	completed
Levi Strauss	1.2b	completed
Metromedia	1.1b	completed
National Gypsum	1.1b	pending
Uniroyal	1.0b	completed
Wometco	977.0m	competed
Denny's	908.0m	completed
ARA Services	883.3m	completed
Households Merchandizing Unit	690.0m	pending
Southwest Forest Industries	650.0m	completed
Dr Pepper	648.0m	completed

Red Lion Inns	**600.0m**	completed
Du Pont/Conoco Chemical Division	**600.0m**	completed
Malone & Hyde	**580.0m**	completed
Harte-Hanks	**575.9m**	completed
City Investing (Motel Division)	**565.0m**	completed
Diversifoods	**525.0m**	completed
Blue Bell	**469.0m**	completed
ACF Industries.	**469.0m**	completed
Scott & Fetzer	**440.0m**	pending
Amstar	**439.0m**	completed
Warnaco	**408.3m**	pending
Weirton Plant	**386.0m**	completed
Mary Kay	**280.0m**	pending
Sybion	**255.4m**	pending
Alamito	**251.0m**	pending
Papercraft	**240.0m**	approved
Swift Independent	**135.0m**	approved
Olin's Ecusta Unit	**125.0m**	completed
Easco	**105.0m**	pending
Datapoint	**100.0m**	pending

Success and frustration

In February 1984, Dr Pepper, fourth largest US soft-drinks firm, changed hands in a $648 million leveraged buyout, in which the investment group headed by Chairman Woodrow Wilson Clements put in around $30 million as equity and borrowed some $620 million. By selling off assets, the group reduced this debt to $170 million. Then, in February 1986, Coca-Cola announced plans to acquire the company, for $478 million, giving the investors some $300 million, or around ten times their initial investment. Clements was expected to receive $20 million for his original stake of $2 million. But in June 1986, the US Federal Trade Commission moved to block the merger, because it would have raised Coca-Cola's share of the soft drinks market from 39 per cent to 46 per cent.

Forked tongue

'What the buyout phenomenon illustrates, above all, is the endlessly ingenious creativity of American capitalism.'
Fortune, January 1984

'The auction atmosphere has inevitably sparked concern among lenders and investment bankers that the pricing may be getting extravagant and the leveraging excessive.'
Fortune, January 1984

New depths of debt

The gobbling frenzy is increasing alarmingly the burden of debt, as companies or groups of individuals increase their borrowings for the purpose.

In 1984 in the US, the debt of non-financial companies rose by $176 billion to some $1,300 billion.

Liabilities of the top 500 US industrial companies as a percentage of assets

1960	35
1984	55

Short-term debt of non-financial US companies as a percentage of total debt

1960	30
1985 (end of 1st quarter)	52

Interest payments of non-financial US companies as a percentage of cash flow

1960	8
1985 (end of 1st quarter)	20

GROWTH OR DECLINE

No man is an island

Sales penetration by foreign-owned companies, 1978, percentages

percentage shareholding to qualify as control
percentage sales penetration by foreign-controlled companies

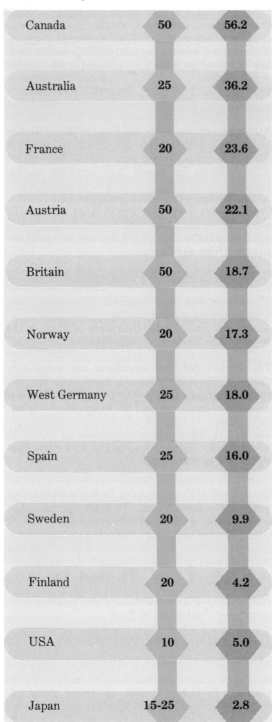

Canada	50	56.2
Australia	25	36.2
France	20	23.6
Austria	50	22.1
Britain	50	18.7
Norway	20	17.3
West Germany	25	18.0
Spain	25	16.0
Sweden	20	9.9
Finland	20	4.2
USA	10	5.0
Japan	15-25	2.8

CONGLOMERATES

Geographic diversification can only go so far. But the opportunities for product diversification are almost limitless, and the thrust toward it is often irresistible.

Beyond a certain point, a diversifying company becomes a conglomerate, active in a number of unrelated or only barely related sectors, and often with the bulk of its operations in no particular one. Conglomerates are on the increase.

Composition of the top 500 US industrial companies, percentage of companies

	1950	1960	1970	1980
single businesses	26	10	9	-
dominant businesses	23	34	39	21
related businesses	28	38	37	45
conglomerates	4	7	15	34

Composition of the top 200 British companies, percentage of companies

	1950	1960	1970	1980
single businesses	35	21	11	9
dominant businesses	41	41	30	26
related businesses	20	31	50	47
conglomerates	4	7	9	18

■ a single business gets no less than 95 per cent of its sales income from one basic business
■ a dominant business gets 71-95 per cent from one major constituent
■ a related business gets no more than 70 per cent from any one of its constituents
■ a conglomerate gets no more than 70 per cent of its sales income from any one series of related businesses

THE BOARDROOM
M·E·N·U

Fruit Cocktail	*Del Monte fruits by Reynolds Tobacco*
Spaghetti Bolognaise	*pasta by Grace; meatballs by Volvo*
Fish	*by Imperial Tobacco Group*

Beef	*by Volkswagen*
Ham	*by Ling-Temco-Vought*
Turkey	*by Greyhound*
Artichokes	*by Purex*
Carrots	*by Tenneco*
Potatoes	*by Boeing*
Spring salad	*lettuce by Dow Chemicals*
	tomatoes by Gulf & Western
Mushrooms	*by Clorox*

Cheeseboard	*by Grand Metropolitan*
Swedish Crispbread	*by Sandoz*
Chocolate Cream Pie	*by ITT*
Strawberries	*by Walt Disney Productions*
Terry's Chocolates	*by Colgate Palmolive*

Chateau Latour	*by Pearson*
Chateau Rausan	*by Lonrho*

CHARMED CIRCLE

As a group, big business is secure. The bigger the business, the more secure it is likely to be. Despite depressions, war, conquests, many big businesses have shown themselves scarcely less resilient than the nation state.

Only 30 of the top 500 industrial companies in the US in 1980 did not exist 25 years before. Going back even further, of the top 10 industrial companies in 1982, four were already there 53 years previously, and three 65 years previously.

Fortune's favourites

The top 500 US industrial companies, 1955 and 1980

	1980's top 500 in 1955	1955's top 500 in 1980
on the list	262	262
too small	147	29
absorbed by merger	-	185
privately held	35	6
not industrial	26	14
out of business	-	4
not yet formed	30	-

The longer run

The top ten US industrial companies by sales, 1917-83

1917	1929	1945	1955	1966	1979	1983
US Steel	Standard Oil (NJ)	General Motors	General Motors	General Motors	Exxon	Exxon
Swift	General Motors	US Steel	Standard Oil (NJ)	Ford	General Motors	General Motors
Armour	Ford	Standard Oil (NJ)	Ford	Standard Oil (NJ), later Exxon	Mobil	Mobil
American Smelting	US Steel	General Electric	US Steel	General Electric	Ford	Texaco
Standard Oil (NJ)	Swift	Bethlehem Steel	General Electric	Chrysler	Texaco	Ford
Bethlehem Steel	Armour	Swift	Swift	Mobil	Standard Oil (California), later Socal	IBM
Ford	Standard Oil (Indiana)	Armour	Chrysler	Texaco	Gulf Oil	Socal
Du Pont	General Electric	Curtiss-Wright	Armour	US Steel	IBM	Du Pont
American Sugar	Western Electric	Chrysler	Gulf Oil	IBM	General Electric	Gulf Oil
General Electric	Chrysler	Ford	Socony-Vacuum, later Mobil	Gulf Oil	Standard Oil (Indiana)	Standard Oil (Indiana)

BIG WOUNDS

Not all businesses, of course, make money. And some big businesses may record big losses.

The ten biggest loss-makers, inside and out

Among the top 500 industrial companies outside the US, 1984

YPF, Argentina (petroleum)	*$3.6 b
Renault, France (motor vehicles and parts)	*$1.4 b
Sacilor, France (steel)	*$920 m
Usinor, France (steel)	*$846 m
British Steel, Britain (steel)	*$382 m
Texaco, Britain (petroleum)	$367 m
British Shipbuilders, Britain (shipbuilding)	*$346 m
EFIM, Italy (metal manufacturing)	*$324 m
Michelin, France (rubber, plastic products)	*$256 m
Adam Opel, West Germany (motor vehicles and parts)	$244 m

*also lost money in 1983

Among the top 500 US industrial companies, 1985:

LTV (metals)	*$724 m
AMAX (mining, petroleum)	*$621 m
Diamond Shamrock (petroleum, refining)	$605 m
Union Carbide (chemicals)	$581 m
Control Data (computers)	$568 m
International Harvester (vehicles)	*$364 m
BF Goodrich (rubber products)	$355 m
Warner-Lambert (pharmaceuticals)	$316 m
Wheeling-Pittsburgh Steel (metals)	*$303 m
Reynolds Metals (metals)	$292 m

*also lost money in 1984

Individually, all-businesses are vulnerable. But some businesses are just too important - in strategic areas of employment or technology - for them to be allowed to die.

THE SOFTER THE FALL

Massey-Ferguson

Massey-Ferguson is no street corner business. It was – and is still claimed to be – the world's largest producer of tractors and second largest producer of combine harvesters.

In the mid-1970s, the company was riding high. Then came the deepest and most protracted downturn in the farm machinery business since the 1930s. For farm machines are durable, and cautious farmers, hit by the rising costs of money, fertilizer and fuel, or by the falling price of agricultural produce, could defer replacement purchases almost indefinitely.

Massey-Ferguson's declining sales, 1976-83

	agricultural tractors	combine harvesters	industrial tractors
1976	849,300	87,100	62,400
1983	611,600	46,100	34,900
decline	28%	47%	44%

Furthermore, while the market shrank, competition grew from national producers fighting for market share with price cuts. For Massey-Ferguson, disastrous year followed disastrous year.

Massey-Ferguson losses, 1977-84, $ million

1978	167.5
1979	35.4
1980	199.7
1981	194.8
1982	413.2
1983	110.0
1984	68.0

Few, if any, companies could sustain such losses. But Massey-Ferguson was too important in too many countries: as a producer of strategic industrial equipment, as an employer, and not least as a debtor, to be left to die.

In January 1981, the company was rescued from collapse with a $579 million package put together by bankers, with the involvement of the Canadian and British governments.

In June 1982, the company was for a second time forced to suspend payments on its accumulated debts to twenty-four US and Canadian banks. One US banker commented that he didn't know why the company had ever bothered to resume payments, since 'they need the money more than we do'.

In March 1983, a further rescue operation was mounted which involved the Canadian, British and French governments as well as numerous banks, and which was estimated to be worth some $600 million.

Meanwhile, since 1976, Massey-Ferguson has:
■ cut its worldwide employment from 68,000 to 25,000
■ sold or closed permanently 35 manufacturing plants
■ reduced manufacturing space by about 40 per cent
■ divested itself of peripheral businesses
■ reorganized so as to concentrate production on its four core businesses: tractors in Britain and France; combine harvesters in Canada; diesel engines in Britain; industrial machinery in Britain.

```
Massey-Ferguson

Toronto
rank in top 500 non-US
industrial companies 327
sales $1.5 billion
loss $68 million
workers 23,751

(1984)
```

DOWN AND OUT

The incidence of business failure increases markedly during recessions. At such times, problems that might otherwise be capable of a solution may become overwhelming.

Some of the seemingly most successful businesses can stumble - spectacularly - and sometimes there is no one to lend a helping hand.

The tumbling House of Esch

Horst Dieter Esch created IBH (Internationale Baumaschinen Holding) in 1975. By 1983, IBH was the third or fourth largest building machinery

company in the world, with 7 per cent of the market - behind Caterpillar, 50 per cent; Komatsu 17 per cent; and slugging it out with J I Case.

Major shareholders in the House of Esch, percentages

General Motors, US	**19.6**
Dallah Establishment, Saudi Arabia	**19.6**
Powell Duffryn, Britain	**13.2**
Babcock International, Britain	**10.1**
Schröder Münchmeyer, West Germany	**9.1**
Horst Dieter Esch, West Germany	**8.6**

The dream was: a worldwide company built from medium-sized independents and parts of the majors, acquired for little, and rationalized to avoid duplication.

The reality was built from:
■ The longest and deepest slump in the construction market in living memory: between 1979 and 1983, the demand for major products fell 30-50 per cent; between 1979 and 1982, US shipments of bulldozers fell from 20,000 to 8,000; cutbacks in public works made the Yacutreta hydro dam (on the Parana River between Argentina and Paraguay) the only new major construction project in the world.
■ The growth of Japanese competition from Komatsu, Hitachi and Mitsubishi.
■ The failure to take drastic rationalization measures immediately after each takeover. In some markets, three IBH brands of wheeled loaders competed against one another as well as their 'real' competitors. Sales personnel used to dealing in one type of market were not trained to extend into others.
■ A failure to win over the big German banks which forced IBH to rely on, and almost bring down, the relatively small Schröder, Münchmeyer, Hengst (SMH), a Frankfurt private bank.

'On Tuesday, 2 November [1983], I flew home from New York without the faintest idea that anything was wrong.'
Horst Dieter Esch

On landing in Frankfurt, Esch learned that SMH had been taken over the previous day by a consortium of banks. The takeover had the blessing of the German regulatory authorities, who were aghast at its overexposure to IBH.

4 November

Other German banks withdrew IBH's remaining lines of credit.

5 November

IBH applied for court protection from its creditors, and one by one its foreign subsidiaries toppled into bankruptcy.

November 1984

Horst Dieter Esch was charged in Frankfurt with breach of trust and contravention of company law. He was subsequently sentenced to three and a half years in jail.

January 1986

Two former partners of SMH were found guilty of fraud, and one former senior employee was found guilty of aiding and abetting, in connexion with the bank's links to IBH.

'In the 1950s, Esch would have been one of those creating the economic miracle, and we would probably have been proud of him. Times change.'
Senior Frankfurt banker

Sinking ships

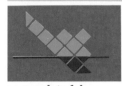 In August 1985, Sanko Steamship, the world's largest operator of oil tankers, became Japan's biggest-ever bankruptcy. In the years 1983-85, it had accumulated losses of 168 billion yen ($715 million), and its total debts by the end of July 1985, to banks and financial institutions alone, were at least 520 billion yen ($2.2 billion).

Hit by the world slump in shipping, Sanko had managed to weather one storm after the other, perhaps because its principal stockholder was the minister for external economic relations. But when the government refused to continue subsidizing shipping by buying all the surplus oil tankers, the banks opened the hatches; they were too exposed already. Loans to Sanko by Daiwa Bank alone amounted to 90 billion yen ($383 million), six times the bank's net annual profit and close to 2 per cent of its total loan portfolio.

The banks had to write off such losses. But still more seriously hit, in such troubled times for the shipping market, were the foreign shipowners from whom Sanko chartered many of its 263 ships and who could expect virtually no compensation.

MAKE OR BREAK

RULES

The game is played with one die and by two or more people. Within reason, the more who play, the better the game.

Each player starts from the square in the centre with 100 points from the bank. The winner is the player who, while in possession of at least 200 points, first throws a six and can exit, through one of the passages marked, into the Fortune Top 50 or into Government Protection.

A player who lands on a Make square (coloured green) receives 20 points from the bank; a player who lands on a Break square (coloured red) surrenders 10 points to the bank; and a player who lands on a Restructuring square (coloured amber) pays 5 points to the player on the right.

A player may move only horizontally or vertically, unless moving to a square already occupied, when a diagonal movement is also allowed.

A player who moves to a square already occupied takes 25 points from the occupier; sends the occupier back to the start; and may ignore any instruction on the relevant square.

Since players possess no security, they may not borrow from one another or from the bank. A player without the points to meet any liability is accordingly bankrupt and out of the game.

GAMES

GOVERNMENT PROTECTION

Cheap imports flood market		Military use found for product
	Main product matures	Loss of biggest customer
	Industry giant notices competition	High dollar raises foreign debt burden
Strikes for shorter working week	Labour shakeouts tame unions	Industry leader slashes prices
Trade unions accept wage freeze	Managing Director turns Buddhist	
Friendly politician indicted for corruption		Energy boom collapses
Inflationary wage settlement		Russia orders hi-tech equipment
	New product found unsafe	Dumping measures hit export sales
Populist regime in major market	Scarcity of key components	Price war erupts
Auditors query accounts	Advertising campaign misfires	Foreign war feeds sales

	Health scare hits sales		Bank lends more against better judgement		R & D costs out of control		Revalued currency hits exports
	Defence Department tests supplies		Market hit by recession	New technology displaces traditional producers		State subsidy negotiated	Costs of bribery increase
Sole survivor of national hi-tech industry	Boardroom row	Foreign giant links with domestic rival	Monetarist government under electoral pressure		Company faces product liability suits	Interest rates leap	
	Industry leader raises prices	Faulty product recalled		Critical comment in financial press			Import restrictions imposed
Low-cost foreign producer starts	Green protest threatens operations	Expansion into textiles	Slump hits major customers		Foreign competitors dump		Main shareholder dies intestate
Expansion causes cash flow crisis		**START**			Widely used product legalized	Under-bidding proves costly	
	Whizz-kid director killed in plane crash	Foreign bills unpaid	Cash crisis follows takeover spree	Toxic prawns served at AGM	Price-fixing ring uncovered		Stock market booms
US vetoes hi-tech exports to Russia		Chief rival's spies stung		Property market boils over		US veto on hi-tech exports vetoed	
Falling currency helps exports	Company moves to grander head-quarters	Distress sale of inventory	Computer code broken	Foreign import tariffs lowered	IMF imposes austerity programme	Sales tax raised	Public spending cut
	China offers joint venture	Cartel talks fail	Coal strike strengthens nuclear lobby		Head of Defence Purchases sacked	Explosion at main chemical plant	
	Company sued for discriminatory practices		Directors indicted for insider trading	Bank refuses further loans		Rights issue flops	Rich states decide to reflate

GOVERNMENT PROTECTION

'One should start looking for alternative ways to reduce the debt burden of developing countries . . . or those countries with large endowments of natural resources or profitable state-owned enterprises; the sale of some national assets to creditors is certainly an option worth considering.'
   Dr Fritz Leutwiler, chairman of the board of directors and president of the Bank for International Settlements, Basle, 1983

Extracts from the BMP Journal,
September - December 1991

BUSINESS MONEY AND POWER

BMP JOURNAL
The Takeover of Romania

International		25
Romania 62	USSR	16
Switzerland 13	Albania	51
Netherlands 87	UK	
US	47	Kuwait 10
Algeria 16		

ROMANIA
IN LIQUIDITY
CRISIS
Paul Ziegler, Zurich, Friday
Bankers here are showing increasing concern at the steep fall in Romania's credit rating. In the past week, the free market new leu has dropped from 2,070 to 4,630 to the US dollar, and Moody's has dropped Romania's credit rating from triple B to C-.

Adversity and opportunity in Roma

Attempts by Romania's management to force an unconditional return to work are understandable but, given the current fragility of the business, are ill-considered.

A combination of bad luck and bad judgement has reduced a once prosperous operation to near bankruptcy. Romania's strategy of concentrating on capital goods production to the exclusion of nearly everything else always seemed risky. But its decision to build at enormous cost a petrochemical subsidiary, despite clear indications that its oil reserves were rapidly running out, was asking for trouble.

Romania might none the less have won through, were it not for the current depression which has made idle some 47 per cent of world intermediate goods capacity, and 62 per cent of such capacity in its medium-sized units.

Given sufficient management skill and support from outside, Romania might still avoid liquidation. Even heavily discounted in real terms, Romania's gleaming new assets are currently worth three to four times their market value. Furthermore, its management is tough and experienced in settling labour disputes at home and in steering a clever, competitive course abroad.

The immediate danger is that the USSR will take advantage of Romania's current difficulties and make an unwelcome bid for the operation. There are reports of intense discussions having taken place between the Kremlin board with their Swiss advisers, and a minority faction of Romania's. Whether well-founded or not, such reports ought to prompt Western firms to mount a counterbid, on less onerous terms perhaps, for the faltering, but still basically sound, Romanian business.

BOARDROOM ROW IN BUCHAREST

Martin Zanuc, Bucharest, Monday

At an extraordinary meeting of the Romanian board last night, directors representing the controlling family interest were outvoted and forced to resign. The remaining members elected Stefan Georgescu as Chairman with a mandate to solve the firm's liquidity crisis and, as a matter of urgency, to open negotiations with foreign banks for a new line of credit. One board member in an exclusive interview said: 'This is a sad day, but we had no choice.'

The boardroom changes came as no surprise. Chairman Nastase has been held personally responsible for the fateful decision to build the huge petrochemical facilities. Romania is now a net importer of oil, making its petrochemical products among the most costly in the world. The Communist Party holding company has been forced to accept regular cuts in the dividend, and was told only last month that this year's payment was to be passed altogether.

Crucial in the boardroom decision was the desertion from the Chairman's camp of the director representing the employees' pension fund. The problem remains: Romania needs a renewed and enlarged line of credit from the banking system. The Governor of the Bank of England has flown to Basle for his usual meeting with colleagues of the Bank for International Settlements.

Western consortium in bid for Romania

Our economics editor, Thursday

At a press conference called hurriedly at midnight in the Hofstatter, Dusseldorf, a representative of the Deutsche Bank announced the formation of an international consortium to bid for a minority shareholding in Romania. The bid comes in response to yesterday's offer of US $16 billion by the USSR for a 51 per cent stake in the equity.

The Dusseldorf Consortium consists of 87 banks led by Deutsche Bank, Morgan Guaranty, Barclays International, Union Bank of Switzerland and Algemene Bank of the Netherlands, together with Royal Dutch Shell, General Electric of the US, Hitachi, BAT Industries, and the Kuwaiti Investment Office.

No further details are currently available.

Romania joins the Fortune 1,000

Gerry Rombold, New York, Friday

An unintended result of last September's successful takeover, by the Dusseldorf Club, of a controlling minority stake in Romania is the firm's inclusion in Fortune's new listing of the world's top 1,000 industrial corporations.

The investment of $16 billion, plus a yet undisclosed amount in loans, enabled Romania to climb out of its liquidity crisis, to rationalize its operations by closing its petrochemicals subsidiary, and to take over the core operations of Albania, just at a time when the world market was pulling out of its worst ever depression.

Romania weighs in at no. 13 on the new Fortune list, with sales of $57.8 billion (1990), assets of $63.2 billion, net income of $2.1 billion and a payroll of 10.1 million.

The Dusseldorf Club, with 33.3 per cent of stockholders' equity, has not yet exercised its option to raise its stake to 51 per cent.

Ousted chairman flies to Moscow

Our special correspondent, Percival Chambers, reports, Tuesday

Sources close to the Kremlin have revealed that ex-Chairman Nastase of Romania is in lengthy talks with the Politbureau. In broadest outline, the Kremlin appears prepared to offer a substantial rouble credit line and 25 million tonnes of oil a year for ten years, in return for 51 per cent of the Romanian equity.

Romani

3

MARKETS
AND
MARKETING

Markets are made whenever and wherever un-committed buyers regularly pay - usually with money; sometimes with goods - for something provided by uncommitted sellers. The exchange takes place at a price which neither party can better in the circumstances.

There is an enormous variety of markets. Some markets are very competitive, while in others competition is more limited.

Markets, like businesses, may grow, decline or even disappear. Some markets - such as the labour market - are very old. Others, especially that for electronics, are new but have grown spectacularly in a very short time.

The discovery of new markets and the exploitation of existing ones is the business of marketing, which promotes the image of companies as well as the appeal of products.

YOU NAME IT

There is a market for virtually everything.

■ For the 70 tonnes of water-soluble paper exported every year by Mishima Paper of Japan: bought, it is thought, by the world's spies.

■ For brides and concubines, such as the 750 women from Yunnan province in China, recovered in 1982 from distant Shandong and Henan provinces.

■ For bridegrooms, 500 of whom were kidnapped to order, in spring 1982, in Bihar state, India, when the going rate for dowries soared beyond what fathers of eligible daughters were able or willing to pay.

■ For future legacies, as at the Auction Mart, London, where H E Foster & Cranfield, established 1843, conduct monthly sales of 'reversionary property' receivable on the death of the testator or testatrix.

■ For 'grannies' who will queue, or stand in line, for goods in short supply, as in Warsaw where they charge the equivalent of $3-$5 a week.

■ For human eggs 'and a little use of her uterus', as in the surrogate mother business, by which the host mother gets $12,000 of a $17,000 fee for conceiving, developing, giving birth to - and losing - the child of a strange man married to a sterile woman.

■ For 'burials' in space, at $50,000 for a 2-kg parcel of remains launched in permanent orbit or $3,900 for a 30-gram sample in a gold-plated casket, to be put in orbit for a guaranteed 63 million years.

■ For the right to run a trouble-free shareholders' meeting in Tokyo, where half the companies listed on the stock exchange pay the Sokaiya - professional disrupters of corporations - a fee to facilitate proceedings or not to obstruct them.

■ For state decorations and service medals in the USSR, despite the punishment of up to one year in a labour camp for first offenders and three years in jail for persistent dealers. Major political decorations, such as the Order of the Red Star, change hands for half a rouble; Tsarist service medals, for more than a hundred roubles.

■ For the handcuffs, ankle straps, body belts, canvas jackets and padded cells used in prisons and mental institutions.

■ For computerized astrology; Future Forecasts, a leading firm, has shops in Los Angeles and London.

■ For insurance against kidnap and ransom, with the value of premiums worldwide at an estimated $75 million. One company, Control Risks, fields a team of 30 specialists, most with a military or police background, to deal with extortion attempts, and provides an information service to clients on the likely terrorist threat in different countries.

■ For after-births. Some 15 tonnes a day of human placenta, from 5,000 hospitals in 30 countries, are processed into disease-fighting blood derivatives at the Institut Mérieux, a French medical group 50.2 per cent owned by the chemical company Rhône-Poulenc. The main source of the placenta is the US, with some 400 tonnes a year (670,000 births), followed by France (350 tonnes), the UK (300 tonnes), the USSR and West Germany.

■ For butterflies, to meet the demand from local authorities and conservationists. The Guernsey Butterfly Farm, with estimated production of 100,000 butterflies in 1985, has other production facilities in Jersey and Britain. In 1983, the value of overall production was £850,000. Tropical varieties of butterfly cost £2 or £3 an insect.

■ For equipment to survive the apocalypse. The survival business, worth more than $150 million in the US alone, offers a Bacterial Warfare Clothing Set (up to 7 days' protection) for $14.50; a Portable Chemical Toilet ('an absolute must') for $44.50; a PVS-100 Starlight Weapon Scope, for shooting by moonlight, at $3,250.

THE LABOUR MARKET

The largest market of all is the market for labour and skills. It is a primary market: an essential source of business profit and of the revenues by which the state lives. Its very size reflects the high and increasing specialization of its components.

The labour market is segmented by scope as well as skill.

There are international labour markets, in which jobs are brought to people; people stream to jobs; and jobs and people are brought together at particular sites – with total disregard for geography, national frontiers or local custom.

There are national labour markets, in which the terms of sale and purchase are partly governed by legislation affecting wages and conditions.

There are local labour markets, in which choices are much more limited and the terms of trade are set by locally powerful people.

In most of these market segments, potential workers (the sellers) and potential employers (the buyers) deal with each other directly. In some the sellers are intermediaries, inserting themselves between the potential workers and employers; they are trade unions or, more commonly, specialist businesses: labour-contractors, labour-brokers, headhunters, bodysnatchers and government departments.

THE STOCK MARKET

At the other end of the market spectrum is the stock market, where business itself is bought and sold.

It is in the stock markets:
■ that the value of a business is assessed through the price of its shares
■ that shifts in control over a business are accomplished through the purchase or sale of shares
■ that a business, or a state, raises new funds and tests its support in the broader business community, by selling shares or bonds at a given price
■ that speculation and gambling take place legitimately.

Stock markets, however, do not always fulfil all these functions; and in so far as they do so they are not unique. Their character is changing: they are becoming more volatile, and along with business itself, increasingly international.

Home to stock markets

Stock markets do not reflect the size of their domestic economies. In some countries, like West Germany, much of the finance for investment flows directly from banks to other businesses, without the mediation of the market; in others, like the USSR, finance derives directly from retained profits and taxes.

Estimated total value of stock market shares, October 1985, $ billion

Europe	700
Britain	302
West Germany	118
Switzerland	63
France	58
Italy	45
Netherlands	42
other	72
Japan	731
USA	1,783

Proportion of adult population owning ordinary shares (equities), 1985 percentages

Britain	14
Japan	16
West Germany	17
France	17
USA	19
Sweden	20
Hong Kong	35

The heavy brigade: pensions and insurance move in

Stock markets are changing in character and conduct. In general, private investors are losing market share to institutions, such as pension funds and insurance companies.

Pension funds dispose of huge and growing financial resources through the retained and postponed wages of business employees; insurance companies, through the growing number of those seeking professional management of their savings.

Market shares, London Stock Market, percentages

	1963	1975	1981
private shareholders	54.0	37.5	28.0
pension funds	6.5	17.0	27.0
insurance companies	10.0	16.0	21.0
unit trusts	1.0	4.0	4.0
investment trusts and other financial companies	11.0	11.0	7.0
other*	17.5	14.5	13.0

* (including industrial and commercial companies, banks, charities, public sector, etc)

Apart from the growing power that this gives the institutions, it increases the volatility of the market. Professional managers of funds, all too aware that they are judged on their performance, follow one another in a veritable stampede, so as not to be left behind by a shift in the market.

The volatility is increased by the growing importance of professional traders who operate on a very short term basis and are similarly given to the herd instinct. This behaviour has already acquired a principle in the maxim sported by New York stock traders: 'The Trend is Your Friend'.

A distressed New York stockbroker was about to end it all when he heard a quiet voice say: 'Cheer up, my friend. Things could be worse.'

So he cheered up - and sure enough, things got worse.

Tides across the frontiers

Huge flows of investment money exist outside the countries of their origin and move both rapidly and anonymously from one refuge to another, often through the stock markets. This flow has increasingly been joined by direct institutional and individual diversification into foreign stocks. US pension funds, for instance, increased their investments abroad from $15 billion at the end of 1984 to over $25 billion at the end of 1985.

One notable manifestation has been the emergence of 'The Nifty Fifty', a collection of major companies in various countries, which attract large sums of migrating money and show the impact in disproportionately high prices because their size promotes confidence. Overall, some 500 companies are listed on at least one stock exchange outside their home country.

Another manifestation is the growing power of the international security-dealing houses, organized in the Zurich-based Association of International Bond Dealers or the London-based International Securities Regulatory Organization, which are influential enough to threaten the sovereignty of the national exchanges.

COMPETITIVE MARKETS

No two markets are the same, though some may bear outward similarities. There is competition in the motor vehicle market, the market for steel, and the cigarette market: in the vehicle market, sellers compete with one another on price as well as everything else; in the steel market, they also compete on price, while claiming that they do not; in the cigarette market, producers compete, for the most part, in everything but price.

Motor vehicles

Currently in the throes of worldwide upheaval is the motor vehicle market, a fiercely competitive market crucial to the world business system. Of the world's 50 largest industrial companies, 11 are motor vehicle manufacturers.

Buffeted since 1973 by large rises in the price of oil, by a slump unprecedented since the 1930s, by a surge in new suppliers and tremendous changes in production technology, the motor vehicle market has changed from being a series of loosely connected national markets to a truly global market, in which, outside of the specialty car sector, the overriding need is for vastly increased volume to spread fixed costs.

In the early 1970s, big national markets were supplied primarily by big national producers. By the 1980s, the biggest national markets - with the notable exceptions of Japan and the USSR - had been invaded by foreign companies abroad and at home. Many established producers went under; others (such as British Leyland in Britain and Chrysler in the US) stared bankruptcy in the face and had to be rescued.

The Americans, primarily Ford, had been manufacturing cars abroad for a long time. But it was the Japanese who did most to create the world market. With cars selling for $1,300 to $1,700 less than those of the established US or European producers, Japanese exports swelled in the 1970s.

The established producers tried to choke off the flow with controls: export restraint agreements, market share agreements, tariffs and quotas. The Japanese countered by setting up manufacturing and assembly plants in their competitors' home markets.

The established producers met the Japanese advance with a gigantic modernization programme. Halfway through the $150 billion binge - $80 billion in Europe (1980-87) and $70 billion in the US (1980-85) - after plants have been closed, workers sacked, wages and overheads sheared, they could claim considerable success. Chrysler's breakeven point was reduced from 2.4 million vehicles a year in 1979 to 1.1 million in 1983; Ford's, from 4.2 million to 2.5 million; General Motors', from over 5.5 million to 4.3 million.

The stronger amongst them also took steps to assert a world presence. They set up, or bought into, production facilities abroad, to produce a network of worldwide collaborative ventures against, as well as with, the Japanese.

Even the relatively small - Mercedes Benz, Volvo, Honda - were pressed to operate on a world scale, and found that they were enabled to do so by the trend in production technology.

The development of a world vehicle market provides opportunities for new producers in poor countries and in the Eastern bloc where governments are eager to promote exports of cars and components and to promote feeder industries in steel, rubber, glass, plastics, metal working and ceramics. For their part, the car giants are eager to lodge in any and every space available in the world market. Companies and governments are getting together more and more.

The top ten motor vehicle makers, 1984

Production, millions

General Motors (US)	6.5
Ford (US)	3.9
Toyota (Japan)	2.3
Volkswagen (West Germany)	1.9
Nissan (Japan)	1.8
Fiat (Italy)	1.4
Renault (France)	1.3
Peugeot (France)	1.2
Chrysler (US)	1.2
Honda (Japan)	1.0
total	22.5

The world car park

World car and truck production, millions

1972	35.8
1983	40.4

Shares in the world car park: 1

World car and truck production, percentages

	1972	1984	change
Japan	17.6	27.2	+55
USA	31.6	25.8	−18
West Germany	10.4	9.5	−10
France	9.2	7.3	−21
USSR	3.9	5.2	+33
Italy	5.0	3.8	−24
Canada	3.9	4.3	+10
UK	6.4	2.6	−59
Spain	2.0	3.1	+55
Belgium	0.8	2.1	+163
Brazil	1.7	1.9	+12
other	7.3	7.3	0

Shares in the world car park: 2

World car and truck production, percentages

	1972	1983	change
rich West (including Japan)	85.9	70.1	−18.4
Eastern bloc	4.3	6.8	+58.1
other (notably Brazil and South Korea)	9.8	23.1	+135.7

Foreign shares of car registrations

Imports and foreign-controlled domestic production, percentages

	1973	1984
UK	67.3	82.2
Italy	26.8	37.0
West Germany	42.0	58.6
France	31.2	35.9
USA	13.5	27.3
Japan	1.2	1.4

A rising tide of moving steel

▉ World car exports as a percentage of world production
▉ Japan's car exports as a percentage of its world exports.

1972	27.8	18.5
1973	26.4	18.5
1974	30.6	22.3
1975	29.9	25.0
1976	32.4	28.5
1977	32.2	30.3
1978	31.9	30.8
1979	32.4	31.2
1980	34.2	40.8
1981	32.6	43.4
1982	35.9	39.7
1983	33.6	38.4

Japan's share of selected car markets abroad, 1981

	hurdles	%
Europe		
Spain	high tariffs, quotas	0.1
Italy	pre-EEC quota	0.1
France	imposed market share limit	2.6
Portugal	high tariffs, quotas,	12.6
West Germany	minimum domestic content export restraint agreement	9.7
UK	market share agreement	11.0
Benelux	export restraint agreement	24.5
North America		
USA	export restraint agreement	21.8
Canada	export restraint agreement	13.2

'Abolition of restrictions on Japanese car imports into France, Italy and the UK would reduce car prices in these countries by between 10 and 22 per cent - and put 46,000 domestic car workers out of a job.'
Netherlands Economics Institute, 1984

Bonsai roots abroad

'We must not engage in deluge-like exports: we must not be disliked.'

Shoichiro Toyoda, president, Toyota Motors

1980

Nissan buys 36 per cent of Motor Iberica SA, Barcelona (later raised to 70 per cent) as Spain readies itself for entry into the EEC. Europe's first Japanese-controlled motor company. Production starts in 1983.

Nissan reveals plans for $660 million truck plant on greenfield site in Smyrna, Tennessee. Largest overseas industrial investment from Japan to date.

Nissan agrees joint venture with Alfa Romeo, Italy, for 60,000 small passenger cars (production 1983).

1981

Nissan announces plans for 200,000-a-year car plant in Britain.

1982

Honda spends $250 million on new 150,000 car plant in Marysville, Ohio.

Suzuki wins contract from Udyog Maruti to make small cars and vans in India.

1983

Toyota signs joint venture agreement with General Motors to make 200,000 small cars at Fremont, California.

Toyota invests $243 million in 45 per cent of new car plant in Taiwan.

Nissan's $120 million plant at Aguascalientes, Mexico, comes on stream.

1984

Honda Motors unveils plans to double Marysville plant by 1988 at further cost of $240 million.

Nissan talks with Chinese, over $100 million joint venture with the Second Automobile Works to produce 20,000 Nissan 8-ton trucks a year at a new plant to be built in Hubei province, central China.

Mazda announces plans to assemble compact cars at an idled Ford plant in Michigan.

1985 (January to August)

Honda announces agreement to build an engine manufacturing plant at Swindon, England, to be followed by full car production.

Mitsubishi Motors and Chrysler agree to joint production of American small cars in the mid-West from 1988.

Akebono Brake and General Motors agree to establish a joint venture for making brakes and other components in the US. Production to start in 1987.

Nippondesco, leading Japanese manufacturer of electronic equipment for cars, announces a major expansion of its US production capacity.

Trojan horse-trading

'When I went to Europe in 1983, the British Secretary of Trade and Industry expressed a wish to see me. I asked him bluntly, "You are very eagerly inviting Nissan to advance into Britain. This is very strange to me. What is your reason?"

'He answered in the following way: "Nissan has acquired very new production technology. Nissan is capable of developing highly innovative models. Nissan has high productivity. It has good labour-management relations. Everything is an object of envy for us. We want you to set up your operation in Britain to demonstrate not only to our automakers but also to other industries these aspects of Japanese industrial management."

'When I heard this, I thought in my mind: "Of all things, they just want us to be a tutor at their home. If we are to be that… they should pay us our return air fare, our expenses during our stay in Britain and a very big salary." They are expecting too much in asking us to tutor them at our own expense.'

Katsuji Kawamata, chairman, Nissan motor company

'GM has welcomed the deal [with Toyota] as a way of learning more about Japanese methods - the plant will be run by Toyota and the car based on a Japanese design'

Financial Times

Steel

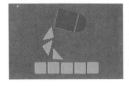

Furious competition on a world scale has swept through the steel market, which is an industry largely regulated by the state.

Aunt Agatha

Dear Aunt Agatha,

The world business in steel is getting out of all control. In 1950, just under 200 million tonnes were produced in 23 countries. Now it is more like 700 million tonnes being turned out by 76 countries.

Steel imports into our country rose by more than half in 1984, to a record 26 million tonnes, or 26.4 per cent of our domestic market; up from 16 million tonnes and 13.4 per cent in 1974. We used to ship steel to the world. Now the world is shipping steel to us. And if you don't believe that we are in serious trouble, allow me to tell you that Wheeling-Pittsburgh, the seventh largest US steel company, was forced in April 1985 to file for protection against its creditors. It had run up losses of $59.4 million in 1984. For 1985, its losses were no less than $303 million.

It is not as though we have not done our best to be efficient. Jobs in the US industry have fallen from some 450,000 in the late 'seventies to about half that number today. Wheeling-Pittsburgh itself undertook an aggressive modernization programme, at a cost of over $500 million in the five years to 1983. And where did this get it?

We in the US have cut our own production ruthlessly. Shipments of our own steel fell, in the three years 1982-84, from 89 million to 73 million tonnes. This is a level last reached in 1962. And we are still losing ground.

Moreover, we are up to our eyes in debt. Bethlehem Steel, one of our largest companies, lost $1.9 billion in the years 1982-85, and the ratio of its debt to its capital nearly doubled to a worrying 52 per cent. Even US Steel, which shut down more than 150 plants to reduce its capacity by around a third, is keeping its head above water only by the earnings from Marathon Oil, the company it acquired in 1982.

I love my business and I love my country. I am sick with worry. What should I do?

Yours appealingly,
Sam Steel

Dear Mr Steel,

You are in a very bad way. I know that you have tried hard. But you must try still harder. Your operations are, simply, not yet efficient enough. In Japan, 86 per cent of all steel is produced by the cost-cutting continuous casting process; in France and West Germany, over 60 per cent; in France and Britain, 45 per cent. In the US, it is still only 26 per cent.

You may say that you are already so deep in debt, you cannot find the money for investment in further efficiency. My answer is that you cannot afford not to find the money. Even with the dollar falling sharply from its over-valued level, your prices are still uncompetitive in the marketplace, because your costs are so high.

This is what you should be talking to your government about, and not pressing for restrictions on imports. You grew rich with free trade and are not likely to do better without it.

If all else fails, you should think about going into a different line of business. One is never too old to move on.

Yours truly,
Agatha

Dear Aunt Agatha,

I read the letter to you from Mr Steel and your very helpful reply, so I decided to write and tell you of our problems also.

We have spent a veritable fortune in subsidies - well over $25 billion - to meet losses, while we dieted our own steel industry into competitive shape.

Allow me to give you some figures.

Between 1974 and 1984, we cut crude steel output, in million tonnes, from:

53.2 to 39.4 in West Germany
27.0 to 19.0 in France
22.4 to 15.2 in Britain
16.2 to 11.3 in Belgium
 6.5 to 4.0 in Luxembourg
 5.9 to 5.8 in the Netherlands

In Italy, output rose slightly, from 23.8 to 24.0 million tonnes. But overall, we secured a cut for our seven major member producers, of 36.3 million tonnes, or 23.4 per cent of the 1974 figure.

The shake-out in labour throughout the industry has been even more ferocious:

21 per cent in Italy
25.5 per cent in the Netherlands
34.3 per cent in West Germany
41.6 per cent in Belgium
46.0 per cent in Luxembourg
46.1 per cent in France
68.2 per cent in Britain

And what is the result? We have a socially disruptive addition to the numbers of our unemployed. The Americans claim that we are dumping steel on them and run to their government shouting about the need for still further restricting our shipments; though we have already done all we could in the interest of protecting free trade. We have recently agreed to accept a limit of 5.4 per cent on our share of the US market. And we took a solemn decision to stop subsidizing our steel industries from the end of 1985. The Japanese dump steel on us and are joined by Brazilians, South Koreans, Taiwanese, in threatening our whole industry. What more can we do? We are at the end of our tether.

Yours in despair,
Baron EEC Commission

Dear Baron Commission,

It is difficult not to be moved by your letter. I wish I could help. But steel is, after all, a competitive market, however you may try to regulate it, and I cannot advise you on how to change the laws of economics.

You have done well, but not well enough. My own information is that you have been operating at an average 65 per cent of capacity and need to cut this capacity by another 25 million tonnes of production, for efficient and profitable functioning.

Keep to the rocky road you have chosen. It is the right one. And remember, it is always darkest before the dawn.

I do have one suggestion. Perhaps you should stop supplying the developing countries with new steel plants which only compete with your own. It may mean rejecting useful new orders now, but you must think of the future.

Yours with understanding,
Agatha

Dear Aunt Agatha,

It is not pleasant for a person to feel that he is everywhere disliked and feared, just because he is doing his best to make an honest living.

We have worked hard in Japan to get where we are in the world steel market and have had to fight against prejudices of every kind. We have tried to accommodate criticism, however unjust we have felt it to be. In 1984, we agreed to reduce our share of the US market from 6.3 per cent to 5.8 per cent. From the way the Americans were carrying on about us, it would have seemed as though we had half their market. Is it our fault that our steel is so much cheaper?

And it is not as though we are having an easy time of it. We have been banking down furnaces and working some of our plants at below 60 per cent of capacity.

Meanwhile, steel from South Korea, Taiwan and other so-called developing countries has begun pouring through our ports. South Korea is especially threatening to us. Please permit me to crave your patience for just four figures, on labour costs per tonne of steel in 1984. In the US, these were around $150; in Japan, just below $70; in the EEC, just below $60; and in South Korea, around $9.

You advised Baron Commission that he should stop selling plants to such countries, and we have taken the step of refusing to supply equipment for such plants, whatever the sacrifice in much-needed export orders. What else can we do?

Yours humbly,
N. Kokan Kawasaki

Dear Mr Kawasaki,

It is most unjust that you should be disliked and feared for the very success you have achieved by honest effort and an intelligent emphasis on efficiency in the steel business. But you must accept that human nature is far from perfect and that the defeated are often envious of the victors. Let them keep their envy, while you console yourself with your victory.

Of course, you are right to be anxious about the pressures coming from the so-called developing countries. But you must also accept that what is sauce for the goose is sauce for the gander. You have shown the way and cannot blame others for following you. Besides, there is still an abundance of opportunity, in this big wide world of ours. The developing countries as a whole still produce only two-thirds of the steel they need. There is a market there, for the truly efficient and enterprising.

You must get used to hearing the Americans complain. They need time to come to terms with the changing world. In the end, they have more to lose than to gain by risking a trade war.

With best wishes,
Yours sincerely,
Agatha

Dear Aunt Agatha,

Why is it that the poor and weak are always the first to be attacked? We are small, and the others are big, yet everybody blames us for the crisis in the steel business. The Americans are especially threatening. And the reason is not hard to find. They are inefficient, uncompetitive and frightened. Yet what sort of threat do we pose? We sold them a mere 1.7 million tonnes in 1983, and they made such a fuss that we have now been restricted to no more than 1.9 per cent of the US market. Is this free trade? The Europeans and even the Japanese now blame us for their own failures. Having made themselves rich, they want to keep other countries poor. What should we do?

We have borrowed money from international banks to develop a competitive modern economy, and now that we are competing, we are abused. If we do not compete, how are we to repay our debts? I am more and more worried.

Yours distractedly,
Steel Pohang

Dear Mr Pohang,

I shouldn't worry, if I were you. You are coming up fast from behind. Let those in front get the shingles. As for your debts, the banks will wait. If they pull out the plug, they will be the first down the drain.

Yours comfortingly,
Agatha

Cigarettes

Even more widespread than steel or cars, the cigarette market is truly universal, while at the same time being effectively controlled.

Its large number of private and state-run producers are dominated by the Big Six transnational tobacco companies; BAT Industries, R J Reynolds, Philip Morris, American Brands, Imperial Group and Rothmans International. These compete strongly amongst themselves and with others in many ways, but seldom, and only in passing, on price.

'A custom loathsome to the eye, hateful to the nose, harmful to the brain, dangerous to the lungs, and in the black stinking fume thereof, nearest resembling the horrible Stygian smoke of the pit that is bottomless.'
King James I of England, 1601-25

'A plague, a mischief, a violent purger of goods, land, health: hellish, devilish and damned tobacco, the devil and overthrow of body and soul'
Robert Burton, Anatomy of Melancholy, 1621

'On average a smoker shortens his lifespan by about 5.5 minutes for each cigarette smoked - not much less than the time he spends smoking it.'
Smoking or Health, Report from the Royal College of Physicians, London, 1977

'And if they (the health lobby) caused every smoker to smoke just one cigarette less a day, our company would stand to lose $92 million in sales annually. I assure you we don't intend to let that happen without a fight.'
William Hobbs, chairman, R J Reynolds

Coughing and wheezing across the Styx

Annual premature deaths in Britain, early 1980s

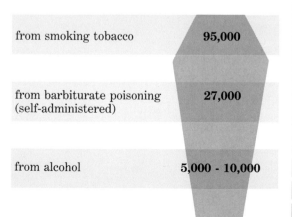

from smoking tobacco	95,000
from barbiturate poisoning (self-administered)	27,000
from alcohol	5,000 - 10,000

Smoking country

Cigarette production, by country

billion pieces, (1984)

state or private ownership, 1984

member(s) of Big Six with licensing agreement with local producer(s)

Country	billion pieces	ownership	Big Six
Albania	6.2	S	
Algeria	18.0	S	~
Angola	2.4	S	
Argentina	38.9	P	~
Australia	28.0	P	~
Austria	14.9	S	~
Bangladesh	14.7	P/S	~
Barbados	0.2	P	
Belgium/Luxembourg	27.7	P	~
Belize	0.1	P	
Bolivia	1.2	P	
Brazil	127.8	P	~
Bulgaria	72.5	S	~
Burkina	0.6	S	
Burma	2.7	S	
Cameroon	2.6	S	~
Canada	61.6	P	~
Canary Islands	30.0		—
Chile	8.2	P	
China	1,062.5	S	~
Colombia	23.4	P	
Congo	0.9	S	
Costa Rica	2.2	P	~
Cuba	30.0	S	
Cyprus	3.6	P	~
Czechoslovakia	26.0	S	~
Denmark	10.6	P	~
Dominican Republic	3.6	P	~

Country	Value		Country	Value	
Ecuador	5.0	P	Madagascar	2.4	S
Egypt	48.0	S	Malawi	1.4	P
El Salvador	2.5	P	Malaysia	14.7	P
Ethiopia	1.3	S	Malta	0.5	–
Fiji	0.6	–	Mauritius	1.3	P
Finland	8.3	P	Mexico	48.5	P
France	60.8	S	Morocco	11.8	S
East Germany	26.0	S	Mozambique	3.4	S
West Germany	160.6	P	Nepal	1.4	P
Ghana	1.3	S	Netherlands	47.3	P
Greece	27.0	P	New Zealand	6.3	P
Guatemala	2.7	P	Nicaragua	2.4	P
Guyana	0.6	P	Nigeria	10.0	P
Haiti	0.9	S/P	Norway	0.8	P
Honduras	2.3	P	Pakistan	40.1	P
Hong Kong	10.0	P	Panama	1.1	P
Hungary	26.2	S	Paraguay	2.0	S
India	86.1	P	Peru	4.0	S/P
Indonesia	99.4	P	Philippines	58.6	P
Iran	12.0	S	Poland	86.4	S
Iraq	8.0	S	Portugal	13.5	S
Ireland	7.3	P	Romania	36.0	S
Israel	6.6	P	Senegal	2.4	S
Italy	80.4	S	Sierra Leone	1.5	P
Ivory Coast	3.7	S	Singapore	3.0	P
Jamaica	1.3	P	South Africa	32.5	P
Japan	306.9	S	Spain	45.1	S
Jordan	4.3	P	Sri Lanka	5.2	P
Kampuchea	4.1	S	Sudan	0.7	S
Kenya	5.4	P	Surinam	0.4	P
North Korea	14.4	S	Sweden	10.5	S
South Korea	76.3	S	Switzerland	25.4	P
Laos	1.1	S	Syria	11.4	S
Lebanon	0.2	S	Taiwan	32.1	S
Liberia	(1980) 0.1	P	Tanzania	4.0	S
Libya	3.5	S	Thailand	29.2	S

Trinidad and Tobago	1.1	‖‖‖ P
Tunisia	6.5	‖‖‖ $
Turkey	56.5	‖‖‖ $
Uganda	2.0	‖‖‖ $
UK	132.5	‖‖‖ P
Uruguay	3.8	‖‖‖ P
USA	668.2	‖‖‖ P
USSR	385.0	‖‖‖ $
Venezuela	20.6	‖‖‖ P
Vietnam	24.0	‖‖‖ $
Yugoslavia	59.2	‖‖‖ $
Zaire	3.5	‖‖‖ P
Zambia	1.4	‖‖‖ P
Zimbabwe	2.3	‖‖‖ P

World total (including others)	4,696.0

In 1983, some $100 billion were spent on cigarettes
and another $10 billion on other tobacco products.
By 1985, more than 1,750 cigarettes were being
smoked annually for every person over the age of
15.

State monopolies, East and West, make half the
cigarettes sold; the Big Six private tobacco transnational companies account for two-fifths; and
other, sometimes very large, private companies,
for about a tenth.

The Big Six

The Big Six reach into cigarette markets controlled by state monopolies and by seemingly independent private companies, through licensing and financial agreements. And they reach beyond
cigarettes to embrace a multitude of other products.

```
R J Reynolds Industries
Winston-Salem, N. Carolina
rank in top 500 US
industrial companies 23
sales $13.53 billion
profit $1 billion
workers 147,513

(1985)
```

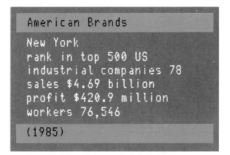

```
Philip Morris
New York
rank in top 500 US
industrial companies 27
sales $12.15 billion
profit $1.26 billion
workers 114,000

(1985)
```

```
American Brands
New York
rank in top 500 US
industrial companies 78
sales $4.69 billion
profit $420.9 million
workers 76,546

(1985)
```

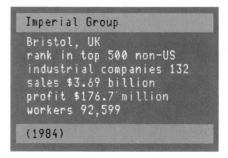

```
Imperial Group
Bristol, UK
rank in top 500 non-US
industrial companies 132
sales $3.69 billion
profit $176.7 million
workers 92,599

(1984)
```

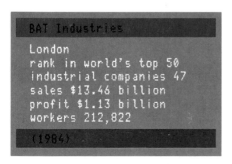

```
BAT Industries
London
rank in world's top 50
industrial companies 47
sales $13.46 billion
profit $1.13 billion
workers 212,822

(1984)
```

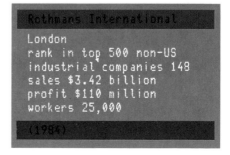

```
Rothmans International
London
rank in top 500 non-US
industrial companies 148
sales $3.42 billion
profit $110 million
workers 25,000

(1984)
```

Launching Barclay, a low-tar cigarette, in the US in 1981, cost BAT $100 million through its subsidiary company, Brown and Williamson. By then the Big Six were spending $2 billion a year on advertising cigarettes worldwide (more than the national income of over half the countries in Africa). Not many outsiders can afford to challenge the Big Six in their markets.

The cigarette market is growing slowly in the rich West, faster in the middle income East, and explosively in the poor South.

The corporate strategies of the Big Six take these trends into account. At home they are diversifying furiously away from tobacco into anything and everything else. Abroad they are making a sustained attack on state monopolies - 'an area of major growth in the future', according to New York stockbrokers Kidder Peabody. And they are driving hard into poor-country markets, where health and other controls are weakest and where they were carried along on a wave of xenophile prejudice.

Riding east across the Gobi

In one week in January/February 1984, R J Reynolds announced the launch of its Camel brand in 'the largest introduction of a foreign cigarette in Japan and one of the largest of any imported consumer product', as well as the early conclusion of a deal with China to set up a $25 million joint venture to produce three billion cigarettes a year, the first foreign step into the protected trillion (million million) Chinese cigarette market.

But not everywhere is welcoming: in South Korea getting caught with an imported cigarette can attract fines of up to $1,250 and imprisonment.

Newest and shyest

Anton Rupert founded his first cigarette company in 1948, the same year the Afrikaner Nationalists won control of the government in South Africa. Rupert's complex empire is now known as Rothmans International and earns half its profits abroad.

It operates in places like Malaysia, Singapore and Jamaica - where South Africa's apartheid is anathema. It exports - from London - to Ghana, Zambia, the Ivory Coast, Ethiopia and Nigeria, countries that do not recognize South Africa and officially boycott its companies and products.

Tightly controlled by an Afrikaner of Calvinist background, Rothmans International earns 72 per cent of its income from tobacco and liquor.

CARTELS

Businesses can collude to stifle competition by carving up markets among themselves, through price-fixing and adjusting their individual or collective outputs accordingly. An association or agreement of this type is called a cartel, and the business houses so combined form a trust or syndicate.

Diamonds

The most successful cartel is the one that dominates the diamond market. It exists because without it, diamonds might lose their financial glitter.

In 1888, Cecil Rhodes wrested control of various competing diamond interests in South Africa to establish a classic cartel in De Beers Consolidated Mines. When demand faltered, the cartel would reduce production. In the slump years of 1932-37, De Beers closed down its own mines altogether.

The CSO

When new diamond producers came on the scene, the real control exercised by De Beers operated less through an association of producers than through an all but complete marketing monopoly, known as the Central Selling Organization (CSO), with its headquarters in London.

Established in 1934, the CSO or Syndicate, as it is often called, handles over 80 per cent of the world's rough or uncut diamond output. De Beers itself produces only around a third of world output but, through its control of CSO, has purchasing arrangements even with producing countries politically hostile to the South African regime under which De Beers operates. Angola and Tanzania are parties to the arrangements. Zaire broke away for a while but returned to the fold. Even the USSR submits surreptitiously; so surreptitiously that, at the request of De Beers, the British government blocked, from the end of 1980, publication of statistics on the flow of diamonds from the USSR to the CSO in London. The value of this flow was £202 million in 1978; £335 million in 1979; and £367 million in 1980.

When the demand for diamonds rises, the CSO supplies the market at manageably rising prices and builds up its cash reserves. When demand falls, the CSO cuts the supply and accumulates stocks, using its cash reserves to continue purchasing from producers and even mopping up excess supplies in the market place. Whenever necessary, De Beers cuts the production of its own mines and encourages - it can do little more - foreign producers to do likewise.

The CSO is, in normal circumstances, imperious towards the trade. It lays down the law on who may buy at its regular sales or 'sights'; what assortment of stones and at what price; traders are barred from future 'sights' if they infringe the rules. And the trade is submissive because the rewards are enormous, with mark-ups of 500-1000 per cent between the cost of rough stones and the $18.5 billion retail market.

We've heard that song before

'Whether this measure of control amounts to a monopoly I would not know, but if it does it is certainly a monopoly of a most unusual kind. There is no one concerned with diamonds, whether as a producer, dealer, cutter, jeweller or customer who does not benefit from it.'

Harry Oppenheimer, when chairman of De Beers

But the very success of the near-monopoly (only the Central African Republic, Ghana, Brazil and Venezuela remain outside), in securing a steady rise in the price of diamonds year after year, nearly proved its undoing. In the high inflation years of 1977-80, prices rose sharply, as cutters and polishers in Israel took the lead in accumulating stocks, and individual investors began speculatively buying diamonds as well. The price of the benchmark gem, the one carat flawless, soared over 600 per cent, and diamond stocks outside the CSO looked set to rival those within. Then the price broke, demand faltered, and De Beers found itself forced to buy from dealers as well as producers to avert panic.

In the event, the CSO cash reserves fell from some \$2 billion in 1979 to around \$200 million, while stocks of diamonds rose to a value of \$1.4 billion in 1982, \$1.85 billion in 1983 and \$1.95 billion in 1984.

Such persistent market support, along with a decline in relatively cheap Russian offerings, led to a brighter outlook for the cartel in 1985. The stocks of Israeli cutters fell to around \$200 million worth, from the \$1.3 billion in 1981. CSO sales in 1985 totalled \$1.82 billion, 13 per cent up on the figure for 1984 and the highest dollar total since the record of \$2.72 billion in 1980.

OPEC - the cartel that failed

No fewer than 20 of the world's top 50 industrial companies are mainly involved in oil.

In the 1950s, and for many years before, the oil market was dominated and effectively regulated by a handful of companies operating worldwide.

In 1960, OPEC (Organization of Petroleum Exporting Countries) was founded with the aim of securing a better deal for the producer countries.

In 1971, Libya made the first break with a 40 per cent price hike for its oil. In 1973, when the Arab producers demonstrated Western dependence on their supplies by stopping exports during the Middle East war, OPEC raised the recommended oil price from \$2.60 to \$11.65 a barrel. During the years that followed, the price was raised time and again, to over \$38 a barrel in 1980.

Widely attacked as a cartel, OPEC was no more than a loose association of producers determining a recommended selling price for their output. Paradoxically, it was only in 1982, when the prices set by its members came under pressure from new supplies, alternative energy sources, energy saving measures and recession - in fact, when its dominance of the market seemed seriously threatened - that OPEC set out to be a classic cartel, and restricted production to maintain prices.

It faced considerable problems. Its five rich states (Kuwait, Libya, Qatar, Saudi Arabia and the United Arab Emirates) pulled one way, and its eight poor (Algeria, Ecuador, Gabon, Indonesia, Iran, Iraq, Nigeria and Venezuela) pulled the other. Neither group was itself united in agreement on output quotas; and not least, important new producers like Britain, Mexico and Norway remained outside the organization. Moreover, slowing industrial growth worldwide shrank the market for oil.

Average market price of a one-carat flawless white diamond, Antwerp, $

Year	Price
1974	6,000
1975	5,500
1976	6,000
1977	7,500
1978	16,000
1979	33,000
1980	55,000
1981	25,000
1982	13,000
1983	10,000
1984	12,000
1985	13,000

OPEC's declining share of world oil consumption, percentages

Year	Percentage
1974	54.7
1976	53.5
1978	49.8
1980	45.2
1982	35.5
1984	32.2

Falling oil production, million barrels a day

	1979	July 1985
Saudi Arabia	9.6	2.7
Kuwait	2.3	1.0
United Arab Emirates	1.8	1.2
Qatar	0.5	0.3
Iran	3.1	2.3
Libya	2.1	1.0
Algeria	1.3	0.7
Venezuela	2.4	1.6
Nigeria	2.3	1.4
Indonesia	1.6	1.3
Iraq	3.5	1.2
Gabon	0.2	0.2
Ecuador	0.2	0.3
total	30.9	15.2

The moving price of oil

Average spot market price of Arabian light crude oil

4th quarter	$ per barrel
1973	4.50
1974	10.45
1975	11.50
1976	11.90
1977	12.70
1978	13.80
1979	38.35
1980	38.40
1981	33.75
1982	31.75
1983	28.35
1984	27.77
1985	27.79

A cartel with such a small and declining share of the world market is no cartel. OPEC had sustained its credibility mainly because Saudi Arabia, the 'swing' producer, had agreed to bear the brunt of cuts.

But as 1985 proceeded, there was mounting Saudi impatience at the enormous cost that this entailed. A current account surplus for the country of $38 billion in 1981 had turned into a deficit of $24 billion (the world's largest after that of the US) in 1984. In late summer, the Saudi government announced its intention to go for market share rather than for price support, and increased production from an average of 2.7 million barrels a day to around 4.5 million.

By January 1986, the price of crude oil had fallen to below $20 a barrel, in February it reached below $15; and by April was testing a $10 level. Amid much rejoicing in the West at OPEC's discomfiture, expressions of alarm came notably from the US, many of whose relatively high cost oil wells were no longer profitable at such price levels and were being taken out of production, in some cases irretrievably.

It's an ill wind...

Ian Clubb, chief executive of leading British oil exploration company Carless, Capel and Leonard, found some source of comfort in the gloom of falling oil prices:

'We don't have a lot of oil production, so we are suffering less because of a lack of exploration success in the past.'

The cartel is dead - long live the cartel?

While the price of crude oil plummeted in world markets, the price of petrol at the pumps dropped relatively little. The smaller oil companies, which might have been expected to seize the opportunity for engaging in a price war, were still nursing the wounds of previous efforts and in no condition to confront the massive promotional campaigns undertaken by the giants. The leaders of the industry denied with indignation even the possibility of pricing agreements. They explained that apparently high prices at the pumps were no more than a return to profitable operations after a long period of forecourt lossmaking. The oil analyst of major London stockbrokers Grieveson Grant declared: 'It seems as if there is a more effective cartel in the petrol market than OPEC has been able to maintain.'

Tin – the market that.overwhelmed the managers

It was the tin market that was to experience the calamitous consequences of price supports in defiance of market realities.

The tremendous tin tumble

From its establishment in the mid-1950s, the International Tin Council (ITC), an association of major tin-producing and tin-consuming countries, set out to promote the common interest of its members by managing the price of tin in the world market. It did this by setting both a ceiling price, at which it would supply tin to the market so as to satisfy demand, and a floor price or support level, at which it would buy tin for its buffer stocks.

In the late 1970s, as the market price of virtually all commodities rose in a climate of high inflation, the ITC floor price was correspondingly raised. And there it remained, even when, in the 1980s, a widespread decline in commodity prices began. And tin was particularly vulnerable to pressures for decline.

The high cost of tin had promoted a search for substitutes - aluminium came increasingly to be used for containers - and consumption of tin plummeted nearly 25 per cent.

The price support for tin had also allowed traditional producers to maintain uneconomic mines and encouraged new producers, outside the ITC, to enter the market.

Brazil, a new producer, increased production from 5,000 tonnes in the early 1980s to 22,000 tonnes by 1985. The supply surplus was further swollen by smugglers who evaded the local quotas of ITC producers. In Thailand, up to 18,000 tonnes a year were reaching the market in this way, mainly through Singapore.

As the surplus mounted, the ITC bought more and more for its buffer stocks to protect the floor price of tin in the London Metal Exchange (LME), the world centre of trading in base metals. When its liquid funds ran out, the ITC borrowed from the banks. On 24 October 1985, the ITC ran out of funds altogether. The floor level, of around £8,500 a tonne, plunged, and the LME suspended all trading in tin.

When the dust began to clear, the dimensions of the crisis emerged. If the ITC were to honour its commitment to buy tin at fixed prices in the forward market, it would have gross debts of about £900 million: £281 million to its 14 banks and the rest to metal traders.

After months of repeated postponement, as one rescue attempt after the other failed, all attempts to negotiate a settlement of the crisis were abandoned on 6 March 1986. The LME authorities set out to limit the damage by organizing a 'ring-out'

which fixed the tin price at £6,250 a tonne for all outstanding contracts: leaving 24 brokers to face a total loss of £180 million. Those left with stocks would face a further loss of £130 million, at a free market price of £4,000 a tonne: and in fact, by 19 March, the price was below that figure on unofficial markets in Europe. The 14 banks which had lent money to the ITC with tin as the collateral faced losses, at £4,000 a tonne, of £100 million.

But this was very far from being the end of the affair. With 100,000 tonnes of tin held by the ITC and by mines - equivalent to eight months of Western consumption - the price was unlikely to recover for some time to come. Bolivia, where tin costs around £10,000 a tonne to produce, and which relies on tin for 40 per cent of its export revenues, seemed set to plunge into still deeper economic trouble. In Malaysia, 200 of the 400 mines were already closed or operating at half-capacity. In Thailand, more than 40 per cent of the mines were threatened with closure.

The failure of governments, including those of rich states such as West Germany, to accept their contractual obligations, looked likely to hasten the collapse of other commodity pacts. Moreover, it raised questions about the financial reliability of other multi-governmental institutions. The only beneficiaries seemed certain to be lawyers, as brokers sued the LME, and banks sued member governments of the ITC.

THE INFORMATION REVOLUTION

Once in a while, a market is created in a big bang that reshapes everything around it. The electronics revolution - a revolution in the storage, manipulation and transmission of information - is such a primeval force.

Already the electronics revolution has affected almost every other market, from labour to arms. It has shifted the domicile of entire industries, broken national autarkies and undermined national attitudes. It has dismembered immense monopolies, state and private, and propelled backroom tinkerers into the highest of financial orbits.

The further consequences are incalculable.

There are three key segments of the electronics market
■ semiconductors,integrated circuits, or 'chips': the cells for the storage of information
■ computer hardware and software
■ telecommunications

The effect of advancing technology and mass production on the price of an electronic product has nowhere been more dramatic than in the declining cost of calculators from Japan's Casio, the world's leading manufacturer of calculators.

The little calculator boom

	production per month units	weight kgs	price $
1957	100	130.0	2,146
1965	500	17.0	1,681
1969	7,000	6.8	487
1972	150,000	0.35	57
1977	1,200,000	0.03	30
1983	2,500,000	0.01	26

Chipping in

The semiconductor market is new, dating from 1967. But already it is huge, worth almost $29 billion worldwide in 1984; having grown furiously from $18 billion in 1982.

Bigger chips, bigger markets

	peak sales	peak year
4K chip	$168 m	1978
16K chip	$910 m	1980
64K chip	$1.6 b	1985
256K chip	(est) $2.5 b	1988

It is a market swept by wave after wave of new products, each cheaper than its predecessor. It is a highly volatile market, with crash following boom at dizzy speed. Prices of some widely-used 'commodity' chips plummeted during the recent slump by as much as 80 per cent.

Price of a 256K D-RAM chip

(D-RAM: Dynamic Random Access Memory, industry standard)

mid-1983	$110
Jan 1984	$84
Jan 1985	$10
Oct 1985	$3

Leading producers oust each other; with Japanese producers quickly racing to the top.

The microchamps

The top ten companies' sales of semi conductors

	1983 rank	$ million	1985 rank	$ million
Texas Instruments (US)	1	1,638	3	1,760
Motorola (US)	2	1,547	2	1,850
Nippon Electric (Japan)	3	1,413	1	1,980
Hitachi (Japan)	4	1,181	4	1,670
Toshiba (Japan)	5	983	5	na
Philips (Netherlands)	6	917	6	na
National Semi-conductor (US)	7	875	9	na
Intel (US)	8	775	8	na
Fujitsu (Japan)	9	688	7	na
Matsushita (Japan)	10	600	10	na

Between 1975 and 1985, the trade balance in semiconductors between the US and Japan moved from around $100 million in the US's favour to around $1.1 billion in Japan's. In June 1985, Micron Technology, an Idaho manufacturer, filed the first-ever anti-dumping action in the US against Japanese suppliers of semiconductor products. In October, United Technologies announced the closure of its memory chipmaker Mostek, eighth largest US chipmaker, which had, ten years before, been in the forefront of semiconductor technology and was celebrated as the pioneer of cheap memory devices. Unfair Japanese competition was alleged responsible for the closure.

Pressure from US producers on the US government and pressure from the US on Japan, resulted in an agreement, in the summer of 1986, to raise the price of Japanese microchips in the US.

SILICON COCKTAIL

Silicon Valley, between San Francisco and San Jose, with a third of total capacity, is still the world's microchip capital.
It is rapidly attracting imitators in both form and spirit.

In the US at:
Albuquerque (New Mexico): Austin (Texas): Boston (Massachusetts): Colorado Springs (Colorado): Dallas (Texas): Phoenix (Arizona): Raleigh-Durham (North Carolina): San Antonio (Texas).
And abroad in:
Brazil: Britain: Canada: France: Japan: USSR (at Zelinograd, north of Moscow).

Mix:
Stanford University's commitment to collaborating with industry
with:
venture capital for hi-tech industry (one-third of which goes to the Valley)

1974 $10 million
1980 $667 million
1981 $867 million
1982 $1423 million
1983 $2000 million

and a consuming interest in making money.

Shake and serve.

The hardware market

The market for computers, the hardware that processes or manipulates information, has also been swept by wave after wave of new products, each cheaper, more adaptable and more acceptable than their predecessors. But it too, is beginning to show a cyclical pattern of boom and recession, with 1985 a recession year for all but a relatively few specialist producers.

The high rollers

Sales of the world's largest computer manufacturers, 1984 $ billion

	total revenue	computer revenue
IBM (US)	45.9	44.3
Digital Equipment (US)	6.2	6.2
Burroughs (US)	4.9	4.5
Control Data (US)	5.0	3.7
NCR (US)	4.0	3.7
Fujitsu (Japan)	6.5	3.5
Sperry (US)	5.4	3.4
Hewlett-Packard (US)	6.5	3.4
NEC (Japan)	7.6	2.8
Siemens (West Germany)	16.0	2.8

PS Moscow

The information upheaval has so far largely bypassed the USSR, once thought to be the natural home for computers, which are surely custom-built for central planning bodies. Yet the USSR can boast of no more than a 7.5 per cent computer penetration of industrial enterprises, or an estimated 3,300 machines in the mid-1980s. Suspicious and fearful of the uses to which computers may be put by those above and below them; aware that Soviet computers crash on average once a week; and frustrated by the inability of telephone lines to cope with the data, Soviet managers have been mutely resisting the electronics revolution.

From the BMP Journal's Moscow correspondent:

This morning, the Party Agitprop Department published a new slogan to encourage and stimulate the Soviet computer industry: 'glory to the Soviet microchip - the biggest microchip in the world.'

Big Blue - the IBM story

'IBM isn't the competition; it's the environment.'
Anon

Immense fortunes are made and lost in the computer market, but there has been one constant factor to date: the dominance and apparent impregnability of IBM or Big Blue, nicknamed such after the traditional colour of its machines.

```
IBM

New York
rank in top 500 US
industrial companies 5
sales $50.06 billion
profit $6.55 billion
workers 405,535

(1985)
```

While only fifth by sales, IBM was by far the most profitable company in the US during 1985. Exxon, second by sales, recorded a profit of $4.87 billion; General Motors, first by sales, a profit of only $4 billion.

'Hail to IBM'

'Our voices swell in admiration
Of T J Watson proudly sing
He'll ever be our inspiration
To him our voices loudly ring'
The company hymn

Thomas Watson, an Ohio farmboy who turned salesman, took over the Computer-Tabulating-Recording Company in 1914. That was the beginning.

During the 1920s and 1930s, IBM totally dominated the market for timeclocks and punch-card tabulators. In the 1930s and 1940s, it pioneered and took command of the electric typewriter market. When Tom Watson Jr, the founder's son, came to head the company in the 1950s, it had annual sales of nearly $600 million and was one of the largest industrial companies in the US.

Then, in 1951, Remington Rand delivered UNIVAC, the first computer designed for commercial use, to the US Bureau of the Census. Suddenly, IBM found some of its machines displaced. It was stunned, but not for long. With plenty of cash for research and with a sales and service organization that covered the country, it proceeded to develop machines that could meet the threat. In the 1960s, it grew to take 80 per cent of the US market and came as close to a monopoly as any single concern in the US.

While revenues grew at an annual rate of 17 per cent during the 1970s, IBM's share of the fast expanding world computer market slipped from 60 per cent in 1967 to 40 per cent in 1980. Already alert to impending decline, in 1977 IBM poured $10 billion into plant and equipment, in a drive to become the industry's lowest-cost producer. As one observer put it, the company turned from a battleship in mothballs to a fleet of killer submarines.

In 1984, IBM's chief executive, John Fellows Akers, declared that by 1994, he wanted to make IBM richer than Australia and New Zealand combined.

IBM's West European sales are more than the combined turnover of its ten closest competitors, and eight times that of its closest rival, Bull of France. In both Britain and France, its turnover is more than double that of the leading 'national' firms, despite the support these have received from their governments over many years.

The IBM way

Special discounts of various kinds have been the prime instrument of IBM's growth.

There are discounts for agreements to buy a set number of units by a given date, so locking out competitors.

There are discounts for bulk purchases. In 1981, a big new computer, the 3081, was initially listed at a price of from $3.7 million to $4.1 million each. IBM sold 50 to AT & T at a discount of $1 million each. Amdahl, previously a substantial supplier to AT & T, posted an operating loss in 1982.

In 1983, IBM offered a new display terminal, priced at $1,700, with a discount of 40 per cent for buyers of 3,000 or more. A trade newsletter promptly called the company's marketing campaign a 'reign of terror'.

The power of IBM was never better displayed than in its reaction to the growth of the market in personal computers. After Apple, Tandy and a host of others had carved out a niche for the personal computer (PC), moving from nothing in 1977 to a combined turnover of $15 billion in 1982, IBM struck back. By late 1984, its share was some 35 per cent, with between 60 and 70 per cent of the corporate market. Along the way, it had launched five versions of its PC and cut the original price by half. An estimated dozen or more makers of competitive models had been, or were being, driven from the market.

In 1985, IBM had around 11.5 per cent of the total world market in electronics, valued at around $400 billion in 1984, and planned to have 17.25 per cent of the $620 billion that this market was predicted to reach in 1990.

IBM's dominant position is not unchallenged. Japanese competitors, in particular, are intent on breaking the company's lock on one of the most lucrative and politically-sensitive markets of all.

The Japanese challenge

As global competitors, the Japanese computer companies are still small fry by IBM standards. Fujitsu is no. 1 in Japan but only no. 6 internationally and around a tenth the size of IBM. In all, Japanese companies have only 2 per cent of the US market for all computers. But as the volume of personal computers soars, Japanese mass production techniques will weigh more heavily in the balance.

The Japanese computer industry is flexing its muscles: in 1980, Japan was a net importer of computers, mostly from the US. By 1983, Japanese exports of computers ($2.75 billion, 57 per cent to the US) were worth four times its imports (unchanged at $637 million).

Japanese computer companies are offering aid and comfort to IBM's enemies wherever they can be found.

Fujitsu owns 49 per cent of Amdahl, the only important US manufacturer of large or mainframe computers compatible with IBM machines, and is closely linked with the British flag carrier, ICL. Hitachi supplies National Advanced Systems, another leading US supplier, with all its machines; NEC is the source of Honeywell's large computers. And Siemens in West Germany, Olivetti in Italy, and Bull in France all sell 'own brand' computers supplied by Japanese companies.

IBM in Japan

'If IBM and other foreign computer companies don't fight it out in Japan, they will wind up battling the Japanese in their own backyards.'

James C Abegglen, Boston Consulting Group, Tokyo office

In 1969, the US Department of Justice filed an anti-trust suit against IBM; seeking to break it up into several competing concerns. In 1982, after many millions of dollars had been expended by both sides, the Department abandoned its suit. Washington wanted an IBM strong enough to maintain its supremacy abroad and force its Japanese competitors into retreat.

IBM is fighting back on three fronts:

■ By forming manufacturing alliances with Japanese firms, it is staying strongly in the market for character-writing machines:

The personal computer plays an increasingly important role in Japanese offices, since it can master the thousands of characters in the written Japanese language, a task that confounds typewriter technology. To assemble components, IBM hired Matsushita Electric. To make the keyboard and printer, it hired two other Japanese companies, Oki and Alps. And to keep in the forefront of development, it bought a 35 per cent stake in

Japanese Business Computer Company, a small firm that helped pioneer the character writing technology.

■ By forming marketing alliances with Japanese outlets:

Marketing in Japan all too often encounters problems of distribution. Hitachi, Japan's electrical giant that is no. 4 in the Japanese computer market, has no fewer than 10,000 exclusive retail dealers.

IBM enlisted Nissan Motor and Nurihiko, a saké distributor with a long list of liquor dealers who may need computers. And in 1984, it landed more than 200 US executives and their families on IBM Japan's doorsteps: one of the largest personnel shifts in its recent history.

■ By using the courts to protect its own technology from Japanese competitors:

In 1983, it humbled Hitachi in a suit claiming industrial espionage: getting not only damages but also the right to open and inspect initial shipments of new Hitachi computer products for five years. Both Hitachi and Fujitsu have signed software agreements with IBM; implying that they were previously freeloading by modifying and selling parts of IBM software.

The Europeans choose sides?

'But IBM, for its part, must also recognize the sensitive political realities in Europe. In particular, it cannot expect Europeans to accept as readily as Americans the argument that dramatically aggressive commercial tactics are justified by the need to meet the challenge from Japan. Most of its European competitors already regard IBM as a far more serious threat than the Japanese.'

Financial Times, 1984

The software market

There is no single giant, dominating the other companies, in the software that regulates the behaviour of the computer. There are, by contrast, more than 4,000 small companies contesting the business.

Given manufacturing costs less than one-twentieth of the retail price and with clever programmers, growth can be funded out of cash flow and profits can be spectacular.

The software industry arrived conclusively when, in 1980, IBM called on Microsoft, a leading firm in the field, to adapt one of its programs for the forthcoming IBM personal computer. IBM designated Microsoft's product the 'primary operating system'. Some 95 per cent of the 300,000 machines that IBM shipped in the first eighteen months used the Microsoft system, and most other computer makers adopted it.

Personal computer software

Market share of major US companies, 1983, percentages

IBM	9
Tandy	9
Apple	5
Commodore	5
MicroPro	5
Microsoft	4
Lotus	4
VisiCorp	4
Digital Research	4
Ashton-Tate	3
MSA (Peachtree)	2
others	46

Telecommunications and information systems

The third big arena for the electronics revolution is the market for telecommunications, the transmission of information. This segment of the market is vast - an estimated $150 billion a year, with some 39 per cent in US hands and almost 12 per cent in Japan's. Market leaders today are not necessarily leaders tomorrow. At one time the preserve of state or state-licensed private monopolies, the market has been invaded by armies of communicators armed with computers.

The top ten in telecommunications

Equipment sales, 1983, $ billion

AT & T Technologies (US)	11.16
ITT (US)	4.86
Siemens (West Germany)	4.49
L M Ericsson (Sweden)	3.16
Alcatel-Thomson (France)	2.74
Northern Telecom (Canada)	2.66
NEC (Japan)	2.41
GTE (US)	2.30
Motorola (US)	2.31
IBM (excluding Rolm) (US)	1.73

The whole industry is being reshaped. AT & T, the largest private sector company in the world, was dismembered in 1984. British Telecom (BT) was the object of the largest ever transfer from state to private ownership in the same year. And NTT (Nippon Telephone and Telegraph), double BT's size, is following, at a slower tempo, the road to privatization.

They are gearing up to cope with a new world-competitive environment. In particular, the two superpowers in electronics, AT & T and IBM, are manoeuvering towards a titanic struggle for supremacy.

The electronic battlefield

Both IBM and the restructured AT & T are now free of anti-trust action in the US and so are aggressively disposed to make inroads on each other's territory. The two companies are more or less evenly matched in muscle power. Above all, the convergence of their respective technologies has made competition between them inevitable.

The centre of the struggle is the field of office automation, where computing (or the power to process information) is merging with telecommunications (or the power to move information around).

Convergent technologies have already produced new services. Video teleconferencing (using closed circuit television techniques) is increasingly in use.

Citibank and Chase Manhattan are among the many large businesses using electronic mail. Messages, electronically transmitted, can be filed in a 'mailbox', with the memory of a computer controlling the system, for retrieval when the recipient returns to the terminal. It is simply the application of computer techniques to telex.

In London's City Business System, telephone, telex and computer terminals are combined with visual display units to meet the communication needs of currency and commodity dealers.

But the most revolutionary development in the market place is of local area networks or LANs, linking together all the constituent parts of the automated office - word processors, work stations, computers, facsimile machines, copiers, file stores, printers - so that information can be passed from one to the other quickly, accurately and cheaply.

The prospect that IBM should triumph here too, is one that alarms some Europeans.

'As a manufacturer and seller of machines, IBM had customers and a few rivals. As a controller of networks, the company would take on a dimension extending beyond the strictly industrial sphere; it would participate, whether it wanted to or not, in the government of the planet. In effect, it has everything it needs to become one of the world's great regulatory systems.'
Report to the President of France, 1978

Eight years after the report was submitted, in February 1986, the first summit gathering of the world's French-speaking states ended in Paris with modest but concrete steps aimed at limiting the dominance of English as the language of computers.

Supertech alliances

Both AT & T and IBM are making alliances, in their own business or that of the other, to position themselves for the campaigns ahead.

By mid-1985, AT & T:

- had a joint venture with Philips, the large Netherlands-based electrical and electronics firm, to sell switching and transmission equipment in Western Europe, the Middle East and parts of Latin America.
- had a 25 per cent stake (with an option to raise it to a total 40 per cent) in Olivetti, the large Italian office products company, for co-ordinated development and marketing of work stations and telecommunications.
- had set up a joint venture with CTNE, the Spanish telecommunications group, to build a micro-plant in Spain.
- and had commissioned Convergent Technologies, of California, to develop work stations for its own use.

By mid-1985, IBM:

- had bought Rolm of California, one of the world's major manufacturers of digital private exchanges (PABXs).
- had an arrangement with Toshiba of Japan, which supplies sub-assemblies for a new facsimile machine.
- had increased to 60 per cent its stake in Satellite Business Systems, the US satellite communications network.
- had concluded an agreement to buy up to 30 per cent of MCI, the biggest of the independent long-distance phone companies in the US (with 2.5 million customers compared to AT & T's 87 million).
- was operating a sophisticated data network, Information Network Services, in the US.
- was in partnership with Merrill Lynch, the leading US stockbrokers, in developing an electronic financial information and trading system. It is planning a venture in home information services with the broadcasting company CBS, and with the retailing and finance group, Sears Roebuck.

But at least one major IBM plan misfired. In 1984, its proposal to launch a UK data network service jointly with British Telecom was vetoed as anti-competitive by the British government.

Both giants have major developments in the convergent technologies. AT & T has a national network, AIS/1000, to carry high-speed communications between the most commonly used types of computer; IBM has a rival system in INS (Information Network Services).

Other alliances

In the shadow of the battle between IBM and AT & T, alliances are rapidly being made between individual firms of different countries, sometimes along with takeovers of local firms.

- France's CGE has joined forces with Philips in the development and marketing of cellular radio, which uses computer power and modern switching techniques to expand vastly the capacity of mobile communications systems.
- L M Ericsson, Sweden's largest telecommunications group, has bought Datasaab, the main Swedish computer manufacturer, and Facit, which makes electronic typewriters and other office products. In Britain, it has a joint venture with Thorn-EMI. In the US, it owns a joint venture with the oil company, Atlantic Richfield, in marketing equipment, producing software, and cable making. It has also agreed with US computer company Honeywell on plans to develop office systems based on the companies' products.
- General Telephone and Electronics (GTE), second only to AT & T in US telecommunications, owns jointly with Ferranti of Britain an equipment manufacturing venture, and in Italy collaborates with Italtel, the state-owned telecommunications equipment manufacturer. It is working with Wang, the US office systems supplier, to make compatible communications products.
- Northern Telecom, Canada's leading telecommunications manufacturer, is working with Hewlett-Packard, Digital Equipment, Data General and Sperry in the US to make their computer equipment compatible with its products. In Britain, GEC makes its large SLI-PABX under licence.
- Mitel, Canada's second telecommunications manufacturer, has an agreement to supply a version of its large PABX, the SX-2000, for distribution through ICL, the largest British-owned computer manufacturer. British Telecom has bought an interest in Mitel.
- Plessey of Britain has bought the US public switching business of Stromberg-Carlson and has links with Scientific Atlanta, manufacturer of satellite receivers and cable TV equipment.
- Cable and Wireless (UK), privatized by the British government in 1981, has bought Hong Kong Telephone and entered several telecommunications joint ventures in China. It is a partner with the US consortium Tel-Optik in a project to lay a transatlantic optical fibre system. It has acquired full ownership of Mercury Communications, which is building a British network to compete with British Telecom, and which operates transatlantic services in partnership with Western Union of the US.
- Italy's Olivetti has a minority holding in some 30 high tech companies, most of them in the US.

In 1983, the French government promoted a major swap of industrial assets between France's two leading nationalized electronics conglomerates, Thomson and Compagnie Générale d'Electricité (CGE). Thomson got CGE's electronic components, consumer electronics and military supply divisions. The telecommunications business of both conglomerates were combined into the CGE subsidiary, Cit-Alcatel. Cit-Alcatel has agreed on technical co-operation in public exchanges with Italy's Italtel and is discussing link-ups with Germany's Siemens. It is also collaborating with Xerox on the production of computer software.

ADVERTISING AND MARKETING

The reach of business into increasingly global markets has both promoted and been promoted by a huge expansion of marketing. At its core is advertising, a $150 billion a year business, more than half of which is spent in the US.

National advertising in the US reached a value of some $87 billion in 1984 and was estimated to reach $96 billion in 1985. By 1990, advertising expenditure is expected to reach $137 billion in the US and $163 billion elsewhere.

Most of the spending goes through very large agencies. In some places they are more than agencies; they exercise a power and influence far beyond that of their clients. The biggest operate worldwide, sometimes in close association with each other.

The world's top ten advertising agencies by annual world billings, 1984 $ billion

Dentsu (Japan)	3.5
Young & Rubicam (US)	3.2
Ogilvy & Mather (US)	2.9
Ted Bates Worldwide (US)	2.8
J Walter Thompson (US)	2.7
Saatchi & Saatchi Compton (Britain)	2.3
BBDO International (US)	2.3
McCann-Erickson (US)	2.2
Foote, Cone & Belding (US)	1.8
Leo Burnett (US)	1.7

In late April 1986, the world's largest advertising agency group, with annual billings estimated at some $5 billion, was formed by the combination of three leading US firms: BBDO International, Doyle Dane Bernbach, and Needham Harper Worldwide.

Hardly had the news of this merger been digested when, in early May 1986, Saatchi & Saatchi vaulted into top place. By acquiring Ted Bates, the major privately-owned US agency, for $450 million in cash, it came to command estimated annual billings of some $7.5 billion.

It is unlikely that this phase of merger mania has run its course. Saatchi & Saatchi itself did not seem satisfied. One of its executives informed the press: 'After all, even in advertising, with billings of $7.5 billion we will only have 4 per cent of the market... That's nothing really, is it?'

Global gloms

Ogilvy & Mather has more than 100 offices in 34 countries, 6,000 staff and more than 1,700 clients.

J Walter Thompson has 100 offices in 32 countries, 7,000 staff and more than 1,200 clients. The group also owns Euro-Advertising (185 clients, with agencies or affiliates in 9 countries), along with Hill & Knowlton, the world's largest public relations concern (800 employees and more than 600 clients).

Interpublic, a holding company, associates three major agencies (McCann-Erickson, SSCB-Lintas, Marschalk Campbell-Ewald), which together had billings in 1985 of $4.7 billion, or more even than Dentsu of Japan.

And in 1981, Dentsu signed an agreement with Young & Rubicam to set up joint ventures in various countries: a new association that represented an alliance of billings at $6.7 billion in 1984.

Note the notes

In 1983, Nabisco, fourth largest food company in the US, laced all its radio and television advertisements for every one of its products, from Bubble Yum to Moosehead beer, with the same three-note motif: G, D, E. The musical composition, the most expensive, note-for-note, in history, was played some 70 billion times during the year.

'My acid test on the issue [of advertising] is whether a housewife, intending to buy Heinz tomato ketchup in a store, finding it to be out of stock, will walk out of the store to buy it elsewhere or switch to an alternative product.'

A J O'Reilly, president and chief executive officer, H J Heinz

Dentsu

Dentsu, the world's largest single advertising agency before Saatchi & Saatchi acquired Ted Bates in 1986, commands a quarter of the advertising market in Japan, or two-and-a-half times as much as its nearest rival. So powerful is Dentsu that it is commonly called the country's kuroko, after the black-clothed stagehand who manipulates puppets in the bunraku theatre. Elsewhere in advertising, competing clients do not generally employ the same agency. Dentsu's 3,000 or so clients, however, include Toyota, Nissan and Honda among automobile companies; Matsushita, Toshiba, Sony and JVC among those in electronics; and the two leading cosmetic firms, Shiseido and Kanebo.

Dentsu also represents the Japanese government, with government billings in 1981 totalling some $67 million. This connection gives it an added appeal to private clients, since it can often iron out bureaucratic wrinkles for them.

Japan's media-saturated society superbly suits Dentsu's operations. There are 125 daily newspapers, with a circulation of 47 million (1.3 papers per household compared to 0.75 in the US), and 2,000 magazines, with aggregate sales of 2.5 billion copies. Television, with almost a hundred commercial stations and five national networks, reaches into more than 99 per cent of all Japanese homes.

Dentsu buys in advance huge blocks of space in newspapers and magazines, along with half of prime time on commercial television. And here, too, there are added dividends for clients. Dentsu's editorial influence has reputedly helped in moderating, if not eliminating, press treatment of particular scandals.

Mechanically, Dentsu is daunting. In its electronically sophisticated test studio, panels of housewives signal reactions to barrages of ads. Computer data banks provide instant detailed information on market share for multitudes of products. But advertising copy is in the main produced by many small, independent 'creative boutiques', clustering around Dentsu as auto-part companies cluster around Toyota Motors.

PUBLIC RELATIONS

Advertising by global companies through global agencies merges into public relations, or selling the company rather than the product.

PR markets the company to the financial sector, in order to safeguard and promote ratings and credit lines; to employees, in order to avoid or solve internal problems; to the general public, in order to underpin product advertising; to government agencies, in order to influence legislation and regulation.

'If people perceive us to be doing something wrong, we have to change that perception.'
Dow Chemicals executive

'The public today cannot be expected to take our word on something without corroboration.'
Paul F Oreffice, president, Dow Chemicals

Merchants of nomenclature

'Most of the real words are gone.'
Joel Portugal of Anspach Grossman Portugal, PR agency

Company name consultants in the US gross an estimated $25 to $40 million a year at $50,000 to $125,000 a time, plus anything between $100,000 and $750,000 for redesigning a company's logo.

The change from Esso to Exxon in 1972 cost the company more than $200 million. But at least the change stuck. Kraft was not so lucky. Kraft begat Kraftco which begat Kraft which begat Dart & Kraft. Then Justin Dart died. The company kept its name and in June 1986 decided to split into two: Kraft, and another company not then named.

The first image maker

The modern commercial public relations business was born in the US in 1914, when John D Rockefeller hired Ivy Lee to improve his public image after a massacre of strikers in Colorado. Rockefeller's image changed subsequently from that of a robber baron to that of a public benefactor, and PR has never looked back.

Today, PR is a growing business. Led by the two US majors, Hill & Knowlton and Burson-Marsteller, it is increasingly an international one. The world centre is the US, where 100,000 people work in the sector, and the top ten specialist agencies bill a total $200 million a year.

In Britain, the 113 members of the Public Relations Consultants' Association recorded fees of over £50 million in 1985; some 22 per cent more than in the previous year, and four times their receipts in 1980.

The Labour Marketeers

Dr. Strange 1985

Fry Brothers 1983

Sheikh Al-Come 1982

Jose Sucre 1984

Clive Lovejoy 1984

THE BUYERS

DR STRANGE, chief purchasing officer of the American medical profession and a frequent traveller. He has been a long-term buyer in the market for Philippino physicians, whose training he monitors closely, and to a lesser extent, for graduates from Hong Kong medical schools. He does not like his job, distrusts his medical imports, but appreciates that they keep the public wards open and enable native Americans to concentrate on private practice. *1985*

THE FRY BROTHERS of Kansas City, US, run a very private 'meat market' company. Roger, on the left, heads the nuclear division (or 'frying squad') which supplies 'glowboys' or 'sponges' to the nuclear power industry to service the reactors. His recruiting pitch: 'Jump with us, only 2.5 rems a day in our clients' plants. I guarantee you won't glow at night and you'll still be fertile when you leave. There's no tingling, no sensation. It will kill a few white cells, but white blood cells die every second of your life'. Ronald, on the right, heads the public sector division whose main business is with US government agencies supplying mercenaries - Israelis at one quarter the cost of US citizens, Central Americans at even less. Ronald dreams of recruiting Vietnamese, currently on $1 a month in their garrisons in Kampuchea. *1983*

SHEIKH AL-COME, of the Saudi Royal family, has imported over 2.1 million workers, 800,000 of whom are from India, Pakistan, Thailand, the Philippines and South Korea. He likes the fact that they are cheap, hard-working and safe, but now that the oil market is soft, feels queasy about the 300,000 more he has on order. His seven Gulf cousins have taken on another million, only 800,000 of whom are on the books. *1982*

JOSE SUCRE, chief executive, Dominican State Sugar Council, painted after his recent business coup: 19,000 Haitians for a total of $2 million a year ($105 each, one tenth of the official minimum wage). 'They get what they want - work. Plenty of it: 13 hours a day.' *1984*

CLIVE LOVEJOY, head of Chipso-Facto, a Silicon Valley semiconductor firm, captured on canvas while convalescing after a severe drop in turnover. He is prone to reminiscing fondly about the years of high recruitment when electronic engineers were bought with stock options, scuba diving lessons in the company pool, jogging tracks, dental insurance, paid sabbaticals, lotteries for Cadillacs, Corvettes and $10,000 bonuses, television courses in advanced circuit theory, Friday afternoon beer busts; $100,000 a year and state-of-the-art research or production. *1984*

Hang Fan-shen 1985

M.R.G. Judder 1982

Abdul Aziz Rahman 1982

Inq og'Nito 1986

John and Giovanni Ordinario 1986

THE SELLERS

HANG FAN-SHEN, president, Guangdong Manpower Service, China, heads a powerful labour-exporting company with contracts worth $2.5 billion for the supply of 40,000 workers (labourers, maids, chefs, engineers, architects) building refineries in Iraq, roads across the Sahara, a bank tower in Libya, a soya sauce factory in Thailand, a palace in the Congo. His cousin runs the National Construction Engineering Corporation with over 300 projects in 50 countries, and contracts worth $400 million. Their charges are low: $2 a day per contract worker, six days a week. Distant relatives run the more upmarket labour exporting organizations in the Philippines (700,000 already abroad, three-quarters of them in the Middle East), South Korea (160,000 abroad at $400 a month on average) and Vietnam (60,000-100,000 in the USSR). *1985*

M R G JUDDER, entrepreneur, licensed by the government of Saudi Arabia, charges £140 a month, which includes the cost of shipping back dead bodies or the injured, but not the cost of repatriating strikers and other troublemakers to their homes in India, Pakistan, Bangladesh, Sri Lanka, Thailand and the Philippines. *1982*

ABDUL AZIZ RAHMAN, PCS, licensed by the government of Pakistan, regrets the passing of the good years, when $3 billion a year were sent home by the two million workers he has helped place in the Middle East. So do his friends and competitors, fellow government appointees in North Yemen ($1.6 billion a year) and Jordan (over half the labour force abroad). *1982*

INQ OG'NITO, the Ordinario's country cousin, is one of the 25 or so million people who live abroad illegally, working at low-paid jobs in farming, construction (men), hotels and catering (men and women), house-keeping and prostitution (women). There could be 8-10 million in the US; 300,000, mainly Zairians, Senegalese and Malians, in France: 300,000 Haitians in the Dominican Republic. Millions more migrate illegally to urban centres within their own countries - above all in South Africa and the USSR. *1986*

JOHN AND GIOVANNI ORDINARIO need to earn sufficient to keep them and their children alive, sane and fit for whatever work is on offer where they live. Wages vary a great deal from place to place and job to job. They are part of an international family, numbering 750 million or so people, one third of whom are women. *1986*

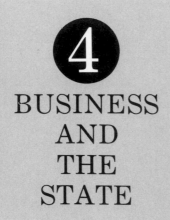

4

BUSINESS
AND
THE
STATE

'The people running the major economies of the world don't know what they're doing.'
Michael Blumenthal, US Treasury Secretary 1977-79 and then chairman of Burroughs Corporation

Business cannot operate without the state, nor the state without business.

Business requires physical security, a solid framework of law, and a supply of usable labour and materials. It expects the state to provide or assure them. All states do, to the limits of their capacity.

But states do more than this. They help business to preserve for itself as much of its home base as it can, and to make as large inroads as possible into markets abroad.

PROTECTIONISM

States impose often high, sometimes punitive, import tariffs. They erect non-tariff barriers of all sorts: bans, quotas, 'voluntary' export restraints, variable levies, minimum import-price arrangements, domestic content requirements – which foreign exporters have to overcome.

They create administrative obstacles and tortuous customs procedures for foreign exporters and condone - if not actively encourage - internal distribution mazes of extraordinary complexity for foreign firms.

The accusation indirect
'Manufactured imports in Japan amount to 2.4 per cent of GNP, compared with 5.6 per cent in Europe and 5 per cent in the US.'
Norman Tebbit, Britain's Trade and Industry Secretary, Tokyo, 1985

The accusation direct
'Japan restricts its imports of leather footwear to one pair per head of population every 200 years.'
M O Fellden, Director General, British Footwear Manufacturers' Federation, 1984

Tit for tat

What the Japanese did for the Renault 5:

'When we first unloaded the Renault 5 in Yokohama, we were told that the cars had to clear customs 200 kilometres away. There were no parking facilities, so we had to buy our own ground. While we went through some extremely complicated and costly legal procedures, the cars had to wait for weeks in bad weather. It took us two years to get the building permit, six months to get it linked to the water mains, and another eight months to get electricity.'
Senior French trade official

By the time the French were in a position to start selling, the Japanese had decided that no foreign company was to be allowed more than eight dealerships in the whole of Japan.

What the French did for the Japanese video recorder:

They routed all imports, running at 500,000-600,000 a year, through a single, small customs post at Poitiers, in the interior of the country, with strict instructions to implement the decree that all trade documents were to be in French, causing every single carton to be opened.

'One morning last week the strict rules were enforced with devastating effect. Customs clearance on a consignment of video recorders . . . ceased altogether while a technician was summoned from Paris, three hours away by train. He was ordered to dismantle a sample video recorder to verify the country of origin of each of its electronic components. The customs officers wanted to satisfy themselves that the full amount of duty on the videos was being paid.'
Sunday Times (London), 1982

Self-interest

States channel their considerable buying power towards national firms and lean on the private sector to do the same.

In 1984, the British Treasury published guidelines which, worded so as not to fall foul of EEC competition rules, suggested that government purchasing officers should not necessarily opt for the lowest priced goods and services.

At about the same time, the Martin-Baker Company of Denham, England, won a contract in open competition to supply ejector seats for the US Navy's F18A war-plane. Congress overruled the award and asked the navy to find a US supplier.

Marconi space and defence systems and Thorn-EMI of Britain both bought US arms contracting companies in order to strengthen their competitive hand in the US. The Pentagon responded by lowering the security classifications of these acquisitions and narrowing their range of biddable contracts.

The Carter administration estimated that the Tokyo Round international trade package would open $20-25 billion a year in foreign-government procurements to US companies: in 1981, only $4 billion of procurements were opened to outside competition, and actual US sales under the agreement seem to have been about $210 million.

Citrus socialism

States reserve large areas of business for themselves in 'lemon socialism', or state owned business, charters.

Eleven of the top 50 industrial companies outside the US, as listed by Fortune magazine, were state owned in 1984. More than a third of the top 100 European companies, as listed by the Financial Times, were wholly or partly owned by the state in 1983.
■ In France, state-controlled companies account for over 30 per cent of the country's industrial turnover and most of its commercial banking. Including energy, commerce, insurance and the media, the state owns around 4,000 companies.
■ In West Germany, Europe's motor of private enterprise, the federal government holds stakes in over 900 businesses, producing half the aluminium, one third the iron ore, one quarter the electricity and one-eighth the hard coal in the country.

■ In Mexico, the state was estimated to own 70 per cent of the economy in late 1982.

States reserve even larger areas in the core economy for national business. At the start of the 1980s, when world trade had flattened out to about $2,000 billion a year, the most common protectionist devices were choking off some $62.5 billion of potential traffic.

Keep off the grass

■ Britain requires official approval for foreign-controlled shareholdings of 10 per cent or more.

■ The US bars foreign investment in domestic aviation, shipping, communications, hydro- and nuclear power, and - in practice, if not in law - military industries.

■ Canada requires official approval for foreign ownership of more than 20 per cent in private companies or 5 per cent in public companies, and discourages foreign control in utilities and the cultural and financial sectors.

■ Sweden bars foreign holdings of over 20 per cent in companies with freehold property.

■ Japan requires to be informed about any share purchase above 10 per cent of a company's equity.

■ Mexico restricts foreign participation to a maximum of 49 per cent except in very special circumstances.

■ France requires Finance Ministry approval for foreign ownership of over 20 per cent. In practice the ceiling is 10 per cent if the money is Arab, except in property.

Arab money is harām

In 1974, when the big rise in oil prices put so many billions in OPEC pockets, only $5 billion managed to settle as direct investments.
Panic struck far and wide:

■ The Deutsche Bank bought control of Daimler-Benz to ward off an Iranian purchase. 'It was a duty we could not shirk', commented Fritz Heinrich Ulrich, president, Deutsche Bank.

■ The leading Swiss banks changed their stock to ensure that control was vested in registered shares, themselves ownable only by Swiss residents.

■ The US Department of Defense instructed all military contractors to avoid investments from Middle East oil producers, after blocking a Saudi

bid for minority holdings in Lockheed and Grumman. Where major investments were allowed, as in Pan Am, they were confined to peripheral spheres, such as Pan Am's hotel subsidiary.

COMPETING FOR FOREIGN INVESTMENT

States also subsidize home producers and pour money into research and development.
States compete vigorously for foreign investment where it promises to plug a gap in employment, technology or foreign exchange, provided that it does not endanger national control. In the West, currently, it is the Japanese who receive most encouragement.
In 1984, the EEC blocked a British government grant to Yamakazi, the Japanese company, to help it build a machine tool plant in Worcester. West Germany objected to the £5.2 million grant, pending an investigation into its possible impact on the European machine tool industry.
Two years previously, West Germany itself had been in hot competition against Britain, France and Belgium for the £20 million plant.
In August 1984, the EEC Commission agreed to the subsidy. In October, Italy and France intimated that they might appeal against the ruling.

Apple pie order

'Loan guarantees, I soon learned, were as American as apple pie. Among those who had received them were electronics companies, farmers, railroads, chemical companies, shipbuilders, small businessmen of every description, college students and airlines. In fact a total of $409 billion in loans and guarantees was outstanding when we made our $1 billion request. But nobody knew this.'
Lee Iacocca, chairman of Chrysler

EXTRATERRITORIALITY

States advance business into foreign territory by:

■ negotiating the framework for multilateral deals through GATT (General Agreement on Tariffs and Trade), UNCTAD (United Nations Conference on Trade and Development), the EEC, Comecon and a host of other forums for settling the international trading order

■ negotiating the framework for bilateral deals between countries, of which there are thousands in any one year

■ negotiating the deals themselves

■ promoting the international spread of state corporations.

Negotiating the deals – or not

Deals clinched by governments are invariably greeted by howls of anguish and accusations of unfair practice from defeated competitors abroad.

The relatively poor British government is frequently accused by business of lacking resolution in the international marketplace. In a review of 29 international contracts for railway locomotives, Hawker Siddeley claimed that its Brush Electrical Machines subsidiary had 'definitely' lost five for lack of matching financial help from the British government. On occasions, the company had not even been invited to tender, because other governments had the customer 'sewn up' with a soft credit package.

It is not only Western states that seed their national companies in foreign soil.

By early 1982, there were about 700 Eastern bloc companies operating outside the East, of which some 400 were in the rich West. Of these about 124 were engaged in production, 28 of them in the West.

They participated in a wide range of activities: commerce, transport, manufacturing, banking, insurance, engineering design and consultancy.

The USSR was involved in 111 companies, Poland in 96, Romania 82, Hungary 68, Bulgaria 44. Most were either fully owned (31.4 per cent of them) or majority owned by Eastern bloc countries (32.4 per cent).

Nor, in the West, is it only the private sector that prospects abroad. In only six months of 1984, French state companies developed considerable US interests:

■ Bull took a 10 per cent stake in Ridge Computers, California.

■ Telic, a subsidiary of Cit-Alcatel, took 20 per cent of Sonitrol, Virginia-based maker of remote control security equipment.

■ Rhône-Poulenc, the chemicals group, formed a joint venture with Siltec, California, to manufacture silicon wafers in France.

■ Sanofi, pharmaceuticals subsidiary of the oil group Elf Aquitaine, took over Dairyland Food Laboratories, the Wisconsin-based biotech company.

■ Thomson, in electronics, agreed on collaboration with two California computer companies, Fortune and Eagle, and joint research and marketing with Diasonics, California.

■ Matra, the defence and electronics group, agreed to joint development and sales of computer terminals with Datapoint.

■ Dalas-Weir, a subsidiary of Alsthom Atlantique, agreed to market power station equipment jointly with Combustion Engineering.

■ Charbonnages de France, the state coal company, agreed to collaborate on solar energy with Chronar.

■ Alcatel-Thomson, the telecommunications group, joined forces with Fairchild Industries to manufacture and market satellite communications services and equipment.

These agreements, between French state-owned and US private sector companies, were mainly in the high-technology fields of computer electronics, telecommunications, engineering and biotechnology.

SOVEREIGNTY v EXTRATERRITORIALITY

The involvement of the state in business and the spread of business internationally have led to an increasing number of brushes between states on the issues of sovereignty and extraterritoriality.

Under US law, foreign subsidiaries of American companies are 'subject to the jurisdiction of the US'.

In most of the world, including Europe, the nationality of a company is determined by its place of incorporation. For Washington to exercise jurisdiction over US subsidiaries abroad is seen elsewhere as an invasion of sovereignty; not to do so is seen in Washington as an abridgement or even abdication of such sovereignty.

The issue has been fought on a number of fronts: shipping and air transport, monopoly or anti-trust legislation, 'trading with the enemy', taxation and, increasingly, investor and consumer protection, civil rights, equal employment opportunities and environmental protection.

At least 19 states have protested to the US about its assertion of jurisdiction in international anti-trust cases. Measures to stop the flow of information demanded by the US authorities from US business subsidiaries and licensees have been taken by many European governments (Britain, Denmark, France, West Germany, Netherlands, Norway, Sweden and Switzerland), as well as by Australia, Canada and India, Japan and South Africa.

The strongest defence was mounted in the British Protection of Trading Interests Act, 1980, which provided for the levying of unlimited fines on firms for failing to obey official directives.

'We can't impose our law within the US and, frankly, they can't impose their law in Britain.'
Norman Tebbit, then British Trade and Industry Secretary

The Soviet gas pipeline

A major row erupted in 1982, when Washington tried to control exports from its trading partners to the USSR. It set out to apply sanctions against companies exporting US-licensed components for use on the giant Soviet gas pipeline being built from Urengoy in Siberia to Western Europe. The action foundered in a storm of rivalry and recrimination.

October 1981

Contracts worth $1.8 billion for Western equipment were signed, after 18 months of negotiations and six years of spasmodic talks. The main European suppliers were AEG-Kanis and Demag, West Germany; John Brown, Scotland; Creusot-Loire and Dresser, France; Nuove Pignone, Italy. Nearly all the equipment involved rested on the technology of three US firms: General Electric, Dresser and Cooper.

December 1981

Following the imposition of martial law in Poland, the US embargoed exports of equipment needed by European companies to fulfil pipeline contracts.

June 1982

The US expanded the embargo to include equipment manufactured abroad by subsidiaries and licensees of US groups.

August 1982

The French government threatened to requisition, under a 1959 decree, the services of Dresser if it failed to fulfil its contract obligations. At stake were £420 million (some $700 million) of exports. President Mitterand described the embargo as 'a restrictive, vexatious, unjust and dangerous' abuse of American power.

Britain invoked the Protection of Trading Interests Act to prevent compliance with the US embargo. At stake were £220 million (some $380 million). The British Secretary of State for Trade described the embargo as 'repugnant in international law'.

West Germany £686 million ($880 million) and Italy £509 million ($1,200 million) instructed their companies to carry on regardless.

November 1982

The US lifted sanctions against European companies unconditionally.

High tech, low results

In 1984, the US again attempted to interrupt the trade of its allies with the USSR, this time over the export of high technology.

January 1984

The US proposed new rules that would require customers for American computers and other high-tech products anywhere to supply Washington with information on their clients and with the identities of all probable clients. The measure would have increased the number of necessary export licences from 90,000 a year to more than a million.

IBM reminded 30 British leasing companies of the need to obtain US official permission for any change in the use or location of equipment supplied by IBM (Britain) anywhere in the world.

'The principal words of guidance I can give the management of IBM Britain are - unless the problem is resolved, it is going to be extremely bad for their business.'

Norman Tebbit, then British Trade and Industry Secretary

John Hadland, a British manufacturer of advanced photographic measuring devices, informed the Prime Minister that applications for US export licences were followed by American approaches to the intended customers in China with offers of US company equipment. Some of the firm's export applications were still 'being considered' by the Americans four years after they were first made.

April 1984

250 US companies and trade associations and several foreign governments protested at the US government's proposals.

'Our industry is fighting for its life against Japanese competition, and our government is threatening to destroy our competitive edge',

Larry Hansen, vice president, Varian Associates of Palo Alto, California

US academics protested at the derailment of scientific and engineering meetings by last-minute government demands to suppress unclassified papers; at surveillance placed on meetings open to participants from the East; at requests to isolate students and researchers from such countries at American universities; at the random searches and confiscations undertaken at ports of embarkation.

President Reagan extended the Pentagon's role in reviewing exports to cover 12 countries in addition to members of the Warsaw Pact and China. Included in the new list were Austria, Sweden and Switzerland, as well as Libya and South Africa.

May 1984

Datasaab Contracting AB (Sweden) was fined a record $3.12 million by a federal judge for providing the USSR with equipment, parts, training and technology used to develop a military air traffic control system.

The US Customs Service revealed the existence of Project Rampart, a plan to place bugs in sensitive computer and electronics equipment shipped abroad. The miniature transmitters would broadcast coded messages on the way to their final destination, providing a check on the accompanying exports.

'If I wanted to illegally export a piece of equipment, which I don't, then why should I knowingly place a bug in it?'

US exporter of hi-tech products

'I would simply remove the bug, place it in a room and move the equipment elsewhere if I wanted to outwit the system. It doesn't make sense.'

Senior industrialist

July 1984

A compromise agreement was reached by the major Western countries, members of the Co-ordinating Committee (Cocom), whereby:

■ most personal computers were freed from export controls;
■ some software was brought under control; and
■ the export of sophisticated telephone exchanges to the East was limited up to 1988.

'The motive of US technology protectionism does not lie in the security field, as is often claimed. The real aim is to protect the domestic high technology industry, which saw its traditional lead endangered in the light of Japanese successes.'

IW (Institute of German Economy), Cologne, August 1984

November 1984

Plasma Technology, Britain, challenged its own government to prosecute it for exporting equipment to China without a licence. It had already lost a vital order to the US company Plasmatherm.

June 1985

The EEC protested at the passage of a new Export Administration Act, authorizing the US President to block imports from any party that violated US national security controls.

July 1985

The British Attorney General protested that US claims were unwarranted encroachments on British jurisdiction and 'are contrary to international law'.

August 1985

The US government blocked a French deal to supply China with a sophisticated business communications system; and entered high-powered talks with Singapore to control the leakage of high-tech products to Soviet bloc countries.

Postscript

In 1985, the US Department of Defense declared that the USSR was forced to spend between $6.6 billion and $13.3 billion in additional weapons development costs as a result of measures taken by the US in 1983-84 to prevent the export of electronic high-tech products.

A secret assessment by the Soviet Military Industries Commission, VPK, put the value to Soviet aviation of Western technology at 18.8 million roubles ($24.6 million) in 1978 and 48.6 million roubles ($64.2 million) in 1979.

Secret secrets

The Militarily Critical Technologies List, which the US Department of Defense has been developing since the mid-1970s, runs to several volumes. These have never been published because publication would benefit the USSR. At the same time their contents cannot be used by exporters as a control, because no exporter has access to them.

Academic cryptographers in the US - the code makers and breakers - have agreed to let the National Security Agency vet anything sensitive they intend to publish. But the NSA dare not tell them openly what it considers to be sensitive. So the academics have to guess.

'The danger is that if the West starts behaving more like the Russians by becoming obsessive about secrecy, it will condemn itself to a Russian rate of innovation.'

Financial Times

BUSINESS V THE STATE

Though the state and business generally work together in world markets, their capacity to bicker is infinite.

Where state and business are one and the same, as in the USSR, these conflicts take place within the bureaucracy and are seldom revealed. In the richer West, where there is greater differentiation in function between state and business, and where the economy and society are more open and change faster in consequence, the conflicts are on permanent show.

Who pays for the state's services to business, how much and for what, are questions that fuel never-ending disputes between them : on tax-levels and subsidies, on civil service payrolls and performance, on trust-busting and -building, and on general economic policy.

In business's view, the state should merely serve - and not do - business. But business cannot always handle its own business. It is often too fragmented; in need of considerable new funds; too weak to cater for the special needs of the 'social sectors' such as finance or defence; unable to withstand international competition or to keep labour sweet.

The state view prevails today in most of the South. For a period after the second world war this view was increasingly influential almost everywhere outside the US, and the state took over many of the classic functions of business in a jamboree of nationalization.

Then, as the world settled down and business grew stronger, there was less need for it to rely so heavily on the state. At the same time, the state was proving increasingly cumbersome in the rapidly expanding and fast changing world market. The public sectors were increasingly eroded by tides of privatization.

Britain showed the way, with the largest disposal of state assets the world had ever seen.

Britain auctions the family silver

State assets sold, £ million

1979-80	
British Petroleum (BP) (5%)	276
ICL (25%)	37
shares in Suez Finance and others	57

1980-81	
Ferranti (50%)	55
Fairey (100%)	22

North Sea oil licences	195
British Aerospace (51%)	43
miscellaneous	91

1981-82	
British Sugar (24%)	44
Cable & Wireless (50%)	182
Amersham (100%)	64
miscellaneous, including Crown Agent and Forestry Commission sales of land and property	199

1982-83	
Britoil (51%)	627
Associated British Ports (49%)	46
oil licences, oil stockpiles and miscellaneous	108
National Freight Corporation	54

1983-84	
British Petroleum (BP) (7%)	565
Cable & Wireless (22.5%)	260

1984-85	
Enterprise Oil	400
British Rail Sealink	66
British Leyland-Jaguar	294
British Telecom (50.2%)	3,700
British Aerospace (48.4%)	363

1985-86	
Britoil (49%)	540
Cable & Wireless (22.5%)	630

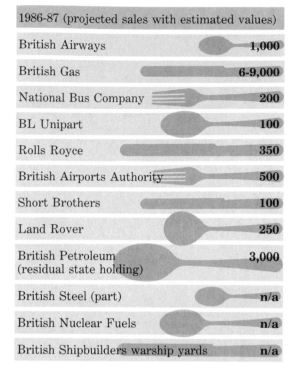

1986-87 (projected sales with estimated values)

British Airways	1,000
British Gas	6-9,000
National Bus Company	200
BL Unipart	100
Rolls Royce	350
British Airports Authority	500
Short Brothers	100
Land Rover	250
British Petroleum (residual state holding)	3,000
British Steel (part)	n/a
British Nuclear Fuels	n/a
British Shipbuilders warship yards	n/a

Privatization fever

Britain is not alone. Special situations apart, the trend is everywhere the same.

■ West Germany is substantially reducing its holdings in major companies, including Volkswagen and VIAG.

■ France's right-wing government, elected March 1986, expects to have privatized some FF200 billions' worth of industrial, banking and other financial assets within five years of taking office. On the list are the three big commercial banks, the three big insurance companies, and six of the biggest industrial companies.

■ Japan ended the state monopoly of tobacco and salt in 1985; and the enormous state-owned telephone company, NTT, is scheduled to become the largest private sector corporation in the country.

■ Canada's state-run Development Investment Corporation is divesting itself of its shareholdings in major aerospace, nuclear, telecommunications and agricultural machinery industries.

■ Mexico is presiding over the largest sale of state assets ever experienced in Latin America : selling shares in 339 companies to the value of $490 million.

■ Brazil has prepared a list of 77 state enterprises to be privatized, merged or closed down.

■ Jamaica has sold or leased most of its state interests in sugar refining and hotels.

■ Turkey, having sold revenue-sharing certificates in the Bosphorus bridge and the Keban dam on the Euphrates, then sold its national airline into majority private ownership.

Morgan Guaranty of New York has drawn up a master plan for privatizing much of the large state sector.

■ Thailand is going in the same direction to ensure 'national survival'.

■ Malaysia, Singapore and Taiwan all have big privatization projects.

■ Bangladesh has privatized nearly one hundred state companies since 1982, including most of the jute, cotton textile, chemical and engineering industries.

■ Pakistan has privatized some 2,000 state companies: mainly rice, flour and cotton mills.

■ China's private business population rose more than fifty fold to 7.5 million in the five years to 1984. By 1985, some 5,500 factories and 52,000 enterprises had been turned over to the private and co-operative sectors.

■ Romanian employees have been granted the right to buy into their places of work.

■ Bulgaria is encouraging foreign investors to participate in small and medium-sized firms.

■ Even in the US, where the state does tend to serve, rather than do, business, the vestigial public sector is being reduced - in communications, in aerospace and in public services, including prisons.

THE ARMS DEALERS

One area of business where the state has not relinquished its hold is armaments. Whatever the formal status of the arms makers and traders in a country, there are few states which do not exercise control over the production, use and sale of weapons.

Arms and the state are inseparable.

Share of world arms exports, 1980-84, percentages

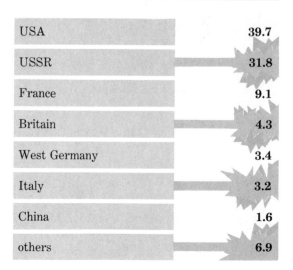

USA	39.7
USSR	31.8
France	9.1
Britain	4.3
West Germany	3.4
Italy	3.2
China	1.6
others	6.9

WORLD WEAPONS WAREHOUSES

ANYTHING, ANYWHERE, ANYHOW

Stunningly presented in the new 3W catalogue is a whole new shopping experience for you, your staff and your advisers to enjoy. A dazzling parade of the most exciting, up-to-the-minute hardware, for a vast choice of missions and tactics, to suit every conceivable need ... a wealth of items for more security...ideas for perimeter defence, concepts for internal peacekeeping - in all, thousands of carefully selected items, each covered by 3W's unique 'No Quibble' guarantee.

All goods are sent on 90 days' approval, and there is free delivery direct to your base. But the best news of all is: with 3W's free credit terms over 12 to 60 months, there's no need to send any money with your first order... What's more, for every million dollars you spend, we give you back $1,000 in commission, placed safely in a bank - and account - of your choice.

How much do you pay?

We in 3W are proud of our reputation for keen pricing, and for passing on to our customers the benefits of our careful selection, fixed-price supplier contracts and fast turnover. But our prices also depend on you: if you order in bulk, you benefit from handsome discounts - up to 50 per cent in some cases; consolidated orders result in large savings - up to 30 per cent; open sales are more economical than camouflaged ones; and the final price of many fast-changing high-tech lines can be a fraction of the cost of early models, if you can afford to wait.

We have found that $25 million is usually sufficient for new clients to make their first selections. However, it may well be that your first selections come to more than this amount. If that is the case, simply inform us of your first orders together with an outline of your requirements.

Credit

We offer a number of schemes. There are standard credits of one to five years' duration, with grace periods of six to eighteen months. And there is the continuous credit facility, an ideal way to buy 'that something extra' when you already have a credit account: we simply add the cost of the latest purchase to the amount you already owe, and spread the new total over a maximum of five years. In many cases you will pay no more than the cash price.

Delivery

Our warehouses hold enormous stocks, and goods are delivered as quickly as possible, either by our own transport or via a reputable international carrier.

Should you require us to arrange special deliveries outside normal schedules or routes, or with unusual cover or documentation, we shall be happy to do so. But in such a case, we shall be obliged to add a delivery surcharge on our warehouse price.

Should you wish to make your own arrangements, we shall reduce our price to take account of that.

All our customers are always right

We are proud of our record in maintaining uninterrupted supplies whatever the difficulties. We can reveal for the first time that we have supplied both contenders in the long Iraq-Iran war that began in 1980 with major items from a number of our suppliers, including the US, USSR, China, France, Italy, Britain, East Germany, Switzerland, North Korea and Brazil.

One of our most enterprising warehouse managers bought captured Iranian equipment - M-47 tanks, howitzers and mortars - from Iraq, and then resold it to Iran.

Special services

This department concentrates on all aspects of your defence needs other than purchases of hardware. It acts as an agent for production licences, and for sales offset and counter purchase agreements; it advises on equipment supply, financial services, technical support and training; it supplies advisers and special agents; it arranges construction, engineering and maintenance contracts; and it liaises between states at every level and at every degree of visibility. Enquiries are welcomed.

GUARANTEE OF SERVICE AND SATISFACTION

We guarantee that every article offered for sale in this catalogue is honestly described and illustrated. If you have any reason to be dissatisfied with any article purchased from us, you may return it in good condition within 90 days of purchase. We will exchange it, or refund any payment made.

Major General Juan Louis MacDroon, Jr.
president, WWW

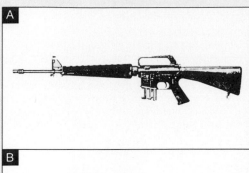

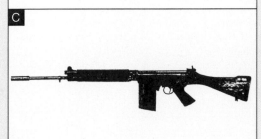

Infantry supplies

The wonders of modern technology have not yet replaced the infantryman as the basic factor on the battlefield.

From our vast stock of standard issue rifles

A 5.56 mm AR-15 (M16) rifle *US made*
A lightweight, low-impulse rifle firing a light-weight bullet at high velocity. Designed in the late 1950s, the rifle was extensively modified in the light of combat experience in Vietnam and a Congressional Inquiry, and is now considered to be at least as reliable as any other in service.

manufacturers: Military Firearms Division of Colt's Industries, Hartford, Conn. Under licence in South Korea, Philippines, Singapore.
status: Currently in production.
service: In service with US forces. Also Chile, Dominican Republic, Haiti, Italy, Jordan, South Korea, Mexico, Nicaragua, Panama, Philippines, United Kingdom, Vietnam.

B 5.45mm AK-74 and AKS Assault Rifles
USSR made
An evolutionary step forward from the highly successful AKM assault rifle, the AK-74 presents no novelties to its users - an important training consideration - and has inherited the reliability of its predecessors alongside their astonishing ability to withstand rough handling and abuse. With its uniquely successful muzzle brake, this is an infantryman's weapon system which is at least the equal of anything in the West and perhaps a half-generation ahead.
manufacturers: State arsenals
status: Currently in production
service: Soviet forces

C 7.62mm FN FAL *Belgium made*
An outstanding success, this rifle has been adopted by over 90 countries and seems likely to continue in first line service until well past the year 2000. Used effectively by both sides in the Falklands war.
manufacturer: Fabrique Nationale (FN), Branche Défense et Sécurité, B-4400 Herstal and licensees.
status: Currently in production.
service: The FAL has been or is still in production not only in Belgium but also in a number of other countries such as Argentina, Australia, Austria, Canada, India, Israel, Mexico, Nigeria, South Africa, United Kingdom and Venezuela.

included amongst the countries using the FN FAL are:
Argentina, Australia, Austria, Barbados, Belgium, Brazil, Burundi, Chile, Cuba, Dominican Republic, Ecuador, Gambia, West Germany, Ghana, Guyana, India, Indonesia, Ireland, Israel, Kampuchea, Kuwait, Liberia, Libya, Luxembourg, Malawi, Malaysia, Morocco, Mozambique, Oman, New Zealand, Norway, Paraguay, Peru, Portugal, Singapore, South Africa, United Arab Emirates and the United Kingdom.

Counter-terrorism and counter insurgency

D 9mm Uzi submachine gun *Israel made*
Arguably the best SMG in production. Fabricated out of metal stampings, it has an unusually short overall length and a remarkable balance which permits handling and firing with one hand. A grip safety catch prevents accidental discharge if the gun is dropped, and a bayonet lug for a short knife bayonet is provided. Proved in combat in continual border clashes in the early 1950s and in the Sinai war of 1956, the Uzi has been widely adopted.
manufacturers: Israel Military Industries, Ramat Hasharon 47100, Israel. Also Fabrique Nationale d'Armes de Guerre, Herstal, Belgium.
status: Currently in production.
service: Israeli forces. Also Belgium, West Germany, Iran, Ireland, Netherlands, Thailand, Venezuela and others.

COMPETITION AND CONTROL

Both business and state strive to strengthen their control over the other. Business does so through deputation and delegation; through seconding its officers to state posts and recruiting state officials on their retirement and, increasingly, in mid-career; through the political process; and ultimately through the threat or reality of a capital strike. The state acts through persuasion, legislation and, as a last resort, physical force.

Neither ever fully trusts the other. The state is seen as inherently slow, inefficient, parochial; business, as self-serving, greedy, irresponsible.

Scandinavian scandal

Disappointed by the government's inability to control inflation, imports, pay settlements, and industrial action, Swedish business went on strike. Early in 1985, it sent growing amounts of money abroad, totalling SKr10 billion by mid-May (a quarter of which went in the last week). The government and the Central Bank were forced to introduce the most far-reaching package of penalties and inducements for decades.

THE ETIQUETTE OF BUSINESS AND THE STATE

'Influencing governments and public opinion was voted the most important new task for chief executives'.

Poll of 300 US chief executives carried out by headhunters Heidrick and Struggles

'There is a right way and a wrong of doing anything, and the best-intentioned people occasionally make trifling lapses from what is regarded as good form. In truth such lapses are most commonly the result of ignorance, and even the best informed long at times for some handbook which, by furnishing details of correct procedure on all important occasions, may be a bulwark of strength.'

The Etiquette of Marriage, London, 1902

A GUIDE TO ETIQUETTE

INTRODUCTIONS

IT IS UNBECOMING, and usually unproductive, for a business suitor to approach an official or politician directly, without being properly introduced. The ways of effecting an introduction are numerous, with local variations. In Italy, for instance, it is useful to join a masonic lodge; in the United States, there are more or less exclusive social clubs; in Britain, there are formal functions, from diplomatic receptions to dinner parties, where a relationship may be initiated. In foreign countries, letters of introduction may be the only means available. But in such instances, the greatest care must be exercised, with exhaustive enquiries advised, if success and even safety are to be assured. The story is told of one British publisher, supplied with a letter of introduction from the former ambassador of an African state, who produced the testimonial during a tedious examination at the airport of the state's capital and was promptly arrested.

COURTSHIP

COURTSHIP is not to be hurried, despite the presumptions to the contrary in the pages of romantic fiction. Impetuous pressure may only produce alarm and the rupture of a prospering relationship. In Britain, it is perfectly proper to entertain a civil servant at a restaurant, for the exchange of pleasantries and information, since the morality of such officials is not the subject of unwholesome public comment. Furthermore, since civil servants are frequently more material in affecting the decisions of departments than are their ministerial masters, wooing is best conducted in this way. In some countries of continental Europe, however, the public entertainment of officials and politicians is somewhat cynically interpreted, and invitation to the discreet enjoyment of private hospitality is more acceptable. In the United States, where the courtship of government by business is a common feature of the political process, attempts to conceal the emerging relationship may well prove less rewarding than the flaunting of it, since they are likely to provoke suspicion that there is something to conceal.

ENGAGEMENT

THE SUCCESS of courtship is generally signalled by a formal engagement, which may be symbolized by the presentation of a gift. But such a gift should never flout the proprieties of the society concerned. In Britain, for instance, the offer of a gift to a civil servant would in general cause unpardonable offence, while gratitude to the party in power would most becomingly be shown by a contribution to its funds. In the United States, gifts may be more personal and offered to the campaign funds of individual politicians who have been helpful and must sooner or later submit themselves to re-election. In other societies, notably those of the so-called developing states, gifts may be made directly to accommodating civil servants and politicians, and are sometimes demanded, even specified, as a condition of the engagement. Such customs

may seem strange, but are not to be altogether condemned, for they provide a stated set of values in what is often a most delicate and ambiguous relationship.

MARRIAGE

THE OBJECTIVE of an engagement is, of course, marriage. And it is a source of celebration when the nuptial knot is duly tied with the appropriate ceremony. In some countries, the ceremony involves the induction of a retired executive into high political office; or the appointment of a retired high official, trailing clouds of influence, to the company board. In others, the attainment of a permanent relationship is not marked by any ceremony, since the marriage is taken for granted, and premarital relations have already been reflected in public expressions of mutual dependence between the business and the government.

DIVORCE

REGRETTABLY marriage is not always as permanent as would appear from the vows which are taken by the parties concerned. Nowhere in the realm of etiquette is the obedience to decorous standards more necessary than in the province of divorce. It is always more profitable to both parties, if a period of separation is chosen in place of a divorce, so as to allow for reconciliation in the future. But if divorce is found to be inescapable, then it should be pursued in the most amicable way, without the slightest evidence of rancour for public entertainment and satisfaction. A suitably worded insertion in the papers, announcing the departure of one or other party with expressions of continuing goodwill and co-operation between the former partners, will prevent much mischief and lend some dignity to an unfortunate occasion.

Making the best of it

The evolution of the giant business into the global business has added a new dimension to the tension between business and the state. Besides its traditional concerns, business now feels it needs to be in a position to influence foreign and military policy. At the same time, the ability of business to shift resources, finance and tax liabilities from country to country, gives the state an irresistible incentive to exercise effective control over such operations.

In the rich host countries of the West, where the state is more powerful than any single company, some form of accommodation is normally reached. In the poorer host countries of the South, the multinationals usually have the whip hand.

The Bechtel connection

The Bechtel Group is the world's biggest international contractor, with contracts valued at $13.8 billion in 1983, or 162 per cent more than its nearest rival, Kellogg Rust of Houston, Texas.

Now

We must not, under any circumstances, seek or appear to seek any special advantage or favour because of the relationships we have with persons who are in or close to government'.

Stephen D Bechtel Jnr, head of Bechtel, member of the Bohemian Club (together with Ronald Reagan; George Bush; Caspar Weinberger, former Bechtel legal adviser; and George Schultz, former president of Bechtel.)

Then

'I dare say that at no time in the history of American business have so few men made so much money with so little risk and all at the expense of the taxpayers, not only of this generation but of generations to come.'

Ralph Casey, Department of Defense, to Senate Committee, on the John McCone-Bechtel partnership which made a profit of $44 million on an investment of $100,000 building shipyards for the US Navy during the second world war. McCone, originally a steel salesman, rose to head the CIA under President Kennedy.

Before then

In 1927, Warren 'Dad' Bechtel was among the members of the Bohemian Club who called on Herbert Hoover, demanding that he announce his candidature for the presidency. Four years later, President Hoover asked Bechtel's company to head the consortium that built the Hoover dam across the Colorado River.

In plain clothes

Episodes from the story of ITT, a political common carrier

■ In May 1970, ITT, through John McCone, board member and former director of the CIA, approached the then CIA director Richard Helms about a joint CIA-ITT operation to ensure the election of a right-wing candidate in the forthcoming Chilean presidential election.

McCone later pledged $1 million to help Jorge Alessandri defeat Radomiro Tomic and Salvador Allende, both of whom had pledged to nationalize ITT's holdings. The Nixon administration rejected ITT's pro-Alessandri plan in favour of a strategy to block Allende, but the CIA helped ITT channel funds to the right-wing candidate.

■ In the early 1980s, Turkey under Turqul Ozal agreed to give ITT a $300 million telecommunications order on one condition: the company should help persuade the US Congress not to couple aid to Turkey with political concessions by Turkey over Cyprus.

Who warns whom?

In 1981, Rhodia, subsidiary of France's Rhône-Poulenc, warned the Brazilian government that, unless price controls over their products were lifted, they would suspend investments, cut exports and repay the company's foreign debts ahead of schedule. Bayer and Nestlé, among others, followed Rhodia's lead.

TAXATION AND THE BLACK ECONOMY

Big government and big business make for big taxes - and for big tax breaks within the law.

Nelson Bunker Hunt, then one of the richest people in the world, paid $9.65 in personal income tax between 1975 and 1977.

General Electric, tenth largest company in the US, paid nothing in federal corporate income taxes between 1981 and 1984, and even racked up a $35 million tax credit in 1983.

Other big US companies, such as Tenneco, Boeing, Dow Chemical and Du Pont also reduced their federal tax payments virtually to nil, through deft use of the 1981 tax reforms introduced by President Reagan.

In 1950, the share of federal tax revenue provided by the corporate sector was 25 per cent; by 1980 it was 12 per cent; by 1984, only 6 per cent.

Most people do not get the tax breaks. They pay, or they seek refuge in the black, grey, informal, underground, submerged, parallel, hidden, irregular, dual, cash, moonlight, twilight, subterranean...economy, where work goes on but is un-recorded by, or is misrepresented to, the state.

The black economy is huge and universal. It has been defined as any sole or secondary gainful, non-casual occupation that is carried out on or beyond the fringes of the law or the terms of regulations and agreements.

Do, dao and don't

'The more laws are enacted and taxes assessed, the greater the number of law-breakers and tax-evaders.'
Lao Tzu LVII

'When governments govern little, people are happy. When government governs much, people are miserable.'
Lao Tzu LVIII

'Those who make their living by collecting taxes cause the people to starve; when the people starve, the tax collectors, having no one to tax, starve also.

'Those who govern people make them discontented with being controlled; and therefore cause them to be uncontrollable.'
Lao Tzu LXXV

The revenue claims its pound, but doesn't get it

The American Internal Revenue Service estimates that under-reporting of income, overstatement of deductions and failure to file tax returns on legal incomes cost the Treasury $100 billion in 1983, up from $30 billion in 1973. Taxes owing on illegal incomes cost the IRS a further $10 billion.

In 1983, Italian shopkeepers declared average incomes of L6.6 million compared with an average L10.5 million for their assistants.

Share of earnings not disclosed to tax inspectors, France, 1984, percentages

self-employed taxi drivers; pastry makers and shoe repairers	52
jewellery makers	44
house painters	42

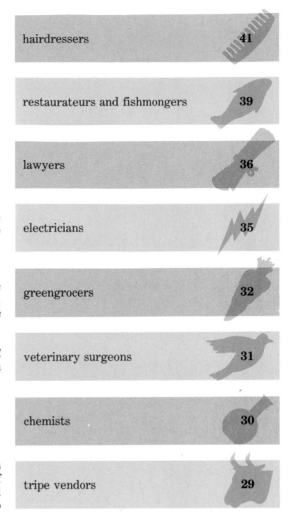

hairdressers	41
restaurateurs and fishmongers	39
lawyers	36
electricians	35
greengrocers	32
veterinary surgeons	31
chemists	30
tripe vendors	29

A trade union survey in the area around Rome found that 46.3 per cent of public sector employees and 51.5 per cent of manufacturing industry workers were moonlighting. Multiple job holding was a widespread practice in all occupational categories, including the clergy. The rates were particularly high among the teaching profession: 65 per cent among university staff and 50-75 per cent among the staff of senior secondary schools.

In Canada, a survey carried out among manual workers found that 15 per cent - or four to five times the rate in official statistics - had multiple jobs.

'The black economy is much bigger than anybody thinks. There is no other explanation for the strong demand in consumer electronics. For example, we are very strong in the Tyne-Tees area, which has had very high unemployment, but we have never noticed any sign of recession.'
David Johnson, managing director of Rum-belows, British high street electricals chain

Share of output and workforce involved in the black economy

Various estimates, percentages

	output	labour force
Australia	10	-
Austria	5+	5+
Belgium	15	15-20
Britain	3-15	3
Denmark	-	11
France	10	3-6
India	18-21	-
Italy	15-25	10-35
Norway	7-17	40
Portugal	10	-
Spain	5+	5+
Sweden	5+	13-14
Switzerland	5+	5+
USA	3-27	25
West Africa	**anything up to half the money supply**	
West Germany	2-13	1.5 +

State-run economies are no exception

In Hungary, the black economy accounts for an estimated 16-18 per cent of total estimated work and involves no less than three quarters of the workforce to some degree (40 per cent of workers in industry and construction, 90 per cent of those in agriculture, 20-25 per cent of the intelligentsia and 40 per cent of pensioners). 250,00 industrial workers organized in 20,000 work partnerships lease state factory machines and equipment for use after normal working hours.

In the USSR and China, it accounts for an inestimable but significant proportion of output, to judge from the growing frequency of trials for 'economic crimes'. In the USSR, 60 per cent of car repairs and 40-50 per cent of the petrol used privately are 'black'.

Closet workers

The principal groups of clandestine workers are:
■ illegal immigrants (for example, 10 per cent of the foreign population in West Germany)
■ undeclared home workers (an estimated 1.7 million in Italy)
■ The working unemployed (from an estimated 15 per cent in the US, through 27 per cent in Italy, to 50 per cent in the Seville area of Spain, and 80 per cent in the Bouches-du-Rhône area of France)
■ Retired persons or pensioners who work (2 per cent of the US labour force and 21 per cent of all old age pensioners and persons on disability benefit in Italy)

Closet sectors

Clandestine employment can be enormously complex, differing from area to area according to the local economy.

In Italy, its growth has been concentrated in certain types of production:
Naples
the manufacture of clothing, shoes and gloves
the Marche
musical instruments and furniture
Emilia-Romagna
pottery
Tuscany
textiles
northern cities
machinery and electronics equipment

In many countries, certain sectors are generally more affected by clandestine employment than others: building, clothing manufacture, the hotel and catering trades, motor vehicle repairs, furniture moving, transport, domestic work (including child-minding) and agriculture.

'It should be emphasized that, according to conservative estimates, almost a third of the houses being built today, particularly second homes, have never been invoiced in accordance with the regulations nor has any relevant notification been sent to the authorities responsible for social security, health insurance or the collection of VAT (value-added tax).'
Official Luxembourg report 1977

Russia's underground capitalists

In the 1960s, Boris Roifman and his cousin Peter Order were arrested by the KGB. Both had been in underground business for about 10 years. One turned over about 200 million roubles' worth of valuables to the authorities and the other about three-quarters that amount.

The chief investigator of the KGB central office asked the wealthier of the two:

'What did you need 200 million roubles for?'

Peter Order replied with a show of bravado: 'Only 200 million! I wanted to make 220 million - one rouble for each Soviet citizen.'

The black economy is the underside of the state economy, which has grown to become the biggest, most pervasive presence in the business system.

USSR INC

Some states are effectively businesses. Some appear to be distinct from business. The USSR is by far the biggest business. It is run by a small committee of people, members and candidate members of the politburo, through the Communist Party and the organs of state.

Like all giant enterprises, the USSR is deeply conservative. Bigger by far than all the others, it is also more leaden-footed. Despite its immense power, therefore, the USSR has been a declining business.

```
USSR Inc

Moscow
rank in world by GNP 2
sales (GNP) $715 billion
net income (gross fixed
investment) $166 billion
workers 149.22 million

(1982)
```

The company in the mid-1970s, and substantially the same today despite occasional reforms

Controlling Trust

CPSU Politburo
14 members, chair Mikhail Gorbachov, 1985-

Party Control Commission

Secretariat

Central Committee

Business
- Agriculture
- Chemicals
- Construction
- Defence
- Heavy industry
- Consumer industries
- Machine Building
- Trade and domestic services
- Transport and communications
- Planning and finance

Public Relations
- Culture
- Propaganda

Military **Education and Science**

Party internal

Party external

Administration
- Organs
- Affairs
- General

Holding Company

Presidium of the USSR Council of Ministers

Service Companies or Agencies

9 Committees or Commissions

Operating Companies

Non-industrial ministries
- All-Union non-industrial ministries 4
- Union-Republic non-industrial ministries 15

Specialized Agencies 3

Other Agencies 5

State Committees 12

Industrial ministries
- All-Union military-industrial ministries 8
- All-Union civil industrial ministries 15
- Union-Republic industrial ministries 16

The decline of USSR Inc

Average rate of growth, percentages

1966-70	**5.3**
1971-75	**3.7**
1976-80	**2.7**
1981	**2.2**
1982	**2.0**

Imports of grain and agricultural products bought with hard currency, $ million

1970	**758**
1975	**4,083**
1980	**9,265**
1982	**9,878**

Cost of foreign support
Soviet aid to client states, $ million

	1970	1980
Economic	**941.5**	**5,030**
Military	**-**	**1,230**
Total	**941.5**	**6,260**

USA INC

In the USSR, business and the state are - and are seen to be - one. In the US, business and the state appear distinct, even hostile to each other. Yet they combine in many ways to form a powerful, subtly articulated entity - US national capital, or USA Inc.

```
Washington DC
rank in world by GNP 1
sales (GNP) $3059 billion
net income (gross fixed
investment) $485 billion
workers 111.9 million
```

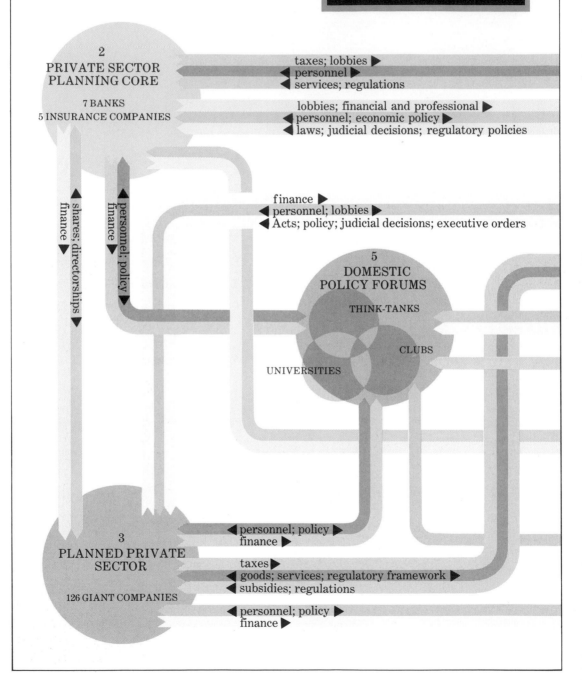

2
PRIVATE SECTOR PLANNING CORE

7 BANKS
5 INSURANCE COMPANIES

taxes; lobbies ▶
◀ personnel ▶
◀ services; regulations

lobbies; financial and professional ▶
◀ personnel; economic policy ▶
◀ laws; judicial decisions; regulatory policies

shares; directorships
finance ▼

personnel; policy
finance ▼

finance ▶
◀ personnel; lobbies ▶
◀ Acts; policy; judicial decisions; executive orders

5
DOMESTIC POLICY FORUMS

THINK-TANKS

CLUBS

UNIVERSITIES

3
PLANNED PRIVATE SECTOR

126 GIANT COMPANIES

◀ personnel; policy ▶
finance ▶

taxes ▶
◀ goods; services; regulatory framework ▶
◀ subsidies; regulations

◀ personnel; policy ▶
finance ▶

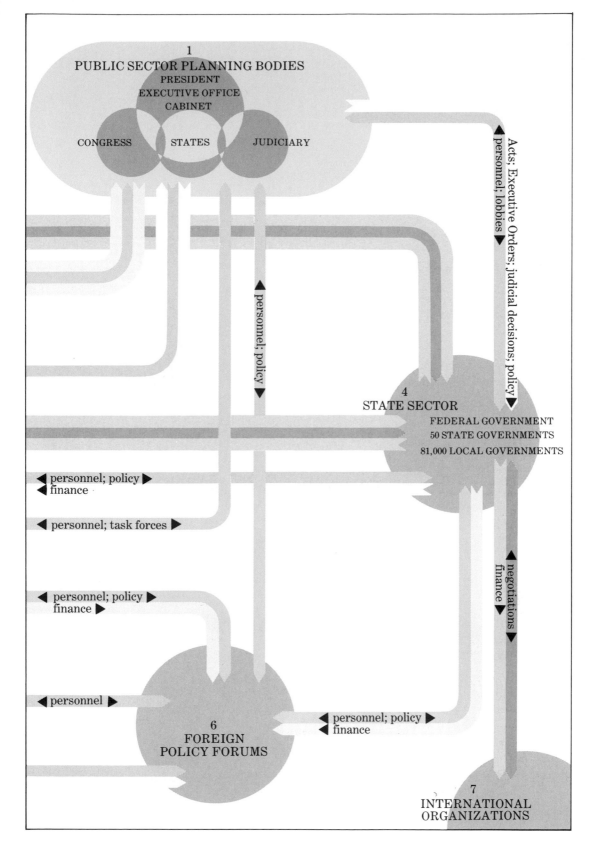

USA Inc is run from two loosely-related centres: a private sector planning core made up of a dozen financial institutions acting through over one hundred giant companies, and a public sector planning core made up of a few key federal departments and agencies acting through the whole range of federal and state public bodies. These centres and their subsidiaries are linked in myriad ways.

1 PUBLIC SECTOR PLANNING BODIES

PRESIDENT

EXECUTIVE OFFICE OF THE PRESIDENT
White House Office
Intelligence Oversight Office
Office of Management and Budget
Office of Policy Development
National Security Council
Council of Economic Advisers
Office of Science and Technology Policy
Council on Environmental Quality
Office of Administration
Council on Wage and Price Stability
Office of the Special Representative for Wage and Price
    Negotiation

CABINET
Agriculture   Interior
Commerce   Justice
Defense   Labor
Education   State
Energy   Transportation
Health and Human Services   Treasury
Housing and Urban Development

CONGRESS
Senate (100 members)
House of Representatives (435 members)
Committees
■ 36 House   ■ 4 Joint House/Senate
■ 29 Senate   ■ 263 Sub-Committees

STATES
50 states
workers 3.7 million
combined budget $198.3 billion   (1981)

JUDICIARY
Supreme Court
lower courts
over 450,000 lawyers

2 PRIVATE SECTOR PLANNING CORE

7 BANKS
5 INSURANCE COMPANIES
assets $409.92 billion
deposits $232.96 billion
trust assets $98.78 billion
workers 322,563   (1978)

In 1978, the seven banks were: Chase Manhattan; Chemical; Citicorp; Continental Illinois; First Chicago; Manufacturers' Hanover; J P Morgan; and the five insurance companies were: Continental Corp; Equitable Life; Metropolitan Life; New York Life; Prudential. Since 1978, changes have occurred. For example, Continental Illinois has shifted from the planning core (2) to the planned private sector (3).

The 263 directors of the planning core met each other 144 times a year in one another's boardrooms; 1512 times a year in the boardrooms of the large-scale planned private sector and on innumerable other occasions on other boards, in government bodies and socially. Representatives of the twelve institutions in the core met at directorial level at least seven times a working day.

3 PLANNED PRIVATE SECTOR

126 GIANT COMPANIES (1978)
assets $661 billion
sales $760 billion
workers 9.8 million

It embraces entire industries: aviation; oil; nuclear power; cars; soap and detergents; agribusiness. It encircles the globe through the so-called multinational companies.

4 STATE SECTOR
FEDERAL GOVERNMENT
50 STATE GOVERNMENTS
81,000 LOCAL GOVERNMENTS
elective posts 526,000
federal government corporations and independent establishments 57 (1981)
workers 18 million (1982)
outlay $1,351 billion (1982-83)
■ defense and international $229 billion
■ labour supply and maintenance $233 billion
■ maintenance of social equilibrium $602 billion
■ production of goods and services $150 billion
■ administration $28 billion
■ other and unallocatable $108 billion

5 DOMESTIC POLICY FORUMS

THINK-TANKS (action-oriented to study-oriented)
American Enterprise Institute   Hoover Institution
Aspen Institute   Rockefeller Foundation
Brookings Institution
Business Council
Business Roundtable
Carnegie Endowment
Committee for Economic Development
Conference Board
Ford Foundation
Heritage Foundation

UNIVERSITIES
Berkeley   MIT
Chicago   Princeton
Columbia   Stanford
Georgetown   Texas
Harvard   Yale

CLUBS
Bohemian (pre-eminently)

6 FOREIGN POLICY FORUMS
American Enterprise Institute   Ford Foundation
Aspen Institute   Hoover Institution
Bilderberg Commission   Rand Corporation
Carnegie Institute   Rockefeller Foundation
Council on Foreign Relations   Trilateral Commission

7 INTERNATIONAL ORGANIZATIONS
IMF
World Bank
Others

Trading places

Japan and US current balances, $ billion

	Japan surplus	USA deficit
1982	+6.9	-7.1
1983	+20.8	-41.6
1984	+35.0	-101.7

JAPAN INC

The most successful national capital of recent years is Japan's. Third after the US and USSR in output, Japan has been the world's fastest growing politically stable economy for more than three decades and is now the world's biggest exporter of industrial products.

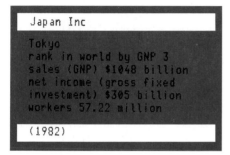

```
Japan Inc

Tokyo
rank in world by GNP 3
sales (GNP) $1048 billion
net income (gross fixed
investment) $305 billion
workers 57.22 million

(1982)
```

After the Second World War, Japan started an export drive, with labour intensive low-tech textiles and metal manufactures. It then moved rapidly to become a world leader in many mass-produced, high-tech products.

■ Between 1965 and 1967, Japan's gross domestic product (GDP) overtook the GDP of the whole of Latin America and the Caribbean area, and then the whole of the rest of Asia.

■ Between 1966 and 1968, Japan's GDP overtook those of Britain, France and West Germany in that order.

■ Income per head in Japan pulled ahead of income per head in Italy 1968-69, in Britain 1974-75, in New Zealand 1975-76, in Austria 1977-78, in Australia 1977-78.

■ In 1953, India and Japan each earned exactly the same amount from exports, $1.2 billion. By 1965, the value of Indian exports had reached $1.7 billion; the value of Japanese exports, $8.5 billion. By 1980, Japanese exports, at $130 billion, were more than 21 times India's at $6 billion.

Faster yet and faster

High-tech exports as a proportion of all exports percentages

	1963	1980
USA	1.29	1.20
West Germany	1.21	0.99
Britain	1.05	0.94
EEC	1.02	0.88
Japan	0.56	1.41

A lot of established producers got hurt. Some died. Many protected themselves by restraining imports from Japan.

Japan countered by shifting some of its manufacturing abroad, first to neighbouring Asian countries and Latin America, where labour costs were lower than at home; then to the US, its largest single foreign market; and then to Western Europe.

Going abroad

Shift to overseas production in Japan's consumer electronics

	production units millions		overseas percentage	
	1979	1982	1979	1982
radios (general)	16.75	16.83	69.0	72.6
mono TVs	8.21	8.30	48.5	49.4
stereo cassettes	4.23	5.57	31.7	44.9
tape recorders	35.95	41.66	33.7	38.4
colour TVs	13.40	14.55	30.1	37.1
speakers	8.79	11.18	11.9	15.2
FM tuners	2.90	3.75	9.3	14.1
video recorders	2.20	4.44	-	-

In general, the Japanese were made welcome abroad. States and regional authorities competed for them with subsidies, tax concessions and other inducements, hoping to revitalize their own industrial base and increase competitiveness.

Japanese holdings abroad

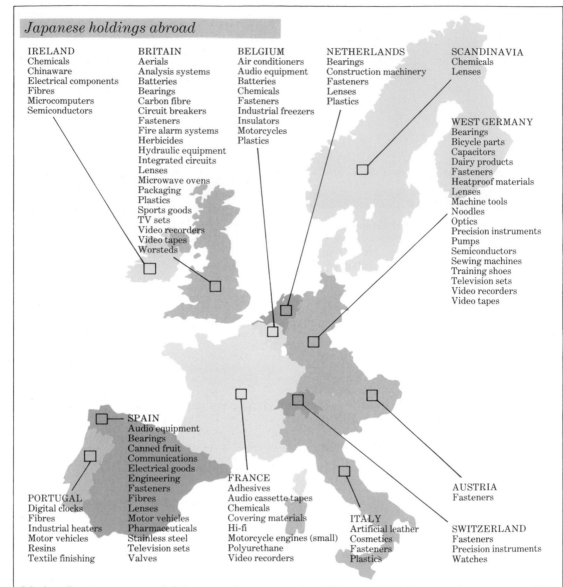

IRELAND
Chemicals
Chinaware
Electrical components
Fibres
Microcomputers
Semiconductors

BRITAIN
Aerials
Analysis systems
Batteries
Bearings
Carbon fibre
Circuit breakers
Fasteners
Fire alarm systems
Herbicides
Hydraulic equipment
Integrated circuits
Lenses
Microwave ovens
Packaging
Plastics
Sports goods
TV sets
Video recorders
Video tapes
Worsteds

BELGIUM
Air conditioners
Audio equipment
Batteries
Chemicals
Fasteners
Industrial freezers
Insulators
Motorcycles
Plastics

NETHERLANDS
Bearings
Construction machinery
Fasteners
Lenses
Plastics

SCANDINAVIA
Chemicals
Lenses

WEST GERMANY
Bearings
Bicycle parts
Capacitors
Dairy products
Fasteners
Heatproof materials
Lenses
Machine tools
Noodles
Optics
Precision instruments
Pumps
Semiconductors
Sewing machines
Training shoes
Television sets
Video recorders
Video tapes

SPAIN
Audio equipment
Bearings
Canned fruit
Communications
Electrical goods
Engineering
Fasteners
Fibres
Lenses
Motor vehicles
Pharmaceuticals
Stainless steel
Television sets
Valves

PORTUGAL
Digital clocks
Fibres
Industrial heaters
Motor vehicles
Resins
Textile finishing

FRANCE
Adhesives
Audio cassette tapes
Chemicals
Covering materials
Hi-fi
Motorcycle engines (small)
Polyurethane
Video recorders

ITALY
Artificial leather
Cosmetics
Fasteners
Plastics

AUSTRIA
Fasteners

SWITZERLAND
Fasteners
Precision instruments
Watches

Major Japanese acquisitions and investments in the US, 1971-84

1971
Kyocera International, the ceramics producer for integrated circuits, builds plant in California.

1972
Sony builds television plant in California.

1973
Fujitsu takes 47 per cent share in Amdahl, the Californian computer manufacturer.
Mitsui and Nippon Steel take 50 per cent in Alumax, the aluminium company.

1974
Matsushita Electric takes over Quasar Electronics, Chicago television manufacturer owned by Motorola.

1977
Sanyo acquires 75 per cent stake in colour television and microwave oven plant in Arizona, opens stereo equipment and refrigeration plant in California.
Sony builds an audio/video cassette tape plant in Alabama.

1979
Sharp opens television and microwave oven plant in Tennessee.

1982
Honda begins car production in Ohio, the first Japanese car factory in the US.

1983

General Motors and Toyota agree on joint manufacture of sub-compact cars in California.

Fuji Bank buys Heller International.

Nissan opens truck plant in Tennessee, later expanded to make cars as well.

1984

Nippon Kokan agrees to buy 50 per cent of National Steel

G M Fanuc, joint company owned by General Motors and Fanuc, announces plans to build robotics manufacturing plant.

Merchants of the world - Sogo Shosha

Even that uniquely Japanese phenomenon, the Sogo Shosha, or giant general trading houses, are slowly spreading beyond the domestic market. Between 1971 and 1982, the domestic trade of Mitsubishi, Mitsui, C Itoh, Marubeni, and Sumitomo declined from 58.1 to 42.3 per cent of their total trade, while their foreign trade rose from 37.9 to 44.9 per cent and their cross trade (between third countries) tripled from 4 per cent of the total to 12.6 per cent.

Nests and nest-eggs

Japan's direct overseas investment, 1983, $ billion

USA	**14.0**
Indonesia	**7.3**
Brazil	**3.5**
Australia	**2.9**
Britain	**2.3**
Panama	**2.0**
Hong Kong	**1.8**
Liberia	**1.7**
Singapore	**1.4**
Canada	**1.3**
South Korea	**1.3**
Mexico	**1.0**

By the early 1980s, Japan had become the third largest international investor, just behind Britain which had been amassing a foreign portfolio for over a century.

Net foreign assets abroad doubled between 1983 and 1984 to $74.3 billion. By the end of August 1985, they totalled some $84 billion, and the country had become the world's largest net creditor.

Japan's success formula

Japan's success in the world has been solidly based on industrial efficiency - the ability to de-liver standard manufactures of dependable quality at a relatively cheap price. That, in turn, has been based on an educated workforce and on an unrivalled concentration of effort by management and the state.

Management is single-minded in its pursuit of efficiency through quality and cost control, down to each assembly worker's performance.

When Hewlett-Packard attempted to introduce standard Japanese statistical controls into some of its US plants, it found that its workers needed remedial teaching in mathematics. At its affiliate in Japan, by contrast, workers with a school-leaving certificate had enough mathematics to pick up the techniques at once. In 1984, three Japanese firms and no US ones met the company's stringent quality standards for 256K D-Ram chips.

Government is single-minded in setting industry goals for products, production and exports.

Sectors that have outlived their usefulness as market-stretchers have been successfully shrunk - shipbuilding by more than a third in one year alone, 1979; aluminium by nearly three-fifths in five years to 1982; petrochemicals by a third in three years to 1985; steel, paper and pulp, chemical fertilizers and oil refining, in varying degrees.

Expanding industries have been set specific targets and pressured into collaborating to achieve them, as in the four-year project launched in 1976 which won Japan world leadership in memory chips; or the current ten-year project, grouping the state telephone corporation and eight private companies in the race for the 'intelligent' computer.

Small businesses are cultivated with finance, technical and managerial help; savings are encouraged; taxes on business are kept low; anti-trust activity is subordinated to the exigencies of international competition.

A key role in co-ordinating this national effort is played by the Ministry of International Trade and Industry (MITI).

Run largely by the elite products of Todai, as the Tokyo University Law School is known, and sharing that distinction with other key ministries (Ministry of Finance, the Foreign Ministry and the Defence Agency), MITI has been able to focus a widely-agreed set of national aims and an armoury of administrative weapons on the battle for world industrial supremacy.

It has presided over Japan's successful conquest of world markets for video recorders, steel, shipbuilding, motorcycles, cars, machine tools, photographic equipment, robotics, watches, telephones, colour TVs, microwave ovens, calculators. But while still the motor of Japan Inc, MITI is declining in power, now that growth requires more the creation of new markets and less the invasion of established ones.

The larger Japan's presence in the world market, the less it can grow without the growth of that market; the more it is compelled to absorb an increasing share of the military and financial overhead expenses incurred in maintaining that market; and the stronger are the pressures on it to make access to its domestic market easier for outsiders. Each of these loads irretrievable costs onto Japanese production; loosens Japan's control of its own resources and direction; impairs the national dedication to industrial growth; and creates openings for the 'new Japans' such as South Korea, Taiwan or Brazil, whose pursuit of market share is now more single-minded than Japan's, and which are moving from 'building the biggest to producing the best'.

Chipping at the old block

At Matsushita's three-year-old video recorder plant in Osaka, Japan, robots do 80 per cent of the work. At Samsung's video recorder plant in Suwon, South Korea, only months old, the work is done by young women whose small incomes are supplemented by 10 cent meals at the company cafeteria and free lodging in company dormitories.

Samsung's women may out-perform Matsushita's robots but this will depend largely on Samsung's ability to keep their wages in check.

Japan's Japan

South Korea is Japan's nightmare. Growing at more than 8 per cent a year in the mid-1980s, with inflation at only 2 - 3 per cent and exports at 10 per cent plus, its income per head broke through $2,000 per head in 1985 and closed on Portugal's or Yugoslavia's.

Its 64K RAM chips are 25 per cent below the US price and 15 per cent below Japan's.

It is now the third country, after the US and Japan, to mass produce 256K RAM chips.

It is in line to manufacture 1.8 million video recorders, selling for $100 less than the cheapest alternative model, in the first year of production.

By 1983 it had three of the top 25 international contractors (nos. 4,16 and 24 in the world) as against Japan's two (nos. 13 and 21).

Japan has reacted to South Korea's emergence into the world market with alarm: half of Korea's exports to Japan - from silk and ginseng products to footwear and cement - are subject to quantitative control.

Japan Inc is still in a category of its own, but the category is becoming less special with every passing year.

CHINA INC

China's national capital is the dark horse.

```
China Inc

Beijing
rank in world by GNP 8
sales (GNP) $301 billion
net income (gross fixed
investment) not available
workers 432.8 million

(1984)
```

Emerging in 1949 from war and civil war, and helped, always grudgingly, by the USSR, with knowhow and equipment for the modernization of its industry and its armed forces, the People's Republic of China at first followed a Russian inspired path to economic growth - at a distance from the world market.

This phase passed. Disputes between the neighbouring giants began at the end of the 1950s and escalated within a decade into military action along their common border. Soon the strain of autarkic growth, culminating in the Cultural Revolution, jeopardized China's cohesion.

After bitter and protracted internal battles, the Chinese leadership under Deng Xiaoping wrenched the country into a declared 'open door' policy in 1978. From then on, growth was to be pursued within the compass of the international market. China's foreign trade doubled in four years, despite the world recession. By 1983 foreign trade was 9.6 per cent of national income, compared with some 5.6 per cent in 1976. China began to borrow abroad: $5.5 billion by mid-1984. It brought in foreign business as partners in huge state-private joint ventures; and allowed foreign minnows - like public relations and advertising agencies, accountancy and legal services, even restaurants - to operate. All told, some $8 billion were invested by the end of 1984; with some $500 million in over 350 joint equity ventures. It set up four special economic zones - tax-free, legislation-light, purpose-built production platforms - and declared fourteen cities open to foreign business.

Behind the bamboo screen

'The open-door policy is now China's fundamental policy. Were any change to occur, it could only be that China would open still wider.'
Deng Xiaoping, 1984

China's new concession ports

● Special economic zones
■ Open cities

China passed legislation to protect patents and copyright, and to enforce commercial contracts. It established a hierarchy of economic chambers within the People's Courts throughout the country and a network of tribunals to arbitrate in commercial disputes. It purged many of its officials and assured foreign business that government initiatives to counter corruption and enforce the law were strictly for the locals. In October 1984, it dismantled most of its planning apparatus of mandatory production and price controls, to promote an enormous private sector with its armies of entrepreneurs, shareholders and creditors. It acclaimed its first millionaires, recruited its first foreign managers for a large state-run enterprise, and assured the 'compatriots' that Hong Kong would remain 'capitalist' up to the second half of the 21st century.

Even its train crews are now wheeling and dealing. The New China News Agency reports that dining car attendants on the Beijing-Changsha line promoted 40 deals worth $180,000 between business people who otherwise would never have met.

It's OK to be a private capitalist also

'I am a capitalist, not a Communist. A very famous capitalist. Tasks have been assigned to me by the central authorities.'
Wang Guangying, founder of the Ever Bright Industrial Company, Hong Kong, and reputed to be China's main business agent in the city, 1983

'What is the difference between owning a television, owning a house and owning stocks?'
Jing Shuping, executive director, China International Trust and Investment Corporation, 1984

In November 1984, Zhang Chengshan, a peasant from Henan province who runs a prosperous cooperative, was declared China's first millionaire. His achievement was hailed with the presentation of a plaque and laudatory national publicity. He owns a colour TV, modern furniture, a car, a lorry, and a motorcycle. The Quangming Daily says that he paid 200,000 yuan in taxes in 1983, when the average urban income was 500 yuan.

During 1985, the shares in at least ten local Shanghai companies were sold to the general public, and in November, China's first stockbroker Jinjiang Trust Company began trading in most of these shares. The largest share offering, in January 1985, was for 100,000 shares in the Yanzhong Copying Industry Company. Valued at around $1.5 million in all, these attracted 18,000 investors within eight hours. Then, in April 1986, the purchase of shares in some state companies was extended to five cities.

China is venturing abroad as an investor. Already the biggest single foreign financial presence in Hong Kong, it is beginning to explore the investment climate in countries as different as Australia, Brazil, Britain, Sweden, and West Germany, and in sectors as different as mining, steel and motorcycles.

China is also becoming a presence in the world arms and nuclear markets, where it keeps company with Brazil, France, Israel, Pakistan and the US, amongst others. It is also seeking a place in the market for space services, such as satellite launchings.

Envoi

China is in transition to modernity. Whether it will be successful in the world of global business depends on three main factors: the ability to find resources sufficient to meet the immense and rising costs of entry into the market for industrial and consumer goods, while meeting also the enormous and rising costs of military security; the ability of China's leadership to shake up its enormous bureaucracy; and its ability to satisfy the whetted appetite of its population.

B L A C K

THE BLACK ECONOMY

Inspector's own cash deposits come out in the wash

BANKING AUTHORITIES
go home

Corrupt arrangement with restaurant trade

IMMIGRATION OFFICIALS
go home

Port authorities found smoking untaxed foreign cigarettes

CUSTOMS OFFICIALS
go home

ENTRAPMENT

Go home whoever you are

Public inquiry into corruption

Don't move till you throw a six

Survey of restaurant trade uncovers irregularities

ILLEGAL IMMIGRANTS
go home

Found asleep at job once too often

MOON-LIGHTERS
go home

Move house next to social security inspector

THE EMPLOYED UNEMPLOYED
go home

RULES

A game for two players. One player represents characters within unofficial, unregistered or illegal trades: the black economy. The other represents corresponding agents of the state.

Each player has six character counters which advance individually towards the opponent's home on the throw of a die. Players may choose to move any one of their characters at a time.

When landing on a square, characters should follow instructions. If a character lands on a square already occupied by the opponent's corresponding character, the occupying character must return home.

A character enters the opponent's home on an exact throw of the die. If a larger number is thrown, the character moves into home and back again as appropriate.

The winner is the player who first gets all his or her characters into the opponent's home.

ECONOMY

Found
moonlighting as a
book-keeper

INCOME TAX
INSPECTORS
go home

Public spending
cuts slash social
services

SOCIAL
SECURITY
INSPECTORS
go home

Kickback racket
discovered

BUILDING
INSPECTORS
go home

Investigative press
report

Don't move till
you throw a three

ENTRAPMENT

Go home
whoever you are

Cheap imported
cigarettes set off
smoke alarm

SMUGGLERS
go home

Builder takes an
inspector as
customer

UNREGISTERED
BUILDERS
go home

Excessive cash
deposits raise
eyebrows

MONEY
LAUNDERERS
go home

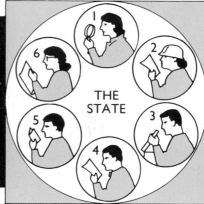

THE
STATE

THE PLAYERS

THE STATE	THE BLACK ECONOMY
1 SOCIAL SECURITY INSPECTORS	1 THE EMPLOYED UNEMPLOYED
2 BUILDING INSPECTORS	2 UNREGISTERED BUILDERS
3 CUSTOMS OFFICERS	3 SMUGGLERS
4 BANKING AUTHORITIES	4 MONEY LAUNDERERS
5 IMMIGRATION OFFICIALS	5 ILLEGAL IMMIGRANTS
6 INCOME TAX INSPECTORS	6 MOONLIGHTERS

· PROTECTED ·

EEC

USA

JAPAN

· LANDSCAPES ·

COMECON

THE SOUTH

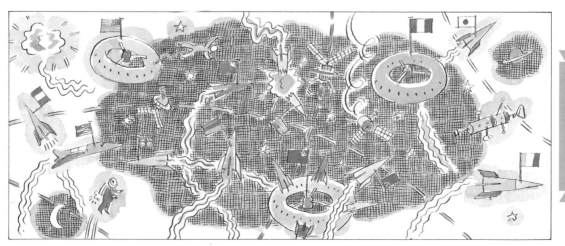

SPACE

5

THE BUSINESS OF MONEY

'Nobody really understands the international monetary system'
H Johannes Witteveen, former managing director of the International Monetary Fund and Finance Minister of the Netherlands

Money is a commodity, since it may be bought and sold. But it is a commodity unlike any other, since it is one for which all other commodities are exchanged. It is accordingly the essential concern of business: the source and product of its operations; the measure of its success or failure.

Almost everywhere, it is a predominant social factor: the impulse and reward of labour; the fuel of government; the criterion of identity.

More than knowledge, it is money that is power. As people become more and more dependent upon one another for the satisfaction of their needs and the supply of their diversions, they use money, in one or other form, more and more.

MONEY

Money is essentially a medium of exchange and a store of value, across space and time. It has taken many forms, from cowrie shells to cigarettes. Until relatively recent times, it was some standardized weight of gold, silver or other metals. Today it is generally a printed piece of paper or a book-keeping entry.

Whatever form money may take, its value depends upon the common acceptance, among those who use it, that it can command goods and services. State authorities attempt to regulate the use and value of their moneys. The market-place delivers its own verdict at home, but especially in the world outside.

The warrior Mongols, unable to pay their soldiers, simply printed military money, and the soldiers had no choice but to accept it. The practice developed into a state monetary system. When Marco Polo visited the court of Kublai Khan in 1271, he found this so remarkable as subsequently to report it:

'All these pieces of paper are issued with as much solemnity and authority as if they were of pure gold or silver...And the Khan causes every year to be made such a vast quantity of this money, which costs him nothing, that it must be equal in amount to all the treasure in the world.'

But the Mongols were obliged to leave China. And by 1358 their paper money had become worthless.

There are national moneys which can command goods and services only within the frontiers of the states that issue them.

There are national moneys with a regional acceptance, such as the South African rand, which circulates alongside the national moneys of neighbouring satellite countries: Botswana, Lesotho, Swaziland.

There are moneys which are effectively international, enjoying widespread acceptability and circulating, sometimes directly, as a means of exchange alongside other national currencies. Supreme amongst these is the United States dollar.

Where has all the money gone?

The US Federal Reserve cannot track down $136 billion, or some 88 per cent of the $154 billion of cash in circulation. It calculates that Americans are carrying around about $18 billion at any one time. It believes that part of the missing cash is held by businesses and part by persons under the age of 18. But there are strong economic and safety reasons why businesses keep little cash, and it is unlikely that American children, however cherished, hold more cash than their parents. Fed officials believe that a big part (between one-third and two-thirds) of the missing 'greenbacks' have gone abroad.

Many states set the value of their own moneys, or 'peg' them, in relation to the dollar. Some other states do this in relation to the French franc.

Other national moneys, varyingly acceptable abroad, if only for the purposes of holding as a store of value, include the West German deutsche mark, the Swiss franc, the pound sterling and the Japanese yen. The Russian rouble, in its transferable form, is a national currency acceptable to certain states for limited purposes.

States whose currencies are pegged to the French franc

Benin
Burkina
Cameroon
Central African Republic
Chad
Comoros
Congo
Gabon
Ivory Coast
Mali
Niger
Senegal
Togo

States whose currencies are pegged to the US dollar

Antigua and Barbuda
Bahamas
Barbados
Belize
Bolivia
Burundi
Djibouti
Dominica
Dominican Republic
Ecuador
Egypt
El Salvador
Ethiopia
Grenada
Guatemala
Haiti
Honduras
Iraq
Jamaica
Laos
Liberia
Libya
Nepal
Nicaragua
Oman
Panama
Paraguay
Romania
Rwanda
St Lucia
St Vincent
Sudan
Surinam
Syria
Trinidad and Tobago
Venezuela
North Yemen
South Yemen

Half-starved in Shenzhen

Liang Xiang, mayor of Shenzhen, a Special Economic Zone between Hong Kong and Canton, cannot eat in about half the restaurants in his town because they do not accept the renminbi in which he is paid. In Shenzhen, a three-tier economy ranks the Hong Kong dollar first, foreign exchange certificates second and the renminbi, exchanging at twice the official rate against the Hong Kong dollar, third.

Less acceptable currencies

Discount on official buying rate for various currencies at a major Swiss bank, 29 February 1984

Discounts for other more acceptable currencies may be less than 1 per cent, and are essentially charges for the services involved.

currency	discount percentages
Europe	
Albanian lek	no price
Bulgarian lev	71
Hungarian forint	16
Icelandic crown	18
Polish zloty	87
Romanian leu	73
Czechoslovakian koruna	78
Russian rouble	78
Asia	
Afghan afghani	65
Bangladeshi taka	78
Burmese kyat	93
Chinese renminbi yuan	20
North Korean won	no price
Indian rupee	21
Iraqi dinar	71
Iranian rial	90
Israeli shekel	55
Laotian new kip	no price
Maldive rufiyaa	64
Nepalese rupee	64
Papuan kina	21
Philippine peso	35
West Samoan tala	82
Syrian pound	46
Tongan ha'anga	39
Vietnamese dong	no price
South Yemeni dinar	60
Americas	
Argentinian peso	87
Belize dollar	26
Bolivian peso	77
Brazilian cruzeiro	22
Cayman Islands dollar	19
Chilean peso	18
Colombian peso	26
Costa Rican colon	60
Cuban peso	no price
Dominican peso	54
Ecuadorian sucre	18
Guatemalan quetzal	49
Guyanese dollar	83
Haitian gourde	31
Honduran lempira	43
Jamaican dollar	27
Nicaraguan cordoba	no price
Paraguayan guarani	78
Salvadoran colon	71
Surinam guilder	75
Trinidad and Tobago dollar	33
Uruguayan peso	37
Venezuelan bolivar	22
Africa	
Algerian dinar	78
Angolan kwanza	no price
Burundi franc	49
Cape Verde escudo	no price
Djibouti franc	40
Egyptian pound	32
Ethiopian birr	no price
Ghanaian cedi	no price
Guinean syle	no price
Guinea-Bissau peso	no price
Kenyan shilling	18
Libyan dinar	56
Malawi kwacha	69
Mauritanian ouguiya	no price
Nigerian naira	84
Rwanda franc	55
Sierra Leonean leone	65
Somali shilling	64
Sudanese pound	55
Tanzanian shilling	83
Swazi lilangeni	22
Tunisian dinar	19
Ugandan shilling	no price
Zaire zaire	61
Zambian kwacha	44
Zimbabwe dollar	61

Some countries have several exchange rates. The official rates are those chosen by the bank concerned in listing the buying and selling rates.

The printing of money may itself be a business. In some countries - generally the major rich ones or those with centralized economies - the state prints the money through one of its agencies. Most countries do not have the domestic facilities and order their money from specialist businesses abroad. The leading such business is Britain's De La Rue, which made £46 million pre-tax profits, on sales of £337 million, in 1985. And in 1986, it bought, for £39 million in cash, its sole British rival, Bradbury Wilkinson. Only two other major specialist companies printing banknotes survive: Giesieke and Devrient of West Germany, and Orell Fuessli of Switzerland.

Metaphysical money

There is still another money that is international but has no physical existence. It is used essentially for book-keeping purposes in transactions among states and increasingly as the currency of commercial borrowings and deposits. Such is the European Currency Unit (ECU) of the European Economic Community; or the Special Drawing Right (SDR) of the International Monetary Fund.

The ECU is rising rapidly in importance. More than two hundred European banks now have ECU denominated accounts for companies and other clients, while in 1983, the ECU was the third most important currency, after the US dollar and the deutsche mark, on the international bond market.

It is made up of variously weighted currencies, adjusted from time to time in their relationship.

ECU, February 1986, percentages

Belgian franc	8.4
Danish krone	2.7
French franc	19.7
Deutsche mark	33.3
Irish punt	1.2
Italian lira	9.5
Luxembourg franc	0.3
Netherlands guilder	10.5
Pound sterling	13.5
Greek drachma	0.9

And there is gold, the one effectively supra-national money. It has a physical existence; is not created by any state but is acceptable to all; and in extreme situations may be the only form of money that is accepted. It is increasingly hoarded, as an ultimate form of money, by private citizens in many states; such hoards in France alone exceed 6,000 tonnes, with a value (at $350 an ounce) of more than $67 billion. Public hoards are enormous, and many states regard it as the ultimate asset in their reserves.

BANKING

The total amount of spendable money in a state - the money supply - is a complex matter. Besides the physical notes and coins in circulation, it includes other forms of purchasing power, such as bank deposits, which may be drawn by cheque to pay for goods and services. And since banks need to keep in cash only a small proportion of the deposits they hold, such deposits represent a great deal of effective money.

The making of money out of the manipulation of money (which the banks themselves help to create) is the peculiar business of banking.

Banks may do some or all of many things:

■ accept deposits of money from the public; and pay interest, generally if such money is deposited for a specified time;
■ transfer funds;
■ trade in different moneys and in precious metals, especially gold;
■ borrow money in the market and from one another;
■ invest the funds at their disposal: on their own behalf; or even, at their absolute discretion, on behalf of customers who agree to accept any risk involved;
■ act as brokers, or as the agents of brokers, in buying and selling equities and bonds;
■ establish and manage unit and investment trusts;
■ act as trustees and as executors;
■ guarantee payments of money on the performance of some work or transaction;
■ act as intermediaries in the raising of loans to businesses and states;
■ lend money in various ways: from loans to states and overdraft facilities for corporate and individual customers, to mortgages, finance for hire purchase or instalment buying agreements, and credit cards;
■ own credit card companies such as Visa and MasterCard.

A child's guide to banking

This is Pamela. She has $1,000 that she has saved from doing odd jobs round the block. She takes it for safety to the First National Whirlpool Bank.

The bank looks like a Greek temple. This is not because Greeks pray in it, but because bankers think that this sort of fancy dress makes people like Pamela feel their money is safe.

This is John. He is a banker. He does not approve of the odd jobs that Pamela does, but he approves of her $1,000 deposit. He puts $50 of it in the till and buys government IOUs for $75.

(John is not altogether boss of his own bank. There are bigger bosses such as those in government, who lay down certain rules for him to follow.)

He then lends $875 of the $1,000 to Paul, who uses the money to buy a motor bike from Max.

Max deposits the $875 in his account with the First National Whirlpool Bank.

John puts $44 in the till and buys government IOUs for $64. Then he lends $767 of the $875 to Basil, who is starting a business in second-hand books.

So, in two loan transactions, John has swollen the supply of spendable money from $1,000 to $2,642. He may go on and on until he creates $8,000.

And what, asks Smart Alec, if Pamela breaks a leg and is no longer able to work, so that she asks for her $1,000 back?

The answer is that meanwhile Sue, who is saving for a holiday in Hawaii, and Jack, who has sold his house to buy an apartment, and Bertha, whose bagels are selling like hot cakes, have all deposited money in the First National Whirlpool Bank.

So Smart Alec is not as smart as he thinks he is. Or is he?

An adult's guide to banking

Banks generally make most of their money by getting, in interest on the loans that they give, rather more than they pay out in interest on the deposits or other funds that they borrow. Overall, their loans are larger than their borrowings.

Much of the money in their keeping may be withdrawn on demand or at very short notice, while much of the money that they lend is due for repayment at some fixed time, often far in the future. Banking is, therefore, an intrinsically risky business.

To complicate matters further, not all those who borrow from banks are able to repay such loans when the time arrives, if ever.

To protect banks against their inclination to lend not wisely but too well, the state has increasingly intervened to regulate their conduct.

To ensure that they are able to meet their likely obligations at any time, the state may permit the banks to lend only a stated multiple of the cash and acceptable equivalent (such as short-term government IOUs) that they hold. This multiple, or liquidity ratio, differs from time to time and from place to place. But a ratio of eight to one has been a British benchmark in recent times.

To meet losses on their operations, as through an excess of bad debts, banks possess capital or money of their own. This consists mainly of the funds provided by the sale of their shares. The ratio of such money to total lending, called the Primary Capital or the Equity Ratio, may be voluntary or imposed by the relevant state authorities. A once favoured benchmark was 1:20 (or 5 per cent), but most banks long considered this to be unnecessarily cautious.

Lending to consumers

Banks are massively involved in lending money to consumers, either directly or through financing others to do so.

Lending to consumers stretches in a cost band: from the interest-free, to rates of usury for which those responsible might well have been burned at the stake in former times.

In October 1985, consumer instalment (hire purchase) debt in the US stood at a record, nearly 20 per cent of all disposable income. In May 1986, the total consumer instalment credit outstanding was some $560 billion.

At the end of 1983, after the subtraction of all assets, the average household in Britain was estimated to have debts of £5,400, or some 60 per cent of all income. In 1970, the total debts of the average household were reckoned to be 40 per cent of its total income.

New consumer credit advanced, UK, £ billion

1982	9.0
1983	10.5
1984	16.1
1985	18.5

The Sarakin

Within the first five months of 1983 alone, more than 200 Japanese committed suicide and more than 7,300 fled their homes to escape the clutches of the Sarakin ('finance for salaried workers'), the loan shark companies in Japan that were charging interest rates up to the legal limit of 109.5 per cent a year and often beyond. Banks charged interest rates of around 14 per cent, when they were willing to provide loans to people in need. But they were readily providing loans to the Sarakin, as were the insurance companies (which are estimated to account for some 25 per cent of the funds that the Sarakin borrow).

The relevant volumes are huge. One expert on loan problems estimated that high interest loans in 1981 amounted to 3,000 billion yen ($12.6 billion); according to another estimate, there are more than 150,000 Sarakin firms, from one-desk operations in front rooms to financial chain stores that advertise on television.

In April 1983, the Japanese parliament reacted to the mounting Sarakin scandal by reducing the lending rate limit by stages, to some 40 per cent by 1988. But this did not deal with the notorious pressures of Sarakin operators who too often react, when repayment is overdue, by calling on borrowers at their place of work, sending notes that threaten them, or hiring gangsters to terrorize them.

Credit and charge cards are an increasingly important form of consumer borrowing.

Plastic

Credit and charge cards issued, early 1980s, millions

world	625
USA	500
UK	22

Cost of consumer borrowing

cheapest

- Interest-free credit provided by business for the purchase of its own goods; credit card accounts settled before the date at which interest payments begin.

- Concessionary rates of interest on credit purchases or mortages, for employees of the companies concerned.

- Loans for home purchase.

- Bank overdrafts, most cheap for those who offer such security that the wonder is their desire to borrow at all.

- Personal bank loans, usually granted to those with little security and carrying correspondingly high interest charges.

- Finance house cash loans; credit card accounts that attract interest payments; the mass of hire purchase contracts.

- Money from loan sharks. Interest rates can reach beyond 200 per cent a year in countries with low rates of inflation.

most expensive

Cost of business borrowing

cheapest

- Loans granted by public agencies to encourage new business or the siting of business in special development areas.

- Short-term IOUs, such as so-called commercial paper. A major source of borrowing in the US - the volume increased five-fold between 1974 and 1984 - but generally available only to the strongest companies.

- Corporate bonds to raise long-term money. Generally a source of borrowing only for larger companies and with some element of risk, since a fixed interest rate may become a costly one if prevailing rates subsequently fall.

- Loans and overdraft facilities from banks: a major source of borrowing everywhere and relatively most important in Britain and West Germany.

- Recourse to loan sharks of various kinds: the fate of small businesses whose banks lose patience with them.

most expensive

Lending to business and the state

Banks are massively involved in lending money to business, through loans, overdraft facilities, and the purchase of bonds. It is ill-fated lending in this sector that has, so far, proved the major cause of bank failures.

Banks also lend massively to the state. They lend to local government and other public authorities, such as those in transport or the power industry, for which the central government acts as formal or effective guarantor.

Business is widely dependent upon borrowing from the banks, but the degree of dependence varies from state to state. In Japan, some 65 per cent of non-financial business debt is represented by borrowings from the banks; in Britain and the US, the proportion is around 25 per cent; and in continental Western Europe, it is somewhere between the two.

Government borrowing

Governments borrow money essentially to meet the shortfall between what they spend and what they gather in tax and in sales of goods and services.

They do so through various instruments in their domestic financial markets:
- tax-free savings certificates
- government bonds of different kinds
- treasury bills or short-term IOUs

Banks are massively involved in lending, through purchase of treasury bills and short-term government bonds. They also lend to the governments of states other than their own, directly through negotiated loans. Almost everywhere, governments have been borrowing more and more: to meet current deficits which are themselves increased by the costs of accumulated debt.

Government budget deficits, 1968-73 to 1984, percentage of GNP

	1968-73	1974-78	1979-80	1981	1982	1983	1984
USA	-0.3	-1.4	-0.3	-0.9	-3.8	-4.1	-3.4
Japan	na	-3.4	-4.1	-4.0	-3.6	-3.5	-2.6
West Germany	-0.2	-3.1	-2.9	-3.8	-3.4	-2.8	-2.3
France	0.7	-1.1	-0.2	-1.8	-2.5	-3.3	-3.3
UK	-0.6	-4.1	-3.4	-3.1	-2.4	-3.5	-3.9
Italy	-5.6	-9.2	-8.7	-11.8	-12.7	-12.4	-13.8
Belgium	-4.9	-7.2	-10.4	-16.3	-14.8	-15.6	-13.8
Switzerland	na	na	-0.6	-0.2	-0.7	-0.9	-1.2

Seeing triple

Some governments, rather than borrow, simply print the money they need. But this is usually recorded in the growth of available cash and worries creditors, domestic and foreign. The late Marcos government in the Philippines determined to bribe a way to victory in the presidential election of February 1986, but reluctant to alarm creditors, found a novel way of increasing the supply of money without appearing to do so. When one newspaper editor came to possess three apparently genuine high denomination banknotes with identical serial numbers, the whistle was blown.

US government borrowing

Putting a particular strain on the world financial system has been the borrowing need of the US government, with an accumulated gross federal debt at the end of 1985 of some $1,800 billion, or around half the country's annual GNP.

Given a relatively low domestic savings ratio, the necessarily huge sums involved could only be borrowed by offering high interest rates. In view of the central role played in the world economy by the US and its money, this affected the availability and cost of lending almost everywhere.

Total annual borrowing in the US - consumer, business and government - grew from just under $400 billion in 1979 to $700 billion in 1984, a rise of more than 75 per cent in five years. In 1984, it rose by 14 per cent, double the average rate in the 1960s, and 3 per cent above the average rate in the 1970s.

The accumulated debt burden rose from 140 per cent of GNP, the average for a quarter of a century, to 152 per cent in 1982 and an estimated 167 per cent by the middle of 1986.

'We are drifting towards a financial system in which credit has no guardian.'
Dr Henry Kaufman, chief economist at New York's Salomon Brothers, and leading Wall Street guru, 1985

Commercial banks

Banks come in all sorts of form and function.

By far the largest number are those that operate as businesses with the primary purpose of making a profit for their proprietors.

These banks may themselves be further distinguished - by size, spread, function and ownership.

The size of a bank is usually measured by the size of its total 'assets', or loans. By this measure, a list of US banks at the start of the 1980s showed the largest as Citicorp of New York, with assets of some $115 billion, and the smallest as the Swift County Bank of Benson, Minnesota, with assets of $36,211.

Size may also be measured by market capitalization, or the total market value of a bank's shares. By this measure, Citicorp was worth some $4.7 billion in 1984; and Britain's National Westminster Bank, some $2.4 billion. Advertised in the same year for 'quick sale' was a bank, complete with cheque books, secretarial services and a boardroom, in the Caribbean crown colony of Anguilla, at just $75,000.

Most banks are commercial banks, whose major business consists in attracting deposits and making loans. Amongst these:

■ There are local banks, with a single place of business, that operate only in the immediate community.

■ There are regional banks, sometimes with many branches but only within a particular part of the country, such as the Swiss cantonal banks.

■ There are banks with branches throughout a country.

■ There are international banks, with branches or agencies beyond their own state borders.

■ There are merchant or investment banks. They are primarily concerned with the investment of capital in business, often through the purchase of equity stakes.

The top five US investment banks (ranked by capital), 1984, $ billion

Merrill Lynch	2.2
Shearson Lehman Brothers	1.9
Salomon Brothers	1.7
Dean Witter	1.2
E F Hutton	1.0

■ There is in the US a general sector of retail banking and a special one of wholesale banking. In this last, large sums of money are raised competitively in the market-place for lending to companies. For instance, Bankers Trust of New York decided in 1976 to abandon retail banking and proceeded to dispose of 80 branches, with $900 million in deposits, to become a wholesale bank.

■ There are 'offshore' banks, whose particular location permits freedom from normal regulation by state financial authorities.

■ There are 'haven' banks that attract funds because of low or no taxation, guaranteed secrecy, and the supposed ultimate safety of deposits.

Many haven banks are also offshore ones; but the most celebrated are the Swiss which are subject to regulation by the state's financial authorities.

■ There are some banks, chiefly the co-operative banks, which operate essentially to support and promote a form of social organization. In France and Germany, the co-operative banks are huge.

The world's largest

Japan's Postal Savings Service, run by the Ministry of Posts and Telecommunications, is the world's largest single deposit taker. With total deposits of some 86 million million yen ($350 billion), it had, in 1984, just over a quarter of all deposits with Japanese financial institutions. Its practice of paying slightly higher interest than that offered by Japan's high street banks is not the only reason. In theory, each Japanese taxpayer can maintain up to 3 million yen in a postal savings account before attracting tax on interest payments. In practice, individuals can maintain multiple accounts; so permitting wholesale tax evasion.

Washing whiter

Haven banking is an important means for the laundering of money, to wash away the criminal origin of funds.

Much of the laundering in the Caribbean offshore financial centres comes from illegal drug operations, and proceeds from such operations have come to be nicknamed 'narcodollars'.

The US Justice Department estimated that in 1983 more than $30 billion were laundered in the area - mainly in the Bahamas, Cayman Islands and Panama.

But such offshore banks are not the only laundries. Sometimes the most prestigious onshore ones may be found to have engaged, perhaps unwittingly but massively, in the business. Boston's First National Bank (founded in 1784 and with assets, two centuries later, of $21 billion) pleaded guilty in early 1985 to having made unreported cash shipments of $1.2 billion to and from foreign banks. According to federal prosecutors, the bank had received $529 million, mainly in small bills (weighing over 20 tons), and had sent out to nine foreign banks (three in Switzerland) $690 million in bills of $100 and upwards. First National was fined $500,999, at that time the highest penalty levied for this type of crime.

It did not hold the record for long.

In mid-1985, Crocker Bank (then a subsidiary of Britain's Midland Bank) agreed to pay a civil penalty of $2.25 million for violations of US laws that require the reporting of cash transactions above $10,000. The US Treasury had claimed 7,800 violations involving a total of $3.98 billion.

Major offshore banking centres
Foreign assets of deposit banks, 1983, $ billion

Bahamas	134.4
Singapore	112.0
Bahrain	62.7
Hong Kong	54.0
Cayman Islands (US bank branches only)	49.0
Panama	37.5
Jersey	25.0

Ownership

There are private banks, owned outright by one person or by a closed partnership. But their numbers have been fast diminishing, even in their Swiss stronghold. In 1983, there were only 21 such banks in Switzerland, compared with 266 in 1903.

Most profit-directed banks are public companies, owned by numerous shareholders, with the shares traded on stock markets.

Other profit-directed banks may be owned by the state, but are still companies of limited liability that function with their own capital resources. The major French banks are a notable example.

A bank may be registered as a company in one state while actually being owned by another. The Moscow Narodny Bank is classed as a British bank but is owned by the USSR.

Banks may be owned by their depositors, as are the co-operative banks.

One bank may be owned by another, in the same or in another country. During 1985, for instance, two of the three main Swiss banks bought banks in West Germany: the Union Bank of Switzerland (UBS), Deutsche Laenderbank; and Credit Suisse, Grundig Bank and Effectenbank-Warburg. The third Swiss major, Swiss Bank Corporation, set up its own German subsidiary in the same year.

And one bank - called a consortium bank - may be owned by several others, essentially collaborating to engage in international wholesale banking.

Swiss banking

Swiss banks hold a special place in the international banking system for a combination of reasons.

Bank secrecy is protected not only by the civil but by the criminal law, so that offenders face public prosecution and imprisonment.

Numbered, or anonymous, accounts are allowed, with the client's identity known only to selected members of the bank's management.

Neither tax evasion nor the contravention of exchange controls is considered a crime, and the Swiss authorities provide information to authorities abroad only where crime is involved.

Switzerland is one of the world's leading financial centres, with a domestic money that is generally considered one of the safest to hold.

It has a high reputation for political and economic stability. In particular, its long commitment to neutrality, which kept it out of two world wars, provides some assurance of refuge even in the event of widespread disorder.

Much of the business conducted by the Swiss banks consists in managing, separately from normal deposits, the money of others.

At the end of 1985, an estimated total of SF500-1,000 billion ($250-500 billion) was being administered on behalf of clients by Swiss banks, which exclude such money from their balance sheets.

The Swiss banks also specialize in what are called fiduciary deposits, or deposits that they administer at the accepted risk of the clients themselves. In mid-1986, the total value of such deposits was estimated at SF245 billion ($135 billion).

Little to the many, much to the few

Loans made by the Union Bank of Switzerland, end 1985

loans in Swiss francs	total millions Swiss francs	number of customers
below 20,000	405.7	119,610
20,001-50,000	889.0	23,935
50,001-100,000	1,873.6	22,744
100,001-500,000	14,262.7	54,064
500,001-1 million	6,956.6	8,890
1-5 million	14,814.7	6,508
5 million and over	23,731.2	1,283
total	62,933.5	237,034

In May 1984, a popular referendum was held on a Swiss Social Democratic Party proposal to modify the law on banking secrecy. Proponents claimed that the law had made Switzerland a refuge for dirty money of every sort, including the fortunes of those who had plundered their own societies, and that the banks themselves disposed of excessive power through the manipulation of so much money and their shareholdings in industry.

The proposal was massively defeated.

Central banks

The central bank is the direct monetary agency of the state.

It does not exist to make a profit but may succeed in doing so through buying and selling foreign currency and the investment of its reserves (for instance, in short-term interest-bearing US government securities).

It performs several functions.

■ It issues domestic money and regulates the supply.

■ It affects interest rates, through the rate at which it lends money to the market.

■ It controls the lending of commercial banks, through setting the ratio between liquid assets and loans.

■ It supervises the conduct of banks, domestic and foreign, within its jurisdiction.

■ It is a lender of last resort, providing funds to domestic banks that run into difficulties.

■ It holds the state reserves of gold and foreign currency.

■ It may buy and sell foreign currencies, to adjust the international value of its domestic money.

Bank for International Settlements

The Bank for International Settlements (BIS) in Basle, Switzerland, is celebrated as the central bankers' bank. It has 473,125 issued shares owned by a number of West European central banks, with a minor part of the equity (mainly the holding originally allotted to the US and then sold) owned by private investors and correspondingly traded. It functions essentially to secure the stability of the financial system. It co-ordinates the activities and policies of the central banks in the Group of Ten leading industrial countries, together with Switzerland and Luxembourg. It acts as a watchdog of international banking. It collates and distributes international banking statistics. It provides emergency bridging loans to central banks in difficulties.

It operates as a business, making a profit and paying a dividend to its shareholders. Most of its income is generated by short-term investments, such as bank deposits repayable in less than three months. For its own accounting purposes, it uses the unit of the gold franc (equal to 0.29 grammes of fine gold). In the year ending March 1985, it made a profit of some 68.4 million gold francs (worth some $133 million).

Development agencies

There are various multi-state agencies operating as banks to promote economic development in poorer countries.

The three main regional aid agencies are the Inter-American Development Bank, Asian Development Bank and African Development Bank. But the capital available to each is inadequate to the scale of the problem of mass poverty and economic backwardness; interest rates on loans are generally close to commercial ones; and special projects are often financed with a view to promoting the exports of the rich.

At the annual meeting of the Asian Development Bank in April 1984, the Finance Minister of Thailand complained that from the outset, only 11 per cent of the $4.4 billion worth of contracts financed by the bank's ordinary capital had gone to developing countries. 'The statistics lead us to the conclusion that our bank is simply a multilateral export bank for its developed member countries.'

World Bank

The World Bank is the largest source of development funds and is the single largest foreign borrower on almost all the financial markets where it obtains its funds (raising around $10 billion a year in this way). The US government is its major shareholder and a decisive influence on its policies.

The World Bank has two major constituents:

The International Bank for Reconstruction and Development (IBRD) is owned by the governments of 139 states, which subscribe the capital ($80 billion in 1985) in the form of guarantees that are used as collateral or security for borrowing. The money borrowed is lent to developing countries at a profit, and only for projects that promise a minimum 10 per cent real rate of return.

The International Development Association (IDA) gets its funds directly from 35 member governments and provides interest-free loans to the poorest countries, but only for projects that satisfy criteria for an adequate rate of return.

In the year to end June 1985, the World Bank made a profit of over $1 billion and by 1986, its income from loans to poor countries exceeded its disbursements.

International Monetary Fund

The IMF is neither an international version of a central bank nor a development bank. But it does perform two functions of central banking. It issues a kind of money, in Special Drawing Rights (SDRs); and it acts as a kind of lender of last resort, to countries in financial difficulties. Its membership is composed of governments from all but a few states in the world. The USSR is not a member, nor are some of its political associates. But Hungary, Romania and Poland are members.

It is not an association of equals. Voting power is distributed according to 'quotas', or the different allocated contributions by member states to the IMF's total resources. Essential decisions require a minimum 85 per cent of the total vote. SDRs are themselves distributed according to quotas, so that the rich members, who tightly control the issue, are the major beneficiaries of such manufactured money.

But its influence extends far beyond the actual funds that it provides. For it lends only on strict conditions, and its loans are accordingly a source of reassurance to the commercial banks. Thus the $3.9 billion facility that it granted to Mexico in 1984 brought with it at least $5 billion of commercial bank credit and $20 billion in the refinancing of existing loans. Its conditions usually involve cuts in public expenditure and currency devaluations. Such measures fall most heavily on the poor and often lead to the sort of popular disorder which reassures the IMF that the medicine is disagreeable and so must be good.

Just nine countries wield 53.78 per cent of voting power in the IMF, with the US alone holding enough to block an essential decision.

Voting power in the IMF, percentages

USA	19.90
UK	6.88
West Germany	6.00
France	4.98
Japan	4.69
Canada	3.27
Italy	3.23
Netherlands	2.52
Belgium	2.31

Getting in on the act

The management of money is too important and generally too profitable to remain the business of banks alone. There are others engaged in various aspects of the business.

THE CAMEL

A cushion-footed quadruped with a hump, in which it stores resources for times of need. Called an insurance company, it usually deals either in life insurance or in risk; but one type has two humps and deals in both forms. There are even camels that are used by other camels to carry part of any risk, and these are known as reinsurance companies.

In the insurance business, policy holders supply premium income, which is then invested to meet claims (for personal accident, property damage or loss, and death) or provide capital after a specified period.

Insurance companies are, accordingly, big investors in the stock markets, in property, and in government debt. In 1984-85, for instance, insurance companies were the biggest institutional holders of Britain's national debt, with £31.8 billion or 22.1 per cent of the total sterling debt, excluding official holdings.

Though operating on a domestic base of investment and risk, insurance companies have become increasingly international in both. Thus, at the start of the 1980s, foreign-controlled insurers had some 22 per cent of the British premium market outside of life insurance; 15 per cent of the West German; 20 per cent of the Dutch; and more than 40 per cent of the Canadian and Australian. In the struggle for expansion, Japan remains the prize; foreigners hold a mere 3 per cent of the insurance business there.

The major reinsurance companies are very large. The Zurich-based Swiss Reinsurance Company, for instance, had a gross premium income in 1984 of SF11.53 billion ($4.46 billion), and investment income of SF1.05 billion ($407 million).

But still the giant of the market is Lloyds of London, which accounts for 20 per cent of the world's marine insurance premiums. In 1970, it had just 5,999 members; by late 1984, it had 23,438. The total personal wealth of members is pledged in the conduct of the business. Since £100,000 is the minimum required for membership, and some members may count their wealth in many millions, the aggregate assets are enormous. But while profits have been generally tempting, there are substantial risks.

Lloyds' members are grouped into 430 insurance syndicates, varying in size, and managed by professionals. In 1985, one group of 1,525 members, who were formerly managed by the PCW Agency, were informed that their total losses could top £130 million.

The US insurance industry has had its own tribulations. One major cause has been the increasingly large damages awarded by courts in product liability and professional malpractice suits. Another has been the failure, in the fiercely competitive climate of the business during the early eighties, to raise premiums sufficiently. Underwriting losses (claims and expenses less premiums) have come to exceed investment income.

US insurance industry, $ billion

	underwriting losses	net investment income
1980	3.3	11.1
1981	6.3	13.2
1982	10.3	14.9
1983	13.3	16.0
1984	21.3	17.7
1985 (est)	25.2	19.7

THE CHAMELEON

An American lizard able to change its colour so as to merge into the background of banking. Known as a money fund, it collects individually small deposits into a considerable sum, which it then lends at relatively high rates of interest, with corresponding benefits to its investors.

Essentially mutual funds for the management of money, money funds were established in the late 1970s, when money placed in the wholesale market could earn far more than banks were paying their depositors in the US. By the end of 1982, money funds had attracted some $230 billion of savings. The banks hit back by paying higher interest on deposits. But the money fund, which offers little risk along with maximum liquidity (easy conversion into cash), has come to stay.

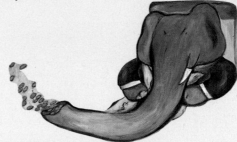

THE ELEPHANT

Otherwise known as a pension fund, it is the largest of the land animals, but is really rather timid. When frightened it can rush about, shaking the financial ground and doing great damage to the vegetation.

Pension funds dispose of enormous funds for investment. British funds totalled around £125 billion in 1984. The top 100 corporations in the US had pension funds in 1983 with a combined asset value of $220 billion; and overall assets of the US pensions industry in 1986 were estimated at $1,000 billion. These pension funds commit substantial portions of their resources to the stock markets. Given the risks as well as the rewards of such freedom, they employ professional managers who are judged on their performance. This promotes caution in never straying from the herd and quickness to take fright, when the weight of collective movement, into or out of certain investments, can be very disturbing.

THE GIRAFFE

A beast with a very long neck that searches for mass deposits of money, which it invests in mortgages, mainly to finance the purchase of homes.

In some countries, especially Britain, where it is known as a building society, the length of its neck is an indication of its success; in others, especially the US, where it is known as a Savings and Loan Association, the length of its neck is a sign of problems, and it needs massage from the game wardens.

In Britain, tax concessions and the ability to raise interest rates competitively with the banks, as well as to raise mortgage rates, have kept the building societies fighting fit. In the US, the Savings and Loan Associations were caught between the requirements to provide fixed rate mortgages and the steeply rising cost of money, with higher interest rates offered by competing financial institutions. Nonetheless in their search to grow, some took to lending most unwisely, with money borrowed, expensively, in the marketplace.

In Britain, the building societies dramatically increased their share of personal sector liquid assets from 25 per cent in 1965 (compared with 35 per cent for the banks) to 45.7 per cent in 1981 (34.6 per cent for the banks). The Halifax, biggest of them all, increased its assets, in 1985 alone, by 19 per cent. In the US, 1985 saw queues of agitated depositors, in both Maryland and Ohio, seeking to withdraw their money from Savings and Loan Associations, whose doors were closed.

In April 1986, US bank regulators closed Mainland Savings, a $1 billion Houston Savings and Loan Association, which had been hit by heavy losses in the much troubled Texan real estate sector. It was one of the largest financial institutions ever allowed to fail in the US.

THE SWALLOW

A migrating bird that pursues the track of the financial sun. Known as a stockbroker, it claims to be careful before committing itself, and is valued for its preparatory explorations.

It makes money both by dealing on behalf of others and by dealing for itself.

Stockbroking, along with the rest of money management, has become increasingly international: moving into London from Tokyo and then winging its way across the time zones to New York. US houses are busy building up a 24-hour global telephone market in top international equities. Goldman Sachs, the biggest block trader of equities in New York, has targeted 150 foreign stocks for its own global trading portfolio, with a quota of between 30 and 40 from Britain. The weight of money that US stockbroking can bring to bear internationally may be measured from the fact that some 62 per cent of the shares in ICI, Britain's giant chemical company, are traded in the US market.

Some dealers in securities are close to being merchant or investment banks, in the extent of the business they do on their own behalf. Salomon Brothers of Wall Street, for instance, usually runs an inventory, in equities and bonds, of well over $20 billion in value, and had capital resources of some $1.7 billion in 1984.

THE WEAVER

A bird that builds elaborate nests with the materials supplied to it by investors. One variety is known as a unit trust or, in the US, a mutual fund (where various shares are bought under professional management, and the shareholders own the trust or fund). Another is known as an investment trust, owned and managed by an institution, where investors simply receive dividends and share in any gains or losses.

Banks themselves build such nests and believe they do it better than the birds. The Union Bank of Switzerland, for instance, operates 24 different investment trusts: 3 in Swiss real estate; 7 in varieties of bonds; 2 in worldwide equities; 12 in equities of particular regions or countries. Total assets in these at the end of 1985 were valued at around $4.2 billion.

The money management upheaval

The business of money is currently in a state of upheaval.

In part, this is because of the revolution in technology, which has dramatically accelerated the internationalization of banking. Banks no longer need branches to reach their customers, and if they cannot transact desirable business in one country, they can find it in another. In part, too, fuelled by this development, governments have been dismantling the regulations that had protected and confined the activity of banks.

The instant transmission of messages between banks across the world, involving transfers of enormous sums, carries corresponding risks of criminal interference to match the convenience. To confront the risks, sophisticated security mechanisms have been developed. SWIFT, the Society for World Interbank Financial Transactions, connects more than 1,500 banks in 39 countries around the clock, with security safeguards.

Very rapidly, the border between banking and other forms of money management, and between money management and business in general, are being swept away.

Banks have been buying stakes in British stockbroking firms. For instance, S G Warburg, a major British merchant bank, merged with Akroyd & Smithers (leading London jobbers or primary market makers), Rowe & Pitman (the Queen's stockbroker), and Mullens (a major dealer in government securities), to form the Mercury International Group, in April 1986. Other moves are taking place across national frontiers, with foreign banks drawn to take a stake in the financial revolution at its centre, the City of London.

Among such important transnational alliances:

- American Express with L Messel

- Bank Bruxelles Lambert (Belgium) with William de Broe Hill Chaplin

- Chase Manhattan (US) with Laurie Milbank and Simon & Coates

- Citicorp (US) with Scrimgeour Kemp-Gee and with Vickers Da Costa

- Girozentrale Vienna (Austria) with Gilbert Eliott & Co

- Hong Kong and Shanghai Banking Corporation (Hong Kong) with James Capel

- Orion Royal Bank (subsidiary of Royal Bank of Canada) with Kitcat and Aitken

- Paribas (France) with Quilter Goodison

- Union Bank of Switzerland with Phillips & Drew

Stockbroking firms have moved into banking. The major innovator was Merrill Lynch, biggest stockbroking firm in the US, which moved into banking by inventing a whole new mechanism of its own, the 'cash management account' (CMA), during the 1970s.

The CMA is a kind of stockbroking, credit card, money fund and bank account rolled into one, with a large overdraft facility. A client can use it to buy securities - borrowing money to buy them on margin, if needs be - while getting a cheque book and a credit card to draw on the account. Any spare cash is automatically invested in a money market mutual fund where it earns relatively high interest. The only requirement is a minimum of $20,000 invested in securities through Merrill Lynch, as collateral for any overdraft and guarantee that Merrill Lynch will get some stockbroking business.

Express vote

When the compilers of the select Dow Jones Index of the 30 leading industrial companies in the US decided to fill a gap by including a service company for the first time, they chose American Express.

1891
American Express introduced its traveller's cheque, which now has 45-50 per cent of a world market worth $35-40 billion.

1958
It introduced its charge card, of which there are now more than 17 million in use.

1968
It bought the San Francisco-based Fireman's Fund, eighth biggest property and casualty insurer in the US.

1981
It bought Shearson Loeb Rhoades, second biggest stockbroking company in the US.

1983
It bought Trade Development Bank Holding, a large Geneva-based private bank.

1984
By 1984, it also owned First Data Resources, one of the largest independent providers of data based services to financial institutions; half of Warner Amex Cable Communications; and a stake in British publishing through Mitchell Beazley (later sold again).

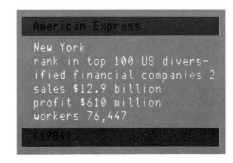

American Express
New York
rank in top 100 US diversified financial companies 2
sales $12.9 billion
profit $610 million
workers 76,447
(1984)

Business into banking

In 1981, Bechtel, the giant US engineering and construction company, bought Dillon Read, the 'aristocrat' of Wall Street securities firms.

In 1983, Britain's BAT Industries, the world's largest tobacco company, bought Eagle Star, one of Britain's biggest insurance companies.

British Petroleum (BP), which moved into banking in 1985, has an annual cash flow of $40 billion, liquid assets of some $3.5 billion, and considerable sums of foreign currency to trade at any one time. BP Finance International, as the new bank is called, will not only handle the financial business of BP but engage in general investment and commercial banking. Its example was followed, a few months later, by Volvo, the Swedish car manufacturer, which unveiled plans for an in-house bank that will rank among the largest financial institutions in Sweden and invade the territory of the conventional banking business.

```
British Petroleum

London
rank in world's top 50
industrial companies 6
sales $50.66 billion
profit $1.47 billion
workers 130,970

(1984)
```

Significant too, has been the fast growing financial diversification of the world's biggest retailer, Sears Roebuck, which now:

- takes money and pays interest

- supplies cheque-writing facilities

- provides loans and mortgages

- issues charge and credit cards

- operates money market funds

- trades in securities (stockbroking)

- sells life, property, casualty and mortgage insurance

- deals in real estate

- provides cash management accounts

- supplies travel agency services

- operates a car rental business.

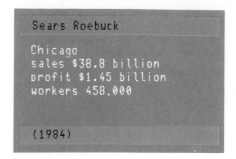

```
Sears Roebuck

Chicago
sales $38.8 billion
profit $1.45 billion
workers 458,000

(1984)
```

Diversifying risks

But the crossing from business to banking, or from banking to business, can be very risky, as some have discovered to their cost.

In 1983, the Allied Irish Bank, Ireland's leading commercial bank, took over Ireland's leading insurance company, the Insurance Corporation of Ireland, for I£86 million (an Irish £ or Punt was worth around a dollar). It soon emerged that the insurance company was in serious trouble from various underwriting misfortunes: asbestos problems in the US, bush fires in Australia, satellite insurance, and costly movements in currency exchange-rates. In March 1985, the Irish government was informed that the Insurance Corporation of Ireland had lost some I£120 milion, which the company could not meet and which threatened to bring down the Allied Irish Bank as well. The government came to the rescue by taking over the insurance company and leaving the bank to meet losses of some I£90 million or about one fifth of its shareholders' funds.

But the affair did not end there. By July 1985, losses by the insurance company were reported to be far beyond the original estimate and perhaps as high as I£1 billion, or I£300 for every man, woman and child in the Republic.

EXPATRIATE MONEY

Other developments are placing the world banking system under increasing strain. For it is a system based on the regulating sovereign state, but which functions more and more in a stateless market of expatriate currencies.

Commonly still called the Eurodollar market, because US dollars constitute the principal currency, the expatriate money market began, reportedly, when a Russian bank in Paris (Banque Commerciale pour L'Europe du Nord) found itself with surplus dollars and lent them within Europe. By 1960 the market was large enough to have been given its name, and it continued to grow as dollars, flowing out of the US to buy European assets and meet the trade deficits that mounted with the Vietnam war, remained in the possession of

Europeans rather than being repatriated in exchange for European currencies. In due course they were joined by other expatriate currencies: marks outside West Germany, yen outside Japan, sterling outside Britain, francs outside Switzerland. The market spread beyond Europe, to encompass footloose currency, mainly dollars, in Asia and in offshore banking centres such as the Bahamas, Cayman Islands, Bermuda and Panama.

The expatriate money market has grown spectacularly through the attractions it possesses.

■ As an essentially stateless market, it escapes common regulation.
■ Banks operating in it do not need to provide related liquid reserves to their central banks, as they would in their home markets, so that loans are correspondingly cheaper.
■ It provides a ready source of major currencies, regardless of attempts by the relevant state authorities to control the supply or employment of their own money.
■ The market ignores such individual state laws as taxation at source or the declaration of income or capital gains accruing abroad.
■ It provides abundant facilities for disguising the source and direction of funds.
■ It has become by far the largest single reservoir of funds for international borrowing, by banks, major industrial companies, and even some international agencies.

But all this carries related risks. The very size of the market dwarfs the resources of individual states. And where there is no regulation, there is also no recognized responsibility. A multitude of borrowers is not matched by a lender of last resort.

Growth of the expatriate money market, 1971-84, $ billion

1971	150
1972	219
1973	315
1974	395
1975	485
1976	595
1977	740
1978	950
1979	1,220
1980	1,515
1981	1,800
1982	1,922
1983	2,028
1984	2,153

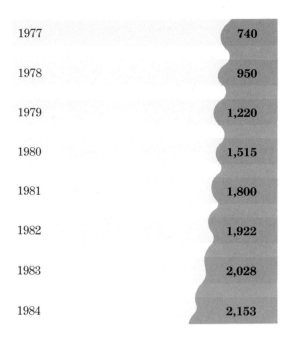

Foreign exchange trading centres
Estimates of daily turnover, $ billion

	1979	1984
London	25	49
New York	17	35
Zurich	10	20
Frankfurt	11	17
Tokyo	2	8
Singapore	3	8
Hong Kong	3	8
Paris	4	5
total	75	150

The City of London is the capital of the expatriate money market, mainly through the operation of foreign banks with branches there, especially US and Japanese.

Overall, Japanese banks have overtaken US ones as the largest aggregate holders of foreign banking assets (essentially, loans), with $640 billion at the end of September 1985 compared to the $580 billion held by US banks. Much of this business is concentrated in London, where Japanese banks hold just over 23 per cent of all banking assets booked in Britain.

Growth in number of foreign banks in London, 1967-83

Year	Directly represented	Indirectly represented	total
1967	114	-	114
1968	135	-	135
1969	138	-	138
1970	163	-	163
1971	176	25	201
1972	215	28	243
1973	232	35	267
1974	264	72	336
1975	263	72	335
1976	265	78	343
1977	300	55	355
1978	313	69	382
1979	330	59	389
1980	353	50	403
1981	353	65	418
1982	379	70	449
1983	391	69	460

▶ Directly represented through office, branch or subsidiary

▶ Indirectly represented through a stake in a joint venture or consortium bank

Expatriate money market bonds

Both states and big businesses borrow money by selling bonds in the expatriate money market, and the volume of business has been growing.

Volume of new issues, $ billion

Year	$ billion
1981	27.5
1982	46.5
1983	46.5
1984	80.2
1985	126.7

The international interbank market

At the heart of the expatriate money market is the huge interbank market - the market in borrowing by one bank from another.

Lending between banks, when one is temporarily short of funds and another is in surplus, is standard practice. But, increasingly, banks have used the international interbank market to acquire general funds for their long-term lending operations.

In 1981, a Bank of England study found that Japanese banks in London were raising three-quarters of their resources in the international interbank market. Other states began encouraging the foreign branches of their banks to tap the interbank market for funds to finance their balance of payments. Brazil is reported to have absorbed some $8 billion in this way. As a result of such operations, interbank trading grew from $5.7 billion a day in March 1980 to $23.3 billion a day in April 1983. At the end of September 1984, cross-border interbank borrowing totalled $1,912 billion.

A dangerous situation arises when banks that are large borrowers in the market run into difficulties and look likely to have problems with repaying the usually short-term (sometimes merely overnight) loans from other banks.

THE BANKING CRISIS

A bank, it is often said but not too loudly, is like an upside down pyramid: marvellously defying gravity, just as long as the air is still. But when the air moves, with suspicions or reports that a bank may be in trouble, the point of the pyramid, or the available resources of the bank to meet withdrawals of deposits, ceases to support the structure.

And the very toppling of the pyramid can so move the surrounding air as to send others crashing.

The British secondary bank collapse

In the early 1970s, the British economy boomed, as the state provided more and more money to promote growth and meet its own borrowing needs. Spectacular beneficiaries were the secondary or 'fringe' banks that attracted deposits by offering relatively high rates of interest and then lent the money at even higher rates to property developers and consumers.

In 1970, one such bank, London and County Securities, had assets (essentially, loans) of £5 million. Three years later, its assets had grown to £129 million.

With the economy threatening to boil over, the government lowered the flame. Property prices reversed direction. Many long-term loans in the sector became or looked like becoming bad debts. Short-term depositors, taking fright, rushed for their money. In November 1973, London and County Securities collapsed.

The panic spread, to overwhelm one secondary bank after the other. Even one of the four major British banks was rumoured to be in trouble, from having made massive loans to the secondary ones. Before confidence was restored, the Bank of England and the more stable members of the banking community had together poured some £2 billion into the system.

The teller tolls

Since banks make their money out of lending and even measure their relative size and success by the extent of their 'assets' or loans, the temptation to lend more and more has increasingly overcome prudence. Meanwhile, stricter monetary policies, pursued by state authorities to keep inflation under control, have put many business borrowers in difficulties.

In October 1984, the US Federal Deposit Insurance Corporation announced that there were 797 banks on its problem list, or 5.7 per cent of the 14,000 total. This was more than twice the previous post-war peak of 385, in November 1976.

Moreover, the number of bank failures in the US has now reached figures unknown since the Depression.

Number of bank failures in the US, 1977-85

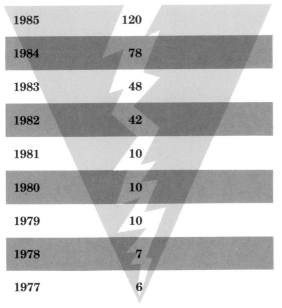

Year	Number
1985	120
1984	78
1983	48
1982	42
1981	10
1980	10
1979	10
1978	7
1977	6

North of the border

In September 1985, two small banks in Alberta collapsed, the first such failures in Canada for 62 years. Subsequently, a third small bank in difficulties was rescued by a merger with National Bank of Canada. Then, a run on deposits threatened Continental Bank of Canada, seventh largest in the country, which was saved in October by a C$2.9 support package from the central bank and the six largest commercial banks. By late March 1986, the central bank had advanced C$4.3 billion (US $3 billion) to various commercial banks in difficulties.

The debt crisis

Domestic banking problems have in general involved relatively moderate sums and been seen as more or less easily manageable by the relevant authorities. But the mounting problems of sovereign debt, or the inability of various poor and middle-income states to repay their loans from banks or pay the interest on such loans, has grown to threaten the whole banking system.

The growth of the crisis

■ The oil price rises from 1973 onwards left many poor states, with little or no oil of their own, facing much increased bills for oil imports.

■ The international banks, encouraged by their own governments, were eager to 'recycle' the deposits of rich oil producers by lending them to needy states.

■ The very availability of so much credit encouraged the needy to borrow, in the belief that growth in economic activity around the world would swell their exports and so enable them to meet their loan commitments.

■ But economic activity around the world did not grow as expected.

■ The terms of trade moved against the poor countries: the cost of manufactured imports rose, while receipts from raw material exports rose by less or even fell.

■ Tight money policies in the rich countries and especially in the US led to rising interest rates, especially for the dollar in which most bank loans were denominated.

■ A mounting proportion of exports was required to meet loan commitments.

■ Quite simply, the borrowers began running out of money or credit.

In 1982, among Latin American borrowers, the ratio of total foreign debt to total exports of goods and services was 300 per cent; of total foreign bank debt, 185 per cent.

The three largest borrowers, Brazil, Mexico and Argentina, were needing to pay some 50 per cent of all export revenue merely in interest on loans. The ratio of their total debt to total export revenue was some 420 per cent; of their banking debt to export revenue some 275 per cent.

Increasingly, the world's leading international banks appeared dangerously exposed. Their equity ratios, or resources available to absorb bad debts, were inadequate to the scale of threatening losses. Their loans to troubled major economies in Latin America alone often exceeded their total primary capital.

The banks exposed

Exposure of top ten US banks to third world debt
Assets (loans) as a percentage of primary capital, 1982

	total	Mexico and Brazil alone
Citicorp	203	158
Bank America	148	105
Chase Manhattan	220	147
Manufacturers Hanover	245	135
Morgan Guaranty	150	102
Chemical	182	144
Continental Illinois	119	70
First Interstate	64	64
Bankers Trust	143	112
Security Pacific	80	69

Exposure of Canadian banks to Latin American debt: Assets (loans) as a percentage of primary capital, 1983

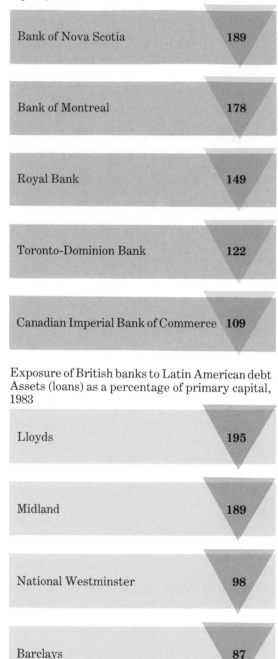

Bank of Nova Scotia	189
Bank of Montreal	178
Royal Bank	149
Toronto-Dominion Bank	122
Canadian Imperial Bank of Commerce	109

Exposure of British banks to Latin American debt Assets (loans) as a percentage of primary capital, 1983

Lloyds	195
Midland	189
National Westminster	98
Barclays	87

Suddenly there were very big banks whose size was no longer an assurance of stability. And a movement in the air from some domestic difficulties became a wind, blowing through the international interbank market, to topple one of the giants.

The Continental Illinois saga

In 1981, Continental Illinois Corporation of Chicago, with assets of $46.9 billion, was ranked among the top ten US banks and 40th in the world. In that year its troubles began, with the crash of a relative dwarf. Penn Square Bank in Oklahoma City had been growing apace, from assets of $34 million in 1974 to $525 million in 1981, by financing new oil and gas ventures in the state's energy boom. To supply large borrowings beyond its own resources, it packaged loans; taking a share for itself and parcelling out the remainder to other banks. Its chief partner was Continental Illinois, which bought roughly $1 billion of these loans.

To fund its own share, Penn Square offered enticingly high interest rates on short-term certificates of deposit, confident that it could still make money from its loans. But energy prices declined; the Oklahoma boom collapsed; and the bank found itself with bad debts. The Comptroller of the Currency discovered that total loan write-offs of $49 million well exceeded the bank's equity or primary capital of $43.7 million. On 5 July 1981, Penn Square crashed, and $250 million of deposits, above the federal insurance limit of $100,000 per loan, were lost.

Continental Illinois found itself with $595 million in 'non-performing' loans purchased from Penn Square: equivalent to 35 per cent of its $1.7 billion in equity or primary capital. But this was not all. Continental Illinois had been lending large sums elsewhere, to businesses either bankrupt now or in mounting difficulties. By the end of 1982, its 'non-performing' loans added up to $1.9 billion, or 5.6 per cent of its total loans.

Throughout 1983, its own difficulties mounted. It was dropped from 'the run', or the top ten US banks whose certificates of deposit are held to be of interchangeable top quality. Increasingly, it turned to the overseas markets for funds. By the end of March 1984, some $18 billion of its deposits came from abroad, with much of the money placed for very short periods. Indeed, it required around $8 billion in overnight funding. Early in May, the confidence of the international banking community, swept by mounting anxieties over sovereign debt and all too aware of the bank's exposure here as well, began to crack. Deposits were withdrawn from Continental Illinois in huge amounts. The US authorities were driven to mount the largest bank rescue operation ever: a $7.5 billion package, along with a pledge to disregard the federal insurance limit of $100,000 and to guarantee all individual deposits, however large, in the bank.

Within a week, the wind had moved against the other US international banks, blowing hardest on Manufacturers Hanover Trust, fourth biggest US bank, one of the world's top twenty, and one of the most exposed to problem loans in Latin America. Only a pledge from the US authorities that they would lend and lend again, to guarantee the liquidity of the major US banks, calmed the market for a while. But the banking system would never be the same again. As large depositors remained wary of Continental Illinois, more and more money was needed to prop it up: by August, more than $8 billion from agencies of the federal government and billions more from banks involved in a $5.5 billion federally arranged 'safety net'.

Other major banks were also shown to be susceptible to a flight of confidence.

'It's frightening. Every single bank in the top ten is sitting on a potential bombshell large enough to create a confidence problem among depositors.'
Senior investment banker in Wall Street

How good are the guardians?

Johnson Matthey Bankers, a subsidiary of the Johnson Matthey precious metal refiner and industrial group, could scarcely have been more prestigious. It was, along with such hallowed names as N M Rothschild, one of the five bullion dealers composing the London gold market. In the three years to 1984, it began boosting its business in commercial loans. Profits rose from £11.6 million in 1980-81 to £24.3 million in 1982-83. Then it all went very wrong.

JMB lent large sums to two Pakistani businessmen who were apparently considerable credit risks - loans that the bank claimed were equivalent to 72 per cent of its capital, but in fact were equivalent to much more than its entire capital of £100 million.

By late September 1984, the bank was facing collapse, and in the early hours of 1 October, the Bank of England, fearing the consequences of a collapse for the delicate functioning of the London Gold Market and for the reputation of the City, came to the rescue. It bought JMB for £1 (one pound), on the agreement of the Johnson Matthey parent to provide £50 million for part of the losses. The four other bullion dealers, along with top British merchant and clearing banks, were pressured into providing £150 million. The Bank of England itself, from its own resources of some £400 million, deposited £100 million in JMB. In May 1985, it emerged that JMB's likely losses would be £245 million, out of a total £450 million of loans. The Bank of England converted its £100 million deposit into fresh capital for JMB.

The question increasingly asked was why the Bank of England, the supervising authority for the banking sector, had not stepped in to rectify matters before it was too late, especially since it had been uneasy about JMB for months. The Chancellor of the Exchequer was prompted to admit, in June 1985, that the Old Lady had 'to some extent fallen down on the job'.

'a tale of banking incompetence on a scale that defies belief'.
Financial Times

The Israeli bank share boom

In 1972, Bank Hapoalim began boosting the value of its shares on the Tel Aviv stock exchange, to prevent its shareholders from suffering losses. By the mid-1970s, the bank was joined by its major competitors - Bank Leumi, Israel Discount, and United Mizrachi - in this risky enterprise. The banks provided loans to their customers for the purchase of their own shares, and with such shares employed as the security for the loans. In addition, through their influence with the stock exchange authorities, they affected trading in their own shares to ensure that they continually rose in value. Not surprisingly, bank shares came to be regarded as the best way for investors to protect themselves against inflation. They continually appreciated, year after year, till they stood at an aggregate market value some three times the registered capital of the banks.

Then, in October 1983, a devaluation scare sent investors rushing to sell their shares and buy US dollars with the proceeds. The banks, fearing a catastrophic fall in the price of their shares, bought back over $1 billion worth, at the cost of the capital base they had built up over the years. With the whole banking system close to collapse, the government moved, to take over $6.9 billion worth of share obligations and guarantees, at their October 1983 value in fixed US dollar terms. Redemptions were to be spread over a ten year period.

The government appointed a judicial Commission of Inquiry, headed by Supreme Court judge Moshe Beijsky. The unanimous report, released April 1986, recommended the removal from their posts, within 30 days, of the Governor of the Bank of Israel (the central bank) and the heads of the country's top four commercial banks. A former Finance Minister and a former chairman of the Tel Aviv stock exchange were strongly criticized for their failure to prevent the scandal. The report stopped short of recommending criminal prosecutions, but noted that the conduct of the banks had come 'close to fraud'.

Rescheduling sovereign debts

During the three years from the onset of the debt crisis in 1982, rescheduling agreements or the effective postponement of obligations, were heralded as having defused the problem, especially for the international banks.

Debt reschedulings, $ billion

	number of countries	value
1982	10	2.2
1983	30	51.1
1984	34	116.2

Under IMF tutelage, several of the major debtors in Latin America pursued policies of domestic austerity that boosted export earnings, and the exercise was helped by a recovering US economy, with an over-valued dollar, that sucked in imports.

But the resolution was more apparent than real.

■ The burden of debt repayments had not been removed. It had merely been postponed, and not for very long.

■ In 1985, the US economic recovery was running out of steam, and Latin American exporters were confronted by protectionist pressures in the US.

■ The big international banks, having lent too well in the past, were now not disposed to provide any new money at all. In 1984, the Bank for International Settlements reported, net bank lending to Latin America actually fell by $8 billion. Yet new money from the banks was precisely what the debtors needed. Mexico, for one, needed as much as $4 billion in new money by 1987, even before the early 1986 collapse in oil prices. With oil providing three quarters of its foreign exchange, the country faced debt service costs of some $11.5 billion in 1986 as well as prospective oil revenues down to merely $6 billion, or half the $12 billion target.

■ Policies of austerity were rapidly meeting the limits of domestic political tolerance. By mid-1985, Brazil, the biggest debtor of all in Latin America, had a government increasingly reluctant to accept debt rescheduling on the terms of domestic policy required by the IMF. For Mexico, 1986 was the fourth year of the worst recession since the 1930s, with the purchasing power of real wages cut by nearly 50 per cent.

■ No less an authority than the huge Morgan Guaranty bank warned, in September 1985, that measures taken since early 1982 to deal with the debt crisis had proved inadequate. Living standards had fallen some 10 per cent below pre-crisis levels; yet, despite pursuing policies of austerity, the debtors had recorded no decline in the key ratio of total debt to exports and only a small drop in the share of export earnings taken by interest payments.

■ The rich in poor countries have continued to export funds, by a variety of illegal means. Morgan Guaranty has estimated that in 1984; some $4 billion moved out of Mexico in this way; $2.7 billion out of Venezuela; and $2.2 billion out of Brazil. The capital flight accelerated during 1985, most notably from Mexico.

The growth of sovereign debt
Debts as a percentage of exports

	1982	1984	1985
Argentina	406	473	483
Brazil	339	322	368
Chile	333	402	442
Ecuador	240	260	254
Mexico	299	293	322
Peru	251	330	370
Venezuela	169	177	201
Nigeria	85	165	180
Philippines	270	312	342
Yugoslavia	167	166	160

In 1985, IBCA, the London-based banking analysis company, suggested that banks should have reserves of at least 20 per cent to meet the discount (or deduction from the face value) at which Third World loans had been changing hands in the secondary market. It reported that the percentage rates, in October 1985, for such loans were:

Peru	32-36
Argentina	63-67
Chile	67-71
Brazil	75-83
Mexico	78-82
Venezuela	81-84

But most large US banks had built up reserves of 5 per cent or less for all problem sovereign debt, and Japanese banks frequently had similar reserve levels. Canadian banks had 10 per cent; the big three French banks 20 per cent; the leading West German banks at least 20 per cent; and Swiss banks 'well above' 20 per cent

IBCA warned that such different reserve levels could cause banks to lose their identity of interest in future negotiations about sovereign debt. Those banks with high reserves were readier to take immediate losses 'than attempt sleight of hand accounting to put off the evil day'.

The limits of adjustment

In May 1985, Peru's new president announced that the country could not pay its debts under present conditions. Its debt service bill in 1985 would total $3.7 billion, against projected exports of $3.1 billion. On taking office, he announced that Peru would limit its debt servicing to 10 per cent of export receipts. For the first time since the beginning of the debt crisis, a government was openly pursuing a policy to pay only what it judged itself able to afford.

In January 1986, the President of Nigeria announced that his country would refuse to spend more than 30 per cent of its revenues from exports on the servicing of debt. Nigeria thus became the second leading debtor to impose a ceiling unilaterally without the agreement of its creditors.

In February 1986, more unsettling still, the President of Mexico, in a nationwide television address, announced that his country was no longer able to meet in full its interest payment obligations on its recently rescheduled $97 billion foreign debt. As a result of the collapse in oil prices, Mexico simply did not have the money.

There are further causes of concern, mainly connected with the US banking sector and with the US economy itself.
■ Of nearly 8,000 banks in the Independent Bankers Association of America, more than half have 25 per cent of their loans in agriculture, and some 1,700 have at least 50 per cent similarly committed. Total farm debt, at $210 billion, is larger than the debts of Brazil and Mexico combined. With high real interest rates to be paid on such debts and the low prices received for their products, US farms overall lost $110 billion in 1984 alone. As the farming community faces the worst financial crisis since the Depression, the value of farmland has plummeted; increasing numbers of farmers have been forced into bankruptcy; and many banks have had to write off substantial loans. Furthermore, the banking sector has yet to feel the full impact from the burst bubble of the energy sector and the bursting bubble of real estate values.

■ The sharp decline in the price of oil during early 1986 has hit not only the major oil producing states. Testifying before a US House of Representatives Banking sub-committee, in April 1986, William Seidman, chairman of the Federal Deposit Insurance Corporation, warned that the volume of problem energy loans was 'expected to expand dramatically'. Most energy loans - about $57 billion worth - were held by large banks, with assets of $1 billion or more. But there would be a 'spillover of loan problems' to smaller banks. Moreover, to augment the difficulties, real estate prices were falling in the most affected states: Texas, Oklahoma and Louisiana.

■ Top class companies are increasingly bypassing the banks and raising loans by the sale of commercial paper. The US market in such paper has risen steeply, from some $184 billion in January 1984, to some $302 billion in January 1986. The commercial banks are, accordingly, being left with the less creditworthy business customers, and the problem loans to energy companies and farmers and ailing Latin American economies.

■ US banks often transmit more funds than they have on deposit each morning, in anticipation of funds they will receive later in the day. The size of such 'daylight overdrafts', has been growing spectacularly, to an estimated average of between $110 billion and $120 billion a day.

The US Federal Reserve is seeking voluntary limits on any bank's total overdraft, in a bid to reduce the risk of a major default in the US money transfer system, which handles some $600 billion a day. Many banks have agreed to support such limits - as long as they are flexible as well as voluntary.

■ More and more international banks are engaged in ways of generating fee income rather than making loans. They guarantee the sale of debt securities by their customers and underwrite exchanges of debt - so called 'swaps' - between borrowers. Such swaps ($80 billion worth were arranged in 1984) and the underpinning of securities sales ($40 billion by the end of 1984) are not included in bank balance sheets but are still obligations which the banks may be called upon to meet. The central banks of Britain, the US, West Germany and Japan have all called attention to the risks involved. And in April 1986, the Bank for International Settlements underlined these concerns.

■ Takeover mania in particular has generated, mainly in the US, so-called 'junk bonds': high-yielding bonds that rank low in the order of repayment in the event of bankruptcy. The higher, if less secure, returns available on these bonds are tempting, not least to already precarious financial institutions, such as the troubled US savings and loan associations.

The increase in the issue of such instruments has provoked corresponding alarm, especially as at least one major issuing company (Global Marine, one of the world's biggest offshore oil drilling contractors) defaulted with debts of $1 billion in early 1986.

Junk bond issues, 1980-85, $ billion

Year	$ billion
1980	1.3
1981	1.4
1982	2.5
1983	7.5
1984	16.4
1985	17.8

One prominent Wall Street investor, James Rogers, has described the whole junk bond market as 'a nightmare just waiting to happen'.

■ Above all, the stability of the world financial system depends on the health of the crucial currency, the US dollar. Since the early years of this century, the US has been a net international creditor. But mounting trade deficits turned the US into a net debtor during 1985. Indeed, by the end of 1986, it is estimated that the US may owe more than $250 billion, or more than the combined borrowings of Brazil, Mexico and Argentina. And on current trends, the country will owe around $1,000 billion (well over the present total debt of all developing countries) by 1990, requiring a trade surplus equivalent to 2.5 per cent of GNP (or the same order as Japan's at present) merely to obviate further borrowing. Then, or well before, the value of the dollar may plummet so far so fast as to unhinge the whole monetary system.

A band aid for pernicious anaemia?

In October 1985, US Treasury Secretary James Baker announced an initiative that reflected his government's growing disquiet at the problems of the world's financial system. He proposed a grant of $20 billion in new commercial bank loans ($13 billion from the US banks), with an equivalent amount in net new lending by the World Bank and the Inter-American Development Bank, to 15 developing countries over the next three years.

The major Latin American debtors, supposedly the main beneficiaries, were less than enthusiastic.

- The plan assumed that debtor countries would continue to run substantial trade surpluses, at the cost of more rapid economic growth and at the risk of rising popular discontent at home.
- The plan involved an annual increase of some 2.5 per cent to 3 per cent in bank lending, or less than half the level of 6 per cent regarded as a realistic minimum by most financial authorities, including the World Bank and the IMF.
- The plan offered nothing towards alleviating the crucial problems: relatively high real interest rates on the accumulated debt and relatively low world prices for the commodities which were the main exports of the indebted countries.

THE PATHOLOGY OF MONEY

The growing instability of the banking system raises the possibility of a financial collapse, when credit sharply contracts and the value or purchasing power of money proceeds to rise. Far more common has been the phenomenon which has itself promoted such rare occurrences - a fall in the value of money.

Inflation

Apart from the Depression years, money has been declining in value virtually everywhere throughout this century. But in some countries, very high rates of inflation seem to be a permanent feature of the economy.

Not so sterling

Purchasing power of the pound, 1920-85

	value of one hundred 1920 pounds £	value of one hundred 1985 pounds £
1920	100.00	8.90
1925	80.00	7.10
1930	73.80	6.60
1935	63.60	5.70
1940	70.30	6.90
1945	89.80	8.00
1950	102.00	9.10
1955	131.70	11.80
1960	151.60	13.50
1965	177.70	15.90
1970	219.20	19.60
1975	373.50	33.40
1980	763.30	68.20
1985	1,119.70	100.00

A primary source of inflation is government itself. When its revenues are insufficient to pay for the goods and services it wants, it creates the extra money to pay for them, in competition for resources with business and the public.

Inflation easily becomes a self-promoting process. Once people begin to believe that their money is bound to drop in value, they become reluctant to hold it. They translate it into goods and services as soon as possible, putting pressure on the supply of such resources, and so on the price.

In the 40 years to 1982, prices in Argentina went up by more than five million times. The Buenos Aires daily, Tiempo Argentino, calculated the inflation rate during the period at 540,115,064 per cent.

In Bolivia, between November 1982 and February 1985, the price of flour rose 50,500 per cent, cooking oil by 111,458 per cent, and a visit to the doctor by 157,745 per cent. Inflation in 1985 was forecast to be 125,000 per cent.

1984 saw Israel struggling with an inflation rate of around 1,000 per cent. At the end of September 1984, a Seat motor car was priced at 4,628,726 shekels. By 21 October, it was 5,313,272 shekels. At 12.29 p.m. on 24 October, it was 5,594,544. At 12.31 p.m. on 24 October, it was 5,673,370. By early November it was over 6,000,000. Things had changed since biblical times. Then the patriarch Abraham bought a field in Hebron for 400 shekels. By late 1984, that would not even have bought him a soft drink.

High rates of inflation are economically damaging. They shift resources from production to distribution and from long to short-term investment. They are socially corrosive. They generally hit hardest the poor, whose meagre income rises more slowly than does the cost of essentials. They hit the weaker sectors of labour, unable to wrest wage rises in line with rises in prices. They hit many, especially in the middle classes, who variously depend on an income from savings. They benefit those, usually the already rich, who know how to exploit the international mobility of money. They feed greed, fear and hatred.

A GUIDE FOR
THE FINANCIALLY PERPLEXED

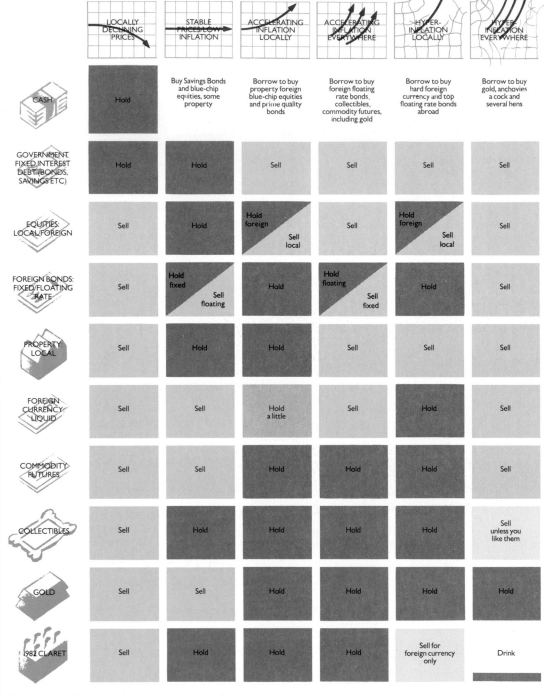

	LOCALLY DECLINING PRICES	STABLE PRICES/LOW INFLATION	ACCELERATING INFLATION LOCALLY	ACCELERATING INFLATION EVERYWHERE	HYPER-INFLATION LOCALLY	HYPER-INFLATION EVERYWHERE
CASH	Hold	Buy Savings Bonds and blue-chip equities, some property	Borrow to buy property foreign blue-chip equities and prime quality bonds	Borrow to buy foreign floating rate bonds, collectibles, commodity futures, including gold	Borrow to buy hard foreign currency and top floating rate bonds abroad	Borrow to buy gold, anchovies a cock and several hens
GOVERNMENT FIXED INTEREST DEBT (BONDS, SAVINGS ETC)	Hold	Hold	Sell	Sell	Sell	Sell
EQUITIES: LOCAL/FOREIGN	Sell	Hold	Hold foreign / Sell local	Sell	Hold foreign / Sell local	Sell
FOREIGN BONDS: FIXED/FLOATING RATE	Sell	Hold fixed / Sell floating	Hold	Hold floating / Sell fixed	Hold	Sell
PROPERTY: LOCAL	Sell	Hold	Hold	Sell	Sell	Sell
FOREIGN CURRENCY: LIQUID	Sell	Sell	Hold a little	Sell	Hold	Sell
COMMODITY FUTURES	Sell	Sell	Hold	Hold	Hold	Sell
COLLECTIBLES	Sell	Hold	Hold	Hold	Hold	Sell unless you like them
GOLD	Sell	Sell	Hold	Hold	Hold	Hold
1982 CLARET	Sell	Hold	Hold	Hold	Sell for foreign currency only	Drink

Where foreign currency, equities, bonds and trading in commodity futures is illegal, buy property or gold.

Where the purchase of bullion is not permitted, buy old coins; where this is not permitted, buy scrap.

Speculation

Instability encourages speculation, or the gambling on movements in prices. Stock markets have long been a major vehicle for such speculation, generally through margin trading, by which only a small proportion of the value involved in a transaction is paid in cash, as an assurance that any loss will duly be met.

But the most spectacular growth in speculation on Wall Street, at least since the late 1920s, has taken place since the 1950s, in the major commodity markets, with trading in futures. These were initially contracts to buy or sell a given quantity of a physical commodity (such as wheat or copper), at a determined price at a determined date in the future, with a cash down payment representing only a small part of the value involved. To these there came to be added financial futures, or contracts in financial instruments, such as treasury bills and foreign currencies. Then trading took flight into the metaphysical, with futures in so-called 'notional' bonds and one or other stock market index. Soon the daily trade in stock index futures would on occasion represent a greater dollar volume than the trade on the New York Stock Exchange. The latest device is for trading in options on financial futures: rights to buy or sell contracts in the future that themselves convey the right to buy or sell contracts in the future beyond.

The flow of speculative money going into the commodity markets has increased enormously during the last few years, to make the markets themselves dangerously more volatile. Huge commodity funds pool the resources of many small speculators. Those in the US alone are estimated to have some $500 million at their disposal, with a trading power perhaps ten times as great through margin dealings. And these compose only a small part of all the private investment funds operating in the markets.

By far the most important markets for trading in futures, by overall volume, are in the United States, where the speculation capital is Chicago.

The US exchanges, 1983

	contracts number	%
Chicago Board Of Trade (CBOT)	62,811,523	44.89
Chicago Mercantile Exchange (CME)	37,830,044	27.04
Commodity Exchange NY (COMEX)	20,014,597	14.30
Coffee, Sugar & Cocoa Exchange (CSCE)	4,876,069	3.48
New York Mercantile Exchange (NYMEX)	3,926,589	2.81
New York Futures Exchange (NYFE)	3,510,285	2.51
MidAmerica Commodity Exchange (MIDAM)	3,166,537	2.26
New York Cotton Exchange (NYCE)	1,703,105	1.22
Kansas City Board Of Trade (KCBOT)	1,693,042	1.21
Minneapolis Grain Exchange (MGE)	379,607	0.27
New Orleans Commodity Exchange	13,542	0.01
total	139,924,940	100.00

Financial futures
Number of contracts traded

	Chicago/ New York	London (Liffe)
1982	33,700,000	246,000
1983	40,900,000	1,400,000
1984	59,600,000	2,600,000

Futures trading most actively traded contracts, first half of 1985

Daily volume, in thousands of contracts

Treasury Bonds, CBOT	151.5
Standard & Poors 500 Index, CME	60.6
Treasury Bonds Option, CBOT	41.8
Eurodollar, CME	36.3
Gold 100 ozs, COMEX	34.4
Soybeans, CBOT	28.2
Deutsche Mark, CME	25.4
Corn, CBOT	24.0
Silver 5,000 ozs, COMEX	22.3
Swiss Franc, CME	17.6
Live Cattle, CME	16.0
Soybean Oil, CBOT	15.7
Crude Oil, NYMEX	15.6
Major Market Index, CBOT	13.4
Soybean Meal, CBOT	12.6
New York Stock Exchange Composite Index, NYFE	12.3
Treasury Bills, CME	11.4
Copper, COMEX	11.3
Sugar, CSCE	11.2
British Pound, CME	10.9
10-year Treasury Notes, CBOT	10.6
Wheat, CBOT	8.1
Heating Oil, No. 2, NYMEX	7.9
Japanese Yen, CME	7.3
Live Hogs, CME	7.1

Massive speculation around the world diverts the resources of savings away from productive investment. The world of business is thus increasingly directed at making money out of manipulating money, rather than out of expanding industry and trade. In the foreign exchange markets, where some $150 billion a day are traded in the financial centres, it was estimated in 1985 that less than 5 per cent - perhaps as little as 1 per cent or 2 per cent - mirror an equivalent transaction in goods and services.

The vast majority of contracts for future delivery are traded not with delivery in mind but with the prospect of trading back the contract at a profit well before delivery is due. In the Chicago grain markets, speculators normally account for over 70 per cent of total trading. The proportion is even higher in financial futures.

Jumping beans

In March 1984, the price of coffee on the London commodity market rose from £1,800 a tonne to £4,000 in just ten minutes. Five traders together held 81 contracts to deliver 405 tonnes of coffee, but without the beans to do so. They had not covered their commitments; presumably on the assumption that those who held the contracts of purchase merely intended to make a profit by selling them on the market. The traders were left collectively facing losses of nearly £750,000.

The most spectacular and costly consequences of demanding physical delivery in a market so accustomed to mere manipulation of future commitments belong to another story.

The great silver bubble

In 1973, Bunker Hunt, the Texan multimillionaire, and his younger brother Herbert, began buying silver and taking physical delivery.

In August 1979, purchasing began on an enormous scale with the intervention of the Bermuda-based International Metals Investment Co., which allied the resources of the Hunts with those of important Saudi and Dubai figures. Silver rose steeply from a price level of $9.60 an ounce.

By 1980, silver had reached $52.50 an ounce in Chicago. In response, the commodity markets in New York and Chicago changed the ground rules. Speculators would be allowed only to sell, not to buy silver. As silver prices fell steeply the Hunts borrowed $1,300 million, in February and March ($12.90 out of every $100 in new loans to US business during the period), to meet their demands for more cash.

At the end of March 1980, Paul Volcker, chairman of the US Federal Reserve, declared publicly that banks should not finance speculation. Swiss and other European banks, which had been lending large sums to the Hunts, toed the line. The Arab associates, asked by Hunt to provide further finance, refused.

On 27 March 1980, 'Silver Thursday', the price of silver fell so far so fast that brokers and banks involved with the Hunts looked as though they themselves might be in trouble. The family's debts were calculated at $1,825 million, an enormous sum, though Bunker Hunt commented, 'A billion dollars isn't what it used to be.'

Fearful bankers, with the reluctant acquiescence of the Federal Reserve, advanced a loan of $1,100 million: on condition that the Hunts mortgaged their possessions, including Bunker Hunt's $34 million art and coin collection, $43 million holdings in real estate, $37 million in cattle and, above all, the family's vast oil interests.

The city jungle

'The trouble is that the world of commodity trading is a jungle, suitable for hunting for large and experienced animals but one in which the small animal is at very serious risk, even though with a degree of luck he might survive.

'The dangers to the small investor, even in the absence of any fraud at all, are frightening.'

Mr Justice Rodney Bax, trying a case at London's Old Bailey in January 1983

The Kuwaiti crash

A case study in the pathology of speculation

In 1982, share fever of a kind probably without parallel since the days of the South Sea Bubble in Britain, 1719-20, seized Kuwait. On the official exchange, as share prices soared, P/E ratios (the number of years at current earnings that would be needed to pay the current price of the share), commonly around 10 in Western stock markets, climbed well into the hundreds and reached 1,000 in one case. Daily turnover sometimes exceeded that of the London Stock Exchange, with $1.5 billion worth of shares traded in a single week at the height of the boom in April 1982.

On the unofficial exchange in the Souk Al-Manakh, a ground floor area in a building that doubled as a five-storey car park, shares were traded in companies located in Bahrain, or other Gulf states to the south of Kuwait. There, P/E ratios often did not exist. Prices soared 500 per cent in the shares of companies which had yet to produce a balance sheet, let alone a profit.

The fever was fed by two contrivances. First, heavily priced shares were split again and again, to encourage buyers, in a parody of such operations elsewhere. One Gulf real estate company, issued a bonus share for every three held; then the right to buy two new shares, at a discount on the market price, for every three held; and finally announced a share split, of three for one - all within a single day. Secondly, as the supply of cash resources for purchasing shares dried up, brokers and customers took to using post-dated cheques, with a premium for the delay in cash payment that rapidly rose to well over double, occasionally to four times, the spot price of the share purchase. The inevitable happened.

Jassim Al-Mutawa, who had once earned 250 dinars a month by stamping passports in Kuwait's immigration department, put his signature on post-dated cheques worth some 3,000 million dinars (more than $10 billion), and was in difficulties.

After the peak of buying frenzy in April 1982, reports of Jassim's difficulties, together with news of Iranian counter-attacks into Iraq and cuts in Kuwaiti government spending, set off a bout of profit-taking on the market. By August, share prices were collapsing, and in due course the extent of the financial disaster was revealed. The mountain of some 28,000 post-dated cheques had a total face value equal to $94 billion, and involved some 6,500 Kuwaiti investors, from the lowest in Kuwait's stratified society to Sheikh Khalifa Abdullah Al Khalifa Al Sabah, nephew of the Kuwaiti ruler.

By early 1984, some 220 people had had their assets seized by the government receiver. Sheikh Khalifa Abdullah, with an estimated deficit on the face value of his cheques amounting to one billion dinars, or $3.4 billion, was provided with a government loan of 278 million dinars (almost $1 billion) or a sum larger than the national debt of Jordan.

When the government withdrew its support for share prices in early April, the stock market index fell 60 per cent over the next 18 months or so : a decline similar to that on Wall Street from 1930 to 1932. In some months, turnover fell to some $6.5 million, compared with the $1.5 billion worth of shares traded in a single week at the height of the 1982 boom.

Jassim Al-Mutawa, who by his own admission owed $10.5 billion, was well on the way to becoming the world's largest ever personal bankrupt. In the end, Jassim declared that he had nothing much to fear, at least in the world he knew. 'I am not afraid of anything or anybody but Allah.'

Countertrade

A clear symptom of sickness in the world financial system is the increasing recourse to barter, or countertrade as it is known in its more developed forms: the direct exchange of goods, in a running backwards of the historical film.

With world trade growing so sluggishly, when at all, countertrade offers an alternative to contracting production.

Countertrade is estimated now to account for anywhere between 8 and 20 per cent of all trade and for some 40 per cent of all Third World trade.

It is increasing because:

■ one or other party to trade does not have the money, or the right sort of money (such as hard, or internationally acceptable, currencies), for simple purchase;

■ one or other party expects to get more for its goods in kind than in cash;

■ one or other party can dispose of its goods only by agreeing to take different goods in their place.

To what point?

The story is told of a US delegation on a visit to Romania that remarked on the unexpectedly large number of factories with busy chimneys. 'What are they making?' a delegate asked the ubiquitous apparatchik.

'They're turning shit into bricks.'

'But that's marvellous. Romania must be doing very well.'

'Not so well. Under a Comecon agreement, we have to supply Czechoslovakia with bricks in return for chemicals.'

'And what is wrong with chemicals?'

'Nothing. But they must go to Hungary in return for machine tools.'

'Well, that really is marvellous. You start with shit, and you get machine tools.'

'Only in passing. The machine tools must go to Poland, and we get back coal.'

'Don't you need coal?'

'Of course we need the coal. But the coal must go to East Germany, in return for optical equipment.'

'And you have no use for optical equipment?'

'But we have a Comecon agreement by which we must supply the optical equipment to the Soviet Union.'

'And what do you get in return from the Soviet Union?'

'We get shit.'

Countertrade involves a variety of arrangements including:

■ partial payment in goods;

■ buy-back agreements by which exporters buy back goods produced with their own machinery;

■ parallel transactions, in which one party delivers goods in return for goods that a third party agrees to accept.

Some countertrade deals are bizarre.
■ Ford trades its cars for thousands of Uruguayan sheepskins.

■ Italy barters frigates for Iraqi oil.

■ Pierre Cardin receives oriental silks for providing consultancy services to China.

■ a Washington law company receives chickens and leather jackets as payment for its advice to a developing country.

■ General Motors and Chrysler trade their cars with Jamaica for raw and refined bauxite.

■ General Electric swaps steam turbines for 8,000 tonnes of Romanian nails.

■ Philippine coconut products go to Romania in return for machinery.

■ Malaysia sends crude oil to Brazil in return for iron ore.

■ Malaysia supplies South Korea with crude oil and refined palm oil in return for naval patrol boats.

■ Sears World Trade, a wholly owned subsidiary of Sears Roebuck, barters US breeding swine for Dominican sugar.

The big time

All such deals were dwarfed by the £5 billion ($7.5 billion) Saudi-British countertrade agreement signed in February 1986. In return for 132 military aircraft from Britain, Saudi Arabia would provide oil, which Shell and BP would refine and sell.

Intermediaries

Money remains the key common denominator, as the basis for arriving at deals, even if its role is secondary, and limited to paying shippers, handlers, consultants and agents.

Countertrade specialists are thriving, and nowhere more so than in Austria, which pioneered the countertrade between West and East. The three main banks (Creditanstalt, Oesterreichische Laenderbank and Girozentrale) all have their countertrade units. But there are smaller banks involved, including specialists in East-West trade such as Bank Winter. There are specialist brokers who make the countertrade practical for the parties concerned. When a French manufacturer sells computers to Hungary, for instance, in return for Hungarian shoes, it may pad the price it demands by 10 per cent, in the knowledge that such might be the price cut it will need to get rid of the shoes. The company then hands the shoes to a broker or countertrade specialist, who splits the premium with a shoe buyer; taking perhaps 2 per cent and passing on the 8 per cent that remains as an enticing price cut.

In all, there are an estimated 250-300 government and private organizations and brokers in Europe involved in countertrade.

Countertrade deals

Product shares of 262 deals with poor countries, 1977-83, percentages

	OECD (rich) countries	'communist' countries	poor countries
agricultural products	5	7	34
oil and oil products	-	11	10
minerals and metals	-	11	11
textiles and clothing	1	2	9
military goods	2	-	-
other manufactured goods and industrial equipment	87	70	15
services	3	-	1
unspecified	2	-	19

THREE FINANCIAL GLOSSARIES

1. Money and credit

Bonds
Historically, institutionalized borrowings by governments or business, with the date of repayment, and the annual rate of interest to be paid meanwhile, fixed at the time of issue. But the mounting need and cost of credit have promoted numerous variations on the theme. There are 'irredeemable' government and corporate bonds, where the interest rate, but no date for repayment, is fixed. There are floating rate bonds, where the interest rate paid is related to the changing rate in the market. There are zero coupon bonds which pay no interest at all but which are issued at a price very much lower than the repayment due on a particular date, so that income effectively takes the form of capital gains. There are index-linked bonds, which pay a small or no rate of interest but whose repayment, at some fixed date, includes compensation for the interim rise in the cost of living. There are convertible bonds, which carry the right of conversion into corporate *equities* (see *3. Market trading*). For further variations, phone your broker.

Bearer bonds
Bonds that are not registered in anybody's name but belong to the holder. Interest is paid on presentation of the coupon, or detachable ticket, accompanying the bond. This is a form of investment much favoured by those who consider their income to be their own business and not that of tax inspectors.

Certificates of deposit
Short-term borrowings of substantial sums by banks; certificates denote the amount of the deposit, the date of its repayment, and the interest payable. A typical CD might be for $1 million, with a maturity up to six months. Most CDs are held by depositors. But billions of dollars worth are also traded in active secondary markets across the world. The CDs of the top ten US banks - nicknamed 'the run' because their paper is held to be interchangeable top quality - are alone eligible for delivery under CD futures contracts.

Commercial paper
Broadly, all salable corporation loans; narrowly short-term borrowings (from one to 270 but usually for 30 to 90 days) made by top corporations.

Gilt edged
The term used for government bonds in Britain. Disappointed investors in them understand why the gilt is apparently only applied to the edges.

Money supply
The amount of money available for the potential purchase of goods and services. But since some of this money is instantly available and other forms involve a measure of delay, there are distinguishing categories. Definitions may differ from country to country, but the three used in the US are perhaps the most important.

M1 is the total of physical money and current account balances or demand deposits at the banks.

M2 is M1 plus most personal savings (such as time deposits at banks or savings and loans associations), and including money market funds.

M3 is M2 plus certificates of deposit and institutional money market deposits.

Treasury bills
Government IOUs (usually for three months) that are regularly auctioned, with the interest rate in the difference between the 100 per cent paid on maturity and the price paid by the successful - that is, the highest - bidders.

Triple A
The highest rating given to the creditworthiness of a borrower or borrowings. The rating is commonly bestowed by specialist credit rating agencies (such as Moody's or Standard & Poor's).

2. Banking and debt

Assets
Overwhelmingly the loans made by a bank. How far they are really to be regarded as assets is another matter.

Default
The failure of a debtor to meet certain commitments specified in a loan agreement; such as to pay the interest on a debt or to repay the principal on the date due. But in the world of banking, the real is not necessarily realized. The lender must 'declare' a default before the default becomes what it is.

Equity ratio
The proportion of a bank's capital (usually funds from the subscriptions of shareholders together with retained profits) to its loans. A variable formula, historically given to erosion.

Liabilities
The money borrowed by a bank, in the form of deposits or of loans, which the bank is required to repay, on a fixed date or on demand.

Moratorium
The declaration by a debtor that he or she needs time to put his or her affairs in order and meanwhile will make no due repayment of debt.

Non-performing loan
A euphemism for a debt whose interest payments are in default.

Repudiation

The declaration by a debtor that he or she simply has no intention of servicing or repaying his or her debts.

Rescheduling

The procedure by which loans, unlikely or unable to be repaid, are rearranged so as to site the burden of repayment some months or a few years away. According to Lord Lever: a 'system for evading formal default which amounts to little more than exchanging an incredible and defaulted promise to pay for another incredible promise to pay later'.

Rescue

The saving of a bank, in difficulties from a withdrawal of deposits or a demand for the repayment of loans, through a takeover by another bank or an injection of funds from the monetary authorities or both (the first commonly being dependent upon the second). The costlier the rescue, the more likely it is to take place, since the bigger the bank in difficulties, the more of a threat its collapse would pose to the survival of other banks.

Restructuring

The procedure by which a debtor is permitted to replace one loan by another, usually involving a later date of repayment.

Servicing

Payment of interest on a loan.

Sovereign debt

The debt incurred by a sovereign state or by one of its agencies.

3. Market trading

Bear

Someone who expects prices to fall and, by extension, takes a pessimistic view of the economic outlook. The term is more commonly applied to someone who sells a commodity that he or she does not have, in the hope of buying it at a profit when the time set for delivery arrives. This conduct is generally regarded as disreputable, if not downright dishonest. (See also *Bull* below)

Bear market

A market in which prices are falling or one dominated by bears.

Bug

Bulls of gold are bears of virtually everything else. For this reason, they are generally held to be at least as disreputable as bears and are given the special derogatory name of Gold Bugs.

Bull

Someone who expects prices to rise and, by extension, takes an optimistic view of the economic outlook. The term is more commonly applied to someone who buys a commodity without paying for it, hoping to sell it at a profit when the time set for payment arrives. This conduct is generally regarded as respectable, since it nourishes optimism and confidence in the system. (See also *Bear* above)

Bull market

A market in which prices are rising or one which is dominated by bulls.

Chartist

A trader or analyst who pays little attention to the news and follows or draws patterns or charts of market conduct; tracking changes in volume, the extent of *open interest* (see below), the trend of price movements. (See also *Fundamentalist* below)

Commodity

Any article of trade; once applied only to physical objects but increasingly now to anything traded, however metaphysical.

Contract

The term given to each unit of commodities traded for future delivery. In New York, on COMEX (Commodity Exchange), such a contract in gold would be for 100 fine ounces. In Chicago, at the Mercantile Exchange (CME), one Treasury Bill contract would be worth $1 million. Such contracts are generally bought and sold on *margin* (see below).

Equities

Shares in the ownership of a company. When the company makes profits, shareholders usually receive some proportionate payment, in the form of dividends. They may also receive dividends from a company that is making losses but has accumulated resources. This is often to keep shareholders from selling their shares or demanding a change in the management. It is a process of limited application.

Financial instrument

A financial article, from the reasonably physical, such as certificates of deposit or a particular foreign currency, to the metaphysical, such as the direction of interest rates through the purchase or sale of a 'notional' government bond.

Fundamentalist

A trader or analyst who believes that market movement is dictated by ultimate changes in the relation between supply and demand, and who examines the news for signs of such changes. (See also *Chartist* above)

Futures

The generic term given to all contracts involving future delivery.

Insider trading

The use of privileged information to trade in the market; as when a company executive uses private information to trade the company's shares. In the US and some other countries, this is an illegal activity.

Margin
That proportion of a contract's total value that must be provided in cash as a guarantee that losses will duly be met. Often around 10 per cent, the proportion may be set well below or well above this figure, depending upon the degree of risk involved in trading a particular commodity.

Margin call
The demand for further cash provision, because the movement in price has consumed, or is rapidly consuming, the guarantee already provided. See also *margin* above.

Market analyst
Someone whose profession it is to explain the conduct of the market rationally. Since the conduct of the market is frequently irrational, such analysis requires considerable imaginative effort and self-deception.

Maximum price fluctuation
The maximum or 'limit' that a price is allowed to move up or down during a single trading session.

Open interest
The total of contracts to buy or to sell that are not covered by reciprocal contracts. Thus, if there are 1,000 contracts to buy September gold at a particular price and only 800 contracts to sell it, there is an open interest of 200 contracts.

Option
The right to buy or sell a particular equity, commodity or contract at a determined price on a determined date for a determined payment. Its advantage is that it allows for a virtually limitless gain while limiting any loss to the cost of the option. Its disadvantage is that any profit only begins to accrue after the cost of the option has been met. A call is an option to buy; a put, an option to sell. A double option allows the holder to buy or to sell at will and is correspondingly expensive.

Short
The temper and conduct of a *bear* (see above). To go short in, or sell short, a particular commodity, is to sell without having it, in the expectation - or hope - of being able to buy it back at a profit.

Speculator
Someone who buys or sells a commodity with the sole purpose of making a profit and at the risk of making a loss; usually by operating on *margin* (see above).

Spot
The term for cash, as in spot price or spot transaction.

Trader
Someone who engages in trade as a profession or who trades for professional purposes (in the course of conducting a business connnected with what is traded). Frequently indistinguishable from a speculator.

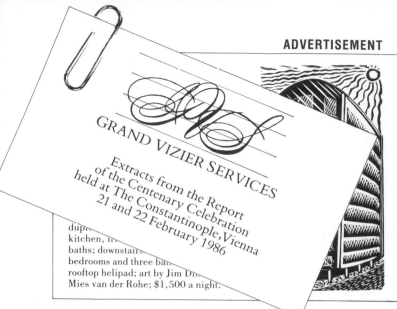
ADDRESS BY THE PRESIDENT, COUNT HERMES BUONAROTTI.

My Lords, Ladies and Gentlemen, Colleagues,

It is a privilege and a pleasure to welcome you here to this special congress of Grand Vizier Services, held so suitably in Vienna, the city of our birth, a century ago.

There have been many changes since then, in our activities and in our organization. There have been times when our members must have wondered whether the world had much use for us any longer. Yet never have we been more in demand, never have we possessed better prospects for expansion, than today.

Fortunately we have always known how to adjust. We have adjusted to a fundamental shift in our clientele, from what, to borrow a term we all appreciate, may be called the 'registered rich' (the Habsburgs, Hohenzollerns, Romanovs, Ottomans, with the lesser nobility of Europe and some of the more cultured Americans), to what may be called the 'bearer rich', or the more anonymous, more mobile, and frankly rather richer businessmen of today.

In keeping with the change in our custom, we have adjusted our own operations: moving our head office from Vienna to London and, in 1914, sheltering in Geneva, before making the happy transition, some 60 years ago, to New York.

Our own membership, as you well know, has also grown considerably, in national origin as well as in skills. Without intending any disrespect to our predecessors, I can say that we have progressed far beyond the activities of individual courtiers, however ingenious. Our multinational teams of bankers and brokers, strategists and social psychologists, publicists and image builders, lawyers and accountants – to name but a few – offer expert and tested advice and services.

The world in which we operate is in considerable turmoil. After a period of steady economic growth and social consolidation, we appear to be entering on a course of severe disruption and change. In the circumstances, it would be advisable for us to define our market and consider how it may develop in the near future.

Our clients are, of course, the very rich. But the very rich are not all of one kind. There are the international rich – the academics among you will know them as the international 'elite' – whose activities, friendships and marriages know no national boundaries, and whose interests and curiosities transcend the narrow confines of race, religion and any particular culture. It is a class that embraces Greek shipowners, German industrialists, English merchant bankers, American dynastic families, and many others in a web of personal and formal contacts.

Eager to join it, and sometimes much richer, are some members of some national elites. The most prominent recently have been ruling families from the Arabian Gulf, whose new-found wealth, beyond the dreams of the Medici, is still very mobile, and whose physical circumstances are not altogether secure. Beside them are aspirants from Japan, Hong Kong, Latin America, and even, less engagingly, certain Americans with Sicilian connections. Some of you may not know that in Japan the annual salaries of the top ten businessmen alone together total $100 million.

These national elites are far from homogeneous. In some countries, they include the old landed rich who have survived the transition to the business society. Almost everywhere they include the so-called 'nouveaux riches' - a term with connotations of belittlement that we do not accept - whose talent lies in shooting the rapids of business or finance.

In catering for the needs of such people, we must never be deceived into taking a narrow national view. We, of all people, know that national circumstances are no indication of personal ones. I can assure you that our own investigations confirm recently reported estimates that some $28 billion is held by Argentinians in foreign bank accounts. We will continue to provide our services, as we have done in the past, wherever there are appreciative clients.

There are also what I would respectfully call the 'community rich', Jews, Marwaris, Patels, Parsees, Ismailis, Lebanese, overseas Chinese: soon to be joined, perhaps, in rather tragic circumstances, by successful entrepreneurs among the Sikhs.

Most significant of all, and of increasing importance, are the state elites, or the people whose wealth, social position and power are inseparable from public office. Of these, the pre-eminent, and certainly one of the most exotic, is the Russian. From a country born in revolution, there has emerged, in great pain and at enormous cost, an elite whose existence is - to say the least - an anomaly, yet which is served in the most intimate detail. Privileged office holders comprise - according to our own sources - some 750,000 officials: together with the members of their families, who share their privileges, they number some three million people, or a little more than 1 per cent of the total population. In the upper reaches, there are those who live better than many high-paid corporate executives in the West. At the very summit of officialdom, such as membership of the Politbureau, there is virtually unlimited disposable income in kind.

But since they are without private property rights of any real meaning, the Russian rich are unusually immobile and isolated; presenting us with something of a problem in marketing our services among them.

Not all the state rich, happily, are so walled in. You will doubtless know of the Bahamas' Prime Minister, Sir Lynden Pindling, who was found by a commission of enquiry to have spent, during a seven year period, eight times more than he earned. More spectacular still, we have the example of Sr. Durazo, merely the police chief of Mexico City, whose two enormous estates, 1,200 retainers and many possessions at home and abroad, provoked irrepressible popular agitation and his subsequent dismissal; ex-President Marcos of the Philippines, whose fortune of several billion dollars, most of which is held abroad, has come under investigation by the new Philippines government authorities; or ex-President Duvalier of Haiti who has a reported $400 million outside his country of origin. Such people have increasingly sought our services, but have in too many instances, and to their cost, ignored our advice.

On a more elevated level, the demand in states of recent creation for accommodation at home and investments abroad, suitable to the prestige and insecurities of high office, has steadily increased. Furthermore, openings are appearing in Eastern Europe and, most promisingly, in China. All in all, we must expect the state rich to compose a growing sector of our clientele.

None of this, of course, is to suggest that we should relax our efforts in the old and tried world of the West, where recent developments have been most favourable to our functioning. In the United States and Britain, most notably, and in France most recently, government is more amenable to the accumulation of large private fortunes than it has been for some time past; though the skills of the lawyers and accountants amongst us are no less necessary to advise in making the most of the opportunity. In particular, advances in technology are generating a multitude of new multi-millionaires, to join the ranks of our customers. Where, as in France, retrograde steps were taken to victimize the rich, the consequences were quickly such as to prompt a change in direction.

Below the national rich, there are the middle classes – the executives, advisers, gurus, ideologues, consultants, experts – in a word, preeminently us. We are in no sense true principals, but we are numerous and rich enough to provide something of a market for one another. Society is coming more to appreciate our services, especially as managers, and to provide corresponding rewards. We, of all people, must show society that wealth should be used and not put away for the moths to corrupt.

Below us, of course, in vast, nay excessive, numbers are the mass who form no part of our market and can be, indeed are - except in times of regrettable social upheaval - ignored. Here I would introduce a caution and a challenge. A body such as ours, with a sense and experience of history, knows how fragile are the arrangements on which our civilization depends, and must observe the current economic and social climate, otherwise so congenial, with trepidation. It is as undeniable as it is deplorable that the vast mass of people are no longer secure in their vocation to serve. Unless they are occupied and once again made to feel relevant to some social purpose, there is a real danger that they will inhibit or even reverse the continued expansion of our market.

It is also true that our clients have an unusual opportunity to shape their circumstances freely in their, and our, best interests. Their most serious rival for social hegemony, the labour movement, is weakened by unemployment, redeployment and the shrinking of its traditional power bases; it has also been castrated by what I like to term the ritualization and growing obsolescence of its most powerful ideological weapon - Marxism.

Its allies, the poor peasantry and the landless, have been much weakened as a force by their headlong rush into unproductive metropolitan slums throughout the world and by their national populist political leadership. That leadership now forms part – a junior but not unimportant part, be it said – of our class, as is evident in this very room.

Our clients' position has also been strengthened by the erosion of traditional distinctions between the control over production which we might term, broadly, business; the control over finance or money; and social control, or power. These three aspects of their traditional responsibilities are drawing together in what we might categorize or classify as power centres.

But we would be foolish to imagine our

clients can seize the time without watching the clock, as our American friends say. There are many weaknesses in their position. Some of them are still falsely loyal to the hostages they have given to history: to popular participation in the public political processes and, even more important, to popular interference in business and economic affairs. Even our Russian comrades, clear-sighted realists to a man, have yet to break openly with their populist image.

There is also grave danger that competition between them, particularly when backed by force, will go beyond the bounds of what is convenient or safe. We owe our existence and power to the efficient workings of a world-wide competitive system. But our common interests go beyond and behind the mechanics of the system. In short, we must do everything in our power to make the system work for us rather than being suborned into working for it, since untempered competition in a world of sovereign states can result only in material ruin for us all or mutual annihilation. I believe I would be right in saying that none of us wants that.

Ladies and gentlemen, danger for us lies not in there being rich and poor in the world. That has always been the case, at least in recorded time, and has come to be accepted by both rich and poor. Rather, danger lies in the rich forgetting that wealth derives from, and belongs to, the exercise of power. Their main preoccupation should be to tend that power rather than exclusively enjoy the wealth. The moment their priorities are reversed, their ascendancy will be threatened and their future obscured.

All of us - not only we the executives, but also the principals, if I may pursue a distinction - must train assiduously in the use of power. We must exercise it constantly, in a manner that is firm, fair and open. In this way we will satisfy the deepest inner needs of humankind, for without social order, without a planned sequence of attainable and spiritual goals for each person, there can be no self-fulfilment and no sense of security. Social harmony and our considerable advantages rest on our providing a framework - however modest it might be - within which that sense might flourish.

Ladies and gentlemen, permit us to end on a narrower note. We ourselves are faced with a particular challenge. We have so far made far less headway than we should in the vast potential market of Japan, with its immensely rich but inward looking national elite, and still less headway among the state rich of China and Eastern Europe, not so rich but vastly more numerous and potentially most lucrative. We are also very weak in the growing sector of the hermit rich: those who set narrow limits on their contribution to our common civilization and who consequently seek refuge in a self-effacement. Unless we find a way to enter and win these markets, not only may we well make less progress in our second century than we made in our first, we may also weaken that cohesion amongst our clients on which ultimately our livelihood depends.

We must, as a matter of urgency, provide tempting, and, we hope, irresistible opportunities for the unassimilated rich to see and experience something of how their counterparts elsewhere act and live. For, as our own corporate culture illustrates, the possession of riches is nothing without the capacity to employ them for profit and pleasure. Indeed, what distinguishes our clients is precisely their capacity to blur the distinction between work and play; to choose between them at will and so stand apart from their differences.

Finally, I wish to commend to your attention our luncheon hampers, provided by courtesy of Escoffier International; to thank all those responsible; and to thank you all for the patience with which you have heard me.

6

THE GOVERNMENT OF BUSINESS

Nobody controls the business system. Yet individual businesses are controlled in the most minute detail.

They need to be. Someone has to define their purposes, and set their targets; someone has to interpret the message of the markets in which they compete; to balance, and constantly adjust, the many internal factors - human, material and financial - which enable them to fulfil their designated purposes.

Control is exercised in many ways, not all of them obvious. Sometimes, but only sometimes, it is through ownership. In the West, millions of shareholders, the legal owners of business, surrender their power in practice to a few of their number, or to the managements whom they, in theory, appoint. In the East, there are virtually no shareholders, yet control is manifestly exercised. Sometimes, this is done through hands-on management, yet even the most entrenched managers are ousted from time to time. Sometimes final control is exercised through law or state administrative devices.

OWNERSHIP AND CONTROL

In the world of business control, the variety is infinite.

Yet there are patterns. At one extreme there are sole owners who manage their own businesses.

Sole owners

As of 1984, David Liederman was director, sole owner and chief executive of David's Cookies, a chain of takeaway cookie stores, with 31 outlets in Manhattan, New York City; another 70 in 22 states of the US; and one in Japan. David Liederman had sole legal title to the 'substantial' net income of the firm.

Not very different from David's Cookies are the royal businesses where control through ownership is reinforced by public arrangements. The Duchy of Cornwall is a prime example.

Charles, Prince of Wales, is the sole legal owner of the vast family of businesses which make up the Duchy of Cornwall, one of the richest private estates in Europe. Based on 130,000 acres in nine counties, it includes about 250 farms, the marble in the rocks of The Lizard, the silver and lead mines of Muhenniot, the oyster beds of Helford, 850 properties in London's Kennington area including the Oval cricket ground, a £3.6 million share portfolio, and the property of all Cornish people who die intestate.

The Duchy, which belongs by right to the eldest son of the monarch, nets Prince Charles some £560,000 a year. In lieu of tax, 25 per cent of the Duchy's profits are paid to the British Treasury, and the provisions of the Health and Safety Act do not apply in the Duchy. In addition, all royal investments are expressly excluded from the legal provisions requiring disclosure of holdings of 5 per cent or more of the shares in a public company.

Vastly richer, but rather more obscure in its articles of association and less secure in consequence, is the royal core of the Saudi economy. Saudi Arabia is presided over by King Fahd, Prime Minister and Head of State, and directed by the six royals in the Cabinet: the Prime Minister and the Ministers of Foreign Affairs, Defence, Interior, National Guard, and Public Works and Housing.

They certainly control, and believe they own, a business with liquid assets in 1983 of over $140 billion.

State companies

The Saudis notwithstanding, ownership of a state is something of a curiosity. More significant by far is the control exercised through exclusive state ownership and management. The state-run economies preside over a quarter to a third of all the business undertaken worldwide. In the mixed economies of the West and South, the state sector is always important, and often predominates, as it does in most of Africa, Latin America and Asia.

Business wholly owned by the state can take different forms:

■ State companies, such as the huge oil or power monopolies, Petroleos Mexicanos and Petrobras (Petroleo Brasileirio); or Elf Aquitaine and Compagnie Générale d'Electricité (CGE) of France; or, less frequently, general manufacturing companies, such as the Rhône-Poulenc chemical firm in France, with its sales of $5.9 billion, profits of $227 million and 79,230 workers in 1984.

■ State holding companies, like the IRI in Italy. IRI is no. 17 in the world's top companies, with sales of $23.4 billion and 504,915 workers in 1984. Its thousand-plus companies include banks, steelmaking, most of Italy's telecommunications companies and their suppliers, Alfa Romeo, Alitalia, shipping, shipbuilding and the autostrada network.

■ State agencies, like the postal services almost everywhere, or many rail networks.

Cooperatives

Formal and beneficial ownership converge more closely with collective ownership of another sort - cooperatives.

There are consumer cooperatives like the 135 member cooperatives of the British Cooperative Union, with their 55 superstores and 1,580 supermarkets, collectively the largest food retailer in Britain until 1982; and worker cooperatives such as ULGOR, in Mondragon, Spain, one of Spain's ten exemplary companies.

ULGOR is the largest domestically-owned manufacturer of household electrical equipment in the country, producing a wide range of goods, from machine tools and microwave ovens to industrial robots. It embraces:

■ 85 manufacturing companies employing an average of 200 workers each

■ a bank, the Caja Laboral Popular (CLP)

■ six agricultural cooperatives

■ 14 housing cooperatives

■ 43 cooperatively owned schools and colleges

■ a social security and pensions cooperative

■ a medical and hospital services cooperative

■ a consumer cooperative

During the recession, which brought widespread closures and mounting unemployment to the region in the early 1980s, not one cooperative went under.

The CLP bank provides management expertise, technical services and 75 per cent of the start-up costs for a new cooperative, as well as sponsoring a research centre for product development. It provides the central direction essential for the group as a whole.

Only workers are members of the producing cooperatives. The ratio between the lowest and highest pay is 1:3.

ULGOR's profits are distributed to the social fund (10 per cent) and the collective reserve (20 per cent), or reinvested on behalf of the worker-owners for their retirement (70 per cent).

'Public' companies

Full ownership is an expensive, and not always an efficient, method of exercising control or imparting direction. Owners with many interests in many fields could not themselves handle the detail and would lose control over individual businesses, if they did not harness the self-interest of others by giving them a stake in the effective direction of these businesses.

Majority ownership – or almost

Under majority ownership, the effective junior partners, whether minority owners or professional managers, are necessarily concerned with the success of the individual businesses in which they have their stake.

Occasionally, control through majority ownership is exercised through a private company, tightly controlled by a single personal or family interest. More often, majority ownership is of a public company, such as Porsche, the West German luxury sports car manufacturer, whose ruling families, the Porsches and the Piechs, sold 30 per cent of its shares to the public, in 1984, in the form of non-voting preference shares.

Majority ownership is often exercised by the state, as in the case of Lufthansa, the West German flagship airline, or VIAG (Vereinigte Industrie-Unternehmungen), the energy, aluminium and chemicals holding company, which (with a turnover of $2.3 billion) was 87 per cent owned by the West German federal government in 1985.

Rupert Murdoch's News International, controlled by a family trust with 46 per cent of the shares in 1984, owns more than 80 magazines and newspapers in Australia, Britain and the US. In the US, it also owns half a film studio, Twentieth Century Fox, and a chain of six major TV stations. And in Australia, it also owns two TV stations, four book publishers, a half interest in the largest private airline, shares in two gas and oil exploration consortia, and a lot more besides.

Minority ownership

More common, and more important, is the exercise of control through minority ownership.

Bechtel is an important example of minority control over private companies. The world's largest private construction and engineering company, it includes amongst its mega-projects: the San Francisco mass transit system; the 1,100 mile trans-Arabian oil pipeline; the world's biggest hydro-electric project at Churchill Falls in Labrador, Canada; and the world's biggest copper complex in Papua New Guinea. Forty per cent of Bechtel stock is owned by a family trust controlled by Steve Bechtel, father and son. The rest belongs to 57 top managers who must sell their stock to the company on departure, retirement or death.

By far the most important form of control through ownership, is the minority ownership of public companies whose shareholding is widely dispersed outside one substantial holding. Even giants amongst public companies are controlled in this way. Shareholdings in such companies can change very quickly. But:
■ E I Du Pont de Nemours, the huge chemicals company of Wilmington, Delaware (in 1985, the ninth largest industrial company in the US), has been controlled by the Du Pont family, with a reported 35 per cent of the shareholding.
■ Corning Glass Works, of Corning, New York (in 1985, the 217th largest industrial company in the US), has been controlled by the Houghton family, with around 30 per cent of the shares.
■ Wrigleys, the Chicago chewing gum manufacturer (in 1985, the 411th largest industrial company in the US) has been controlled by the third generation heir, William Wrigley Jr, through his 25 per cent holding, backed by another 15 per cent family share.

A minority share in a company with otherwise dispersed ownership need not be all that large to be effective in exercising control.

The Keswick family, with only some 10 per cent of Jardine Matheson, the oldest surviving trading company in Hong Kong and still one of the most powerful, ousted the chairman in 1983; had Simon Keswick appointed in his place; and had the company's official domicile moved to Bermuda.

Other means

A controlling minority ownership is sometimes reinforced by other means.

Tata Sons of India, for example, is the holding company for the Tata Group of more than 30 companies, with combined sales in 1980 of $2.2 billion. In most companies of the group, the government is the major shareholder, through investment and financial institutions. In the second largest by sales, Tata Iron and Steel Company, Tata's rival for the leadership of Indian business (the Birla group) has a larger shareholding than Tata. But Tata Sons controls the companies on the basis that the government-appointed board members vote with management 'in the ordinary way'.

Reinforced minority ownership can, and usually does, exist without state intervention, at least in the West. The sheer complexity of the relations amongst businesses provides the opportunity to control them by controlling these relationships, through holding companies or other less formal means, rather than directly.

Alfa-Laval, in 1984, ranked 428 among the largest industrial companies outside the US, ASEA (107), Atlas-Copco (424), Electrolux (114), Ericsson Telephone (136), Saab-Scania (164), SKF (229), Stora Kopparbergs Bergslags (451), as well as one of Sweden's leading commercial banks, Skandinaviska Enskilda Banken (79 among the world's top 100 commercial banks outside the US in 1984), are all in the Wallenberg federation. No formal group exists, but the name turns up again and again on the various boards. Important shareholdings belong to two investment companies, Investor and Providentia, and Peter Wallenberg chairs both. Other significant stakes are held by allied trusts and pension funds.

Recruitment

By far the most important method of control, without ownership or with attenuated ownership, is through appointment to key positions within a self-perpetuating management oligarchy.

General Motors of Detroit, in 1985 the largest manufacturing company in the world, has some 315 million shares dispersed among a million shareholders. Some 38 per cent are held by institutions, but the company is controlled by its highly-paid management.

'General Motors... is a marvellous structure of committees...for administration, sales, engineering, merchandizing, styling, and everything else. The committees are the company, and one of the ways you rise in the company is by being a committee man - preferably secretary of one of the committees.'
Detroit executive

Imperial Chemical Industries (ICI) is Britain's largest manufacturing company, and the 48th largest industrial company in the world. In 1984, there were some 619 million shares in the company, held by 365,000 individual shareholders (not including 25,000 or so American shareholders who owned 16 per cent of the shares). No individual shareholding, personal or institutional, exceeded 3 per cent of the total. Control has long been exercised by its professional management.

Supershares

Reinforcement can take other forms, too. There are supershares - shares invested with disproportionate voting weight.

■ The Nestlé group of Switzerland, for example, has two categories of voting share, one heavier than the other.

■ The Savoy Hotel Group of London is a more dramatic example. It has held at bay its eager suitor, the vastly bigger and more profitable Trusthouse Forte, for years. In mid-1984, Trusthouse Forte had 69 per cent of the shares in Savoy Hotel, but only 42.3 per cent of the votes.

The most telling of special devices to retain control without ownership is the Golden Share, held by British goverment ministers in firms that have been privatized.

There are five of these curious instruments in existence so far: in Amersham International, Britoil, Enterprise Oil, Jaguar Cars, and British Telecom. They carry no dividend rights or votes, and cannot be bought or sold. But they carry the right to veto any takeover, and are a final defence against foreign control.

Families and friends

And there is control through the mutual support that people who share values, insights and opportunities, give to each other. The world of business forms a constantly changing but interconnected whole, whose most durable elements are its controllers. The detail of their relationships changes; the fact of interrelationship does not: in a winning combination of flexibility and durability that makes control possible despite its dispersal.

Italian families

The major private sector companies in Italy are controlled by a very small number of families, the Ala Nobile ('noble chamber'). The Agnellis, who control Fiat, constitute by far the most important centre of industrial power. They exercise influence directly and through Mediobanca, which acts as a clearing house for virtually every transaction between the major private sector concerns, even though state banks hold most of its shares. Their major allies are the Pirelli family.

In 1985, the cosy arrangements of the Ala Nobile came under pressure. An unprecedented conjunction of events - political stability; the inauguration of 30 newly authorized unit trusts, offering an alternative to bank deposits, postal accounts and treasury bonds; the continuation of exchange controls; a huge (35 per cent) increase in corporate profits - encouraged a new generation of businessmen, led by Carlo de Benedetti, chairman of Olivetti, to challenge the established order.

Agnelli family

Some important interests, 1985, directly held percentage of all shares

Toro (insurance)	**51.4**
Fiat (motor vehicles)	**50.0**
Rinascente (department stores)	**48.7**
Gemina (holding company)	**26.9**
Mediobanca (banking)	**below 1.0**

At the same time: Fiat controls 27 per cent of SNIA Textiles and 8.17 per cent of Zanussi; Gemina controls 17.1 per cent of Montedison, 12.26 per cent of Telettra (Fiat Group) and 46 per cent of Rizzoli-Corriere (publishing).

Carlo de Benedetti

Some important interests, 1985, directly held percentage of all shares

Montedison (chemicals)	**17.8**
Gemina (holding company)	**17.6**
SNIA Textiles	**14.97**
Pirelli (rubber)	**11.1**
Zanussi (electrical goods)	**8.17**
Generali (insurance)	**5.1**

A major move came mid-1985, when Mario Schimberni, chairman of Montedison, defied Agnelli, his largest shareholder, and took over Bi-Invest. Agnelli withdrew from Montedison. War looked imminent. But by the end of the year, peace was being declared: Mediobanca showed a willingness to cooperate with de Benedetti; Leopold Pirelli announced that he was acquiring a stake in de Benedetti's empire; and de Benedetti himself revealed that he had been invited to join the shareholders' syndicate that controls Pirelli, as well as the Milan holding company that is the largest shareholder in the Pirelli group.

The new faces were accommodated; the old faces remained.

MANAGEMENT

Control over business reflects social standing and power. It is exercised through management.

Managers are the administrators of business.

They have to deal with states, their own and others; with existing competitors and the ever-present threat of new ones; with organized labour, and with unorganized labour that might be fretful or apathetic; with old and new products, and old and new technologies; with predators and with potential victims; with suppliers and would-be suppliers, customers and would-be customers; with bankers and brokers, and with the need for capital and the pressures of debt.

They must watch their front but also guard their back, for within their own structures there is competition, too.

And they must do all this simultaneously, continually, unrelentingly, and at ever-increasing speed. For the mounting pace of technological innovation affects all business everywhere.

The acid test for managers - the touchstone of managerial success - is to achieve a productive balance between the information they receive and the authority they exercise. They must avoid the use of power in forms that would choke off the flow of information from below, where it is generated, and yet retain sufficient freedom from internal constraints for effective response to the ever-shifting environment in which they operate.

The nature of the business being pursued, and of the society in which it is conducted, affects the terms upon which a productive relationship may be formed between the need for information and the exercise of authority. The more advanced the technology employed, the more important it is to conciliate skilled employees, and the less authoritarian management can safely be. Within the same society, the management of a steel mill can afford to be more high-handed, and is likely to be so, than the management of a pioneering electronics firm.

High risers

'As facts are travelling up the organization, some of them fall off. That's because a guy can't convince his boss that some fact is important, so his boss substitutes another fact that wasn't there before, and his boss does the same. By the time the information gets up here to the 14th floor, you're not seeing what the first guy down there sees.'

Roger Smith, chairman, General Motors

'You usually have a guy way the hell up on the 24th floor and he always has a corner office, and all the stuff filters up, with everybody practising...corporate survival. They manage to filter it a little bit, change it a little bit. By the time it gets there, it's supposedly what he wants to hear.'

Harold Geneen, creator, and for 17 years chief executive, of ITT

A sign of stress

'We've seen a 100 per cent increase in the number of high-level executives coming to us for treatment, compared with five years ago. I'm sure that a year or two from now it'll be another 100 per cent or more. Drugs have taken the business world by storm.'

Dr Joseph A Pursch, director of a US company operating 160 hospitals for the treatment of alcoholism and drug addiction, 1985

The strains of performing effectively and consistently in a constantly-changing, unpredictable market environment, and of marshalling wayward human and other resources, exact a heavy toll of top managers. Unable to sustain the delicate balance between authority and information or understanding, many of the highest managers tend to display manifestations of stress and its relief in an explosive imperiousness.

Within their businesses, top managers wield considerable, sometimes absolute, power. It would be surprising if they did not, as a rule, use such power to perpetuate it.

In the short term, they are subject to little surveillance and less control. What little exists usually comes after the event.

The directors, elected to represent the interests of the owners or shareholders by evaluating the performance of management in general, and of the chief executive in particular, and who are expected to mete out corresponding rewards or punishments, in practice seldom do any such thing.

The board usually meets in the grandest room, around a great polished table, twelve times a year, to hear the chief executive or a selected subordinate report on the success of the management. The board member who insists on asking unwelcome questions is soon labelled a troublemaker. If the chief executive says 'I cannot work with that man', the offender is unlikely to be nominated for re-election.

Board members happily accept perks from the management they are appointed to judge, which raises doubts about the board's independence.

The chief executive is invariably a member of the board; and in three-quarters of the largest industrial companies in the US, he chairs the board. The chairman can scarcely be expected to sit in impartial judgement on his own performance.

Directors run virtually no personal risk for any amount of complacency, cronyism or neglect of their duties. Their responsibility to the shareholders is leniently interpreted by the courts and they are often further protected by insurance and indemnification policies, for which the company pays and which effectively guarantee that any damages assessed against the board member will be paid by the company.

Who manages the managers?

'Among the boards of directors of Fortune 500 companies, I estimate that 95 per cent are not fully doing what they are legally, morally, and ethically supposed to do.'

Harold Geneen

'When you look at it, anybody who runs a company, it's kind of like their own fiefdom. The other management people serve at the pleasure of the chairman, and the board of directors pretty well serves at the pleasure of the chairman. So who really watches the chairman?'

T Boone Pickens Jr, chief executive of Mesa Petroleum

Top managers understandably work hard to cushion the strains of office by enhancing its rewards and, above all, by loosening the bonds between reward and performance.

At the top, managers can pay themselves and some of their colleagues handsomely. Even in Britain, where executive salaries are relatively low, there are riches at the top.

It's alright for some

Chairmen or highest paid directors earning more than £200,000 per year, 1985

	chairman £	highest paid director £
BOC Group	883,100	-
Burton Group	542,000	-
BSR International	-	526,000
Heron	449,000	-
Lonrho	-	322,861
Lex Service	280,970	307,809
Hanson Trust	301,000	-
STC	297,000	-
ICI	287,261	-
British Petroleum	241,547	-

Salary is only part of a chief executive's pay or, as it is increasingly called, 'compensation'. In the 1980s in the US, bonuses and long-term incentives often account for at least as much as basic salary. At the lesser heights of European business, they account for relatively less but are still a significant addition.

Chief executive perks as a percentage of average basic salary

Britain	20.1
Switzerland	17.5
Netherlands	15.4
Portugal	15.1
West Germany	13.7
Belgium	13.4
Italy	9.5
France	8.3

A state of grace

In 1981, J Peter Grace, chief executive of the US conglomerate W R Grace, received:

$549,000 in salary; $1 million in recognition of his accomplishments during his 36-year tenure as the company's chief executive; $265,000 as profits bonus; and $350,000 as the first annual payment of his pension - a total of $2.164 million.

Between 1945 and 1981, stockholders in the company under J Peter Grace's leadership enjoyed an annual return (average annual dividend plus annual average stock appreciation) of 7.4 per cent. The stocks making up Standard and Poor's composite stock index did substantially better, averaging an annual 10.3 per cent return. 'One can only imagine', commented Fortune, 'how much more the directors might have awarded Peter Grace had he succeeded in making W R Grace just average'.

A high flier

Allegheny International reported that chief executive Robert J Buckley, in 1984, had $2,921,840 outstanding in loans from the company, at a mere 2 per cent annual interest, under a corporate stock purchase programme.

On the fringe

Like salaries, fringe benefits are also on the up and up as a form of privileged income. In 1983, Atlantic Richfield spent $120,000 on operating corporate aircraft. A customized Boeing 707 shuttled chairman Robert O Anderson between his residence in New Mexico and the oil company's Los Angeles headquarters.

Of 15 recorded forms of fringe benefit in Britain, ten showed an increase in incidence over the eleven years to 1984. Some of them spread like wildfire.

The spreading fringe

Managers receiving benefit, Britain, percentages

	1974	1984
full use of company car	62.0	77.9
free medical insurance	30.1	68.9
subsidized lunches	64.2	63.2
life assurance up to 3 times' salary	53.1	52.0
life assurance over 3 times' salary	22.2	42.2
bonus	32.6	38.5
free telephone or allowance	-	31.5
share option scheme	4.2	28.9
top hat pension	19.3	23.9
low interest loans	-	10.5
share purchase scheme	4.3	9.4
assistance with house purchase	4.7	8.4
car allowance	12.3	4.4
subsidized housing	0.9	0.3

Ultimately, even at the very summit, management is periodically swept and buffeted by the storms generated in the wider, controlling environment. And the climate is worsening. In the US in 1976-78, there were 21 changes of chief executive amongst the top 500 industrial companies; and in 1979-82, there were no fewer than 36, an increase of 71 per cent. And that was before the latest merger mania overtook Wall Street.

Not surprisingly, top managers will make some effort to secure their future.

The Midas touch

 A favourite device is the 'golden parachute', the special employment agreement, including generous severance pay, that protects the upper echelons of management if control of their companies changes hands. First appearing on the corporate scene in the early 1970s, golden parachutes became prevalent with the surge of takeovers in the early 1980s. In 1982, some 1,500 companies in the US introduced golden parachutes into their by-laws and charters; and some 15 per cent of the top 1,000 companies had them. By 1986, this last figure had risen to 30 per cent.

The cord for opening a golden parachute differs from company to company. Some companies use a percentage of outside share ownership, usually between 20 and 40 per cent.

Golden parachutes, $ million

David J Mahoney, Norton Simon	35.0
Michael Bergerac, Revlon	34.0
William W Granger Jr, Beatrice	7.0
William Agee, Bendix	4.1
Ralph Baily, Conoco	4.0

Golden parachutes are not as widespread elsewhere as in the US. But they do exist in Britain. Bill Fieldhouse (Letraset) received £750,000; and Jack Gill (Associated Communications) £560,000, on parting company with their firms.

In France, Georges Pebereau, managing director of CGE, the state-owned electronics conglomerate, negotiated a payment of FF400,000 a year (about $50,000), for life, index-linked, should he be forced to give up being chairman of the group's telecommunications subsidiary, CIT-Alcatel.

Glittering prizes

Golden parachutes or handshakes are unpopular with those who do not have them, and even with some who do. They 'legitimize giving million-dollar bribes to executives for doing what they were paid to do anyway', wrote Peter G Scotese, chairman, Springs Industries, and current or former director of nine other companies.

'My feeling, very simply, is to forget golden parachutes. I don't like them.'

T Boone Pickens Jr, chief executive of Mesa Petroleum, October 1982

Mesa's proxy statement in 1982 showed that Pickens was provided, at his discretion, with 'a termination fee equal to twice his base salary ($416,000 in 1982) in the event of a change of control not approved by the board'.

Golden hellos

With the increasing internationalization of business, especially in the financial sector, high rates of reward for special skills tend to drive out lower ones. And management simply buys the brains that it cannot itself provide. In the financial revolution that is sweeping the City of London, for instance, spiralling salaries, with so-called 'golden hellos' on appointment (£100,000 is increasingly common), are in such contrast to calls for pay restraint in the wider context as to alarm even a government with a doctrinal devotion to the creativity of material incentives.

Management training

Few managers attain the summit of managerial eminence and reward. But many start on the road, a road full of pitfalls and contradictions.

Big companies adopt military-style management-training programmes for their promising recruits, in which conformity, obedience and predictable reactions are encouraged at some personal cost. Loyalty to the company is the supreme virtue.

Managers are often bent into shape at work, under conditions of stress. Surveillance is strict. Acceptable patterns of behaviour are projected in elaborate detail.

Shaping up

- The company subjects candidates for employment to a selection process so rigorous that it often seems designed to discourage them from taking the job.
- The company then subjects the successful applicants to experiences directed at inducing humility and making them question their prior behaviour, beliefs and values. This usually takes the form of piling on more work than the employee can handle.
- The company sends the newly-humbled recruits into the field and sees that they get lots of carefully monitored experience. Progress is rewarded with promotion at predictable intervals.
- At every stage of the new manager's career, operating results are measured and rewarded or punished accordingly. At IBM, for instance, the cost of violating one of the corporate norms - by handling subordinates too harshly or displaying excessive zeal against the competition - is, typically, a transfer to a fairly meaningless job at the same level, sometimes in a less congenial location.
- All along the way, the company promotes its values, in part by expecting the employee to accept personal sacrifices in their cause. There are long hours of work, weekends apart from the family, bosses who may be difficult, criticism that may seem unfair, job assignments that are inconvenient or undesirable.
- There is a constant harping on crucial events in the company's history, to reinforce the importance of the corporate culture.
- The company assigns role models to promising employees, so that others may be persuaded to follow their example. Proctor & Gamble's brand managers, for instance, display marked consistency in several ways: they are almost all analytical, energetic, and skilled at motivating others.
- The company undermines, as far as it can, the self-image and self-esteem of its employees. No beards, no alcohol at lunch-time, no casual dress and no discussions of certain topics, notably salaries, are the order of the day at Electronic Data Systems, now an offshoot of General Motors.

Dress for success

Together the biggest companies have developed a common cultural environment for which behaviour is defined in exquisite detail.

Dress for Success, first published in the US in 1975, provides a precise guide to correct business attire. It comes complete with photographs, line drawings and diagrams, on such matters as how to tie a tie. It has sold more than 1,500,000 copies. Its sequel, The Woman's Dress for Success Book, first published in 1977, has sold more than 775,000 copies.

John T Molloy, the author of both books, styles himself 'America's first wardrobe engineer'. Use clothing as a tool to help you get ahead is his message; find out what outfits, according to research, go down well with your relevant public and wear them slavishly.

Molloy has gained wide and reputable acceptance on the subject of dress and has reportedly served as a consultant to 380 of the top 500 industrial companies in the US. Business schools, Columbia and Wharton among them, have set up seminars addressed by him.

Under Molloy's influence, enforcement of the managerial dress code has steadily tightened. Proper dress has become a symbol of the young manager's dedication to the company.

Of course, where there is a way, there is also another way:

'There are women who wear our lingerie underneath to take the edge off the uniform - it makes them feel alive and sexual.'
Pam Chadwick of Victoria's Secret, a San Francisco based retailer of expensive ornate underwear for women

Stick and carrot

The punishment meted out to those who conform badly or not at all is ruthless and elaborate. It is measured by the last cent of salary, by the depth of varnish on a desk, by job location and, ultimately, by the existence of the job itself.

The B side

The pitfalls on the road to the top are especially deep for women.

Among the rich industrial countries, it is worst for women in Japanese management, and almost certainly best in American, though the best is pretty bad.

In the US, women account for less than a quarter of business school graduates. Out of 154 places in the Harvard Business School's Advanced Management Program of 1983-84, only four were filled by women.

In the early 1980s, women business school graduates started their company careers earning, on average, just 2 per cent less than their male colleagues. After two years, they had dropped further behind: by 5 per cent in services, 9 per cent in finance, and 30 per cent in manufacturing.

The higher the managerial post, the more difficult it is for women to reach.

'At senior management levels, competence is assumed. What you're looking for is someone who fits, someone who gets along, someone you trust. Now that's subtle stuff. How does a group of men feel that a woman is going to fit?'
Carol Brown, a consultant to several major US companies

'Some departments - like sales and trading, or mergers and acquisitions - are considered more macho than others, and so more prestigious. But if women cannot get the assignments that allow them to shine, how can they advance?'
Frustrated woman executive

The oldest excuse in the book is that women managers may get married, become mothers and resign. Even those who return to work, would do so after several months, representing a loss to the company.

In fact, thousands of women have careers rather than families. A study of women executives showed that 52 per cent of women executives were single (never married, widowed or divorced) compared with 5 per cent of men, and that 61 per cent had no children compared with 3 per cent of men.

Above all, if you are a woman, it is virtually certain that you will never get to the very top of management. Executive recruiters, asked to identify women who might become presidents or chief executives of the 500 top US companies, came up with not a single name. Even companies with women in senior management positions privately conceded that such women were not going to occupy the chairman's office.

Of course there are exceptions.

Katherine Graham heads the Washington Post, the only woman to head a very large US industrial company (ranked 296 in the top 500 in 1985). As she readily admits, this is because her family has a controlling share.

Marisa Bellisario heads Italtel, Italy's leading manufacturer of telecommunications equipment and a state-owned company. There are only three other women among Italtel's 300 executives and supervisory staff.

There are the Jane Fondas, the Mary Quants, the Debbie Moores, but they are notable for being few, rather than few for being notable.

Snakes and ladders

There are snakes attending almost every rung of the managerial ladder. Even if they are eluded, the climber is more likely than not to find the ladder ending in mid-air. For management and training are essentially incompatible. The more successful the training in company loyalty, corporate identity, compatible behaviour and attitudes, the less fluent the trainee becomes in harnessing the uncoordinated impulses pounding the business, from within and without, to its purposes. Management requires the widest possible arc of vision and immediate response. Training narrows the focus and clutters reaction.

Business is fortunate in that most managers arrive rather than set out. Even in the US, where the mystique of management is at its most luxuriant, the vast majority of managers accumulate their operational skills through experience, retain a relatively humble station, middling salaries and a certain sense of proportion.

The trained mind

In some far off newly-independent state the government had decided to nationalize all foreign-owned industry and to execute the top executives. But in fairness, or superstition, the politicians announced that if the blade of the guillotine failed to fall, the particular executive concerned would be free to make his way home.

Scores of foreign executives lost their heads. But one, keeping his head, so to say, came to a financial arrangement with the executioner to save himself, his financial director, and his technical director.

The 'miracle' for which he had paid was duly performed. For both himself and his financial director, the blade failed to fall.

Fearfully, the technical director put his head on the block. Then, looking up at the mechanism, he suddenly cried, 'Stop, I see why it is not working.'

Managerial Snakes & Ladders

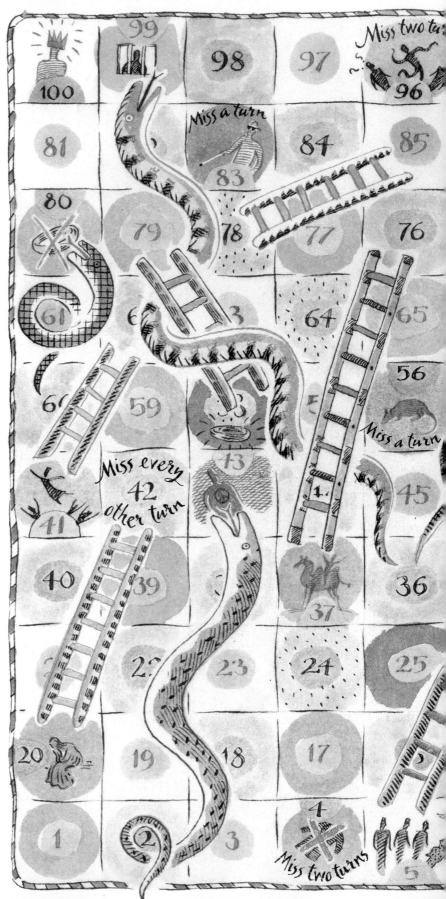

RULES

A game played with a die and counters, by any number of players.

Players move counters up the board, according to the number on the squares, following instructions. A player who lands on a square at the head of a snake, must move his or her counter to the snake's tail. A player who lands on a square at the base of a ladder climbs to its top.

The winner is the player who first reaches square 100 with an exact throw of the die. If a larger number is thrown, the counter is moved to 100 and back again as appropriate.

SQUARES

4 You come to work in a black raincoat.
5 You belong to an ethnic minority.
12 The management introduces aptitude tests and you do well.
13 Your performance is rated low by your colleagues at work in the regular appraisal.
20 You are a woman.
27 Your wife makes no impression at the company party for junior managers.
28 You have been heard to proclaim the virtues of a centralized structure. The Chairman decides on centralization.
37 Your company tenders for a huge contract in Saudi Arabia. You let it be known that you went to business school with a Saudi prince.
41 Your wife performs well at the annual company party for middle managers.

43 The Chairman's daughter saw you at an anti-nuclear rally.
55 You have been heard to proclaim the virtues of a centralized structure. The Chairman decides on decentralization.
56 You decline to buy a ticket for a charitable function. It turns out to be your boss's favourite charity.
58 Your uncle marries the Chairman's sister.
68 Boardroom row. Your patron loses.
70 The company is looking for decisiveness after years of consensus drift. You show suitable signs of self-assurance.
73 You belong to the wrong wing of the right-wing party.
75 Management consultants recommend reorganization. Your division is merged with another.
78 A shift in global strategy gives your division increased responsibilities. You are promoted to the board.
80 Your uncle divorces the Chairman's sister.
83 You fail to recognize the Chairman's sister.
90 You are found to be gay.
94 Japanese multinational takes over your company. A Japanese gets your job, and you get an honorary title.
96 Your negotiating tactics with the union representatives are misunderstood – by both sides.
99 Your company is involved in a major bribery scandal. Someone has to carry the can.
100 You become Chief Executive.

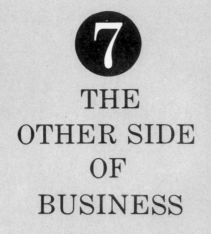

7

THE OTHER SIDE OF BUSINESS

The methods of business are so powerful and the rewards of success so great that many formal and informal inhibitions on behaviour dissolve in its presence.

Crime itself is organized along business lines. Even legitimate business is increasingly transgressing beyond the limits of what is legally or morally acceptable. Its victims may be individuals, other business, or even the state at home or abroad.

CRIME AS BUSINESS

Among the most lucrative businesses are those bound up with crime. Indeed, some businesses, such as drug trafficking, are founded upon wholly criminal activities. Organized crime is big business.

The illegal drug trade

'A typical [drug smuggling] outfit runs $100 million a year in sales. It will employ 25 to 30 people. It will have around five bosses, major shareholders, and they'll call themselves president, vice-president, chief accountant, all that stuff. Half of them will be working on operations and sales and half on finance. The accounts department will have computers and high-speed cash counters. There's a lot of money they have to keep track of. They'll deal with reinvestment, bond funds to bail out guys who get burned, retirement plans and pensions. In the field, you only bust the warehousemen, the pilots, the mules. The principals, they are insurance men, doctors, lawyers...We've convicted Harvard Business School graduates. To get at them, you have to have the same systems you would use on a big multinational that was on a complex tax caper.'

US narcotics agent, 1982

COCAINE
A TRIP THROUGH THE SNOW BELT

The first use of the drug is lost in the mists of the past. Certainly, coca leaves, from which the pure white powder of cocaine hydrochloride is made, have been chewed by the indigenous peoples in parts of South America for all recorded time. The growth of the coca bush now covers some 100,000 hectares in Bolivia, Colombia and Peru, with an increasing expanse in Ecuador. There are three or four harvests a year, producing up to 93,000 tonnes of leaves or enough to make 200 tonnes of cocaine.

The drug was discovered in the West during the second half of the nineteenth century, when it excited much scientific interest. Sigmund Freud, the creator of psychoanalysis, was a regular user; as, in the realm of fiction, was the great detective Sherlock Holmes. Soon after the turn of the century, the US government led others in outlawing the drug, and interest waned until the early 1970s, when cocaine became fashionable among the young of means and soon spread to other age groups of the moneyed classes. By the age of 27, according to a mid-1980s estimate, almost 40 per cent of all young adults in the US had tried the drug.

worth a visit, if time allows	★
site of considerable interest	★★
site of prime importance	★★★

BOLIVIA

The serious traveller should first visit BOLIVIA, the principal country of coca bush cultivation, where the value of the illegal trade is estimated to equal or exceed the legal income of the state. At Cochabamba ★★, the centre of the growing region, we may watch the leaves being picked and observe that the pickers themselves are not among those most prosperously engaged in the business. To the south-east is Shinahota ★★★, a celebrated crossroads for the trade, where every day in the outdoor market thousands of Indian peasant farmers selling their bales of leaves can be seen. At dusk, if we are fortunate, we may be invited to view the process by which 500 kilos of leaves are reduced to 2.5 kilos of the muddy brown coca paste. The paste is then further reduced with chemicals (usually imported from Brazil), to make a single kilo of rather dirty white cocaine base. Prices vary, of course with supply and demand; but a kilo of the cocaine base costs around $11,000, compared to $5,000 for the 2.5 kilos of paste and $1,200 for the original 500 kilos of leaves.

The next stop should be Santa Cruz ★★, a financial centre of the trade and home for many of the so-called cocaine barons, powerful figures who are reputed to have financed the military coup of 1980. So rich are these barons that, reportedly, one of them offered the government a low-interest $2 billion loan in exchange for a free hand in pursuing his business.

Today, Bolivia has a civilian government, but visitors are warned that it is an unstable country, where political upheaval is all too common. Before leaving Bolivia, the traveller may wish to visit the tin mines ★, where the drug is still taken in the old way, through chewing the leaves, to stave off hunger and sustain energy.

Warm clothing is recommended for the high altitudes, and light dress for the low-lying areas.

PERU

PERU is an important area of cultivation and some processing. Iquitos ★★★, in the department of Loreto, is a major crossroads of the country's cocaine trade, receiving coca paste from the Andean foothills and sending it on, sometimes after processing, to Colombia and Brazil. In the crowded suburb of Belen ★★, the drug smugglers hold sway, and the traveller is warned against giving the impression of being unduly curious. But with patience and good fortune, we may observe the fast launches of the smugglers outrunning and often outgunning the Peruvian navy and police who patrol the Amazonian waterways. The intense tropical heat of the area requires the lightest of clothing, and the traveller is strongly recommended to take medical advice before setting out.

Visitors who wish to see the ancient Inca capital of Cuzco ★ can make the necessary arrangements through a local travel agency. General travel is not advised, however, since a guerrilla movement, quaintly called the Shining Path, is active in many parts of the country.

COLOMBIA

Though the final processing, which changes cocaine base into one kilo of pure cocaine, worth around $20,000 at local prices, is increasingly being done in Bolivia and other coca cultivating countries, the processing centre remains COLOMBIA.

Colombia also dominates the crucial export trade with the United States. Estimated to control some three-quarters of this export trade are ten or twelve - the number is uncertain - unregistered Colombian companies. Enquiries into their affairs are not welcomed, and they have their own way of dealing with the inquisitive. They are reported to have placed a $300,000 bounty on the heads of US narcotics agents, dead or alive. The country's crusading Justice Minister, Sr. Rodrigo Lara Bonilla, was assassinated in April 1984 by those suspected of involvement in the $5-billion-a-year cocaine business. In the government backlash that followed, at least 100 air force personnel and 200 national police were discharged for drug connections, and investigations were ordered into 400 judges suspected of complicity in the trade.

Even so, the traveller who exercises some discretion may, with safety, discover much. Medellin ★★★ is the financial centre of the trade. Here, are to be found the unmistakable signs of lavish consumption associated with the repatriation of some of the profits, after suitable measures have been taken to disguise the source. A visit to local estate agents, with enquiries about property prices, cannot but prove to be edifying. In the words of the poet, we can but 'stand and stare'.

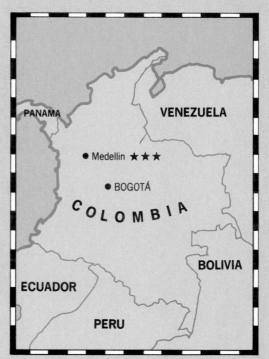

ECUADOR AND BRAZIL

Optional extras

ECUADOR is a latecomer to the Snow Belt, but is already a major point of interest. In 1984, it had no significant production. In 1985, it was producing 15,000 tonnes of the leaf. Flights from Ecuador to BRAZIL, a country which is increasingly important in the trade, are regular and easy. In Brazil, cultivation and processing are on the increase. But the importance of the country lies most of all in its excellent air links, especially with the fast growing market in Western Europe and with the eastern cities of the United States. Brazil is, of course, an enormous country, and much may be hidden there. But the observant traveller will still find much of interest in São Paulo ★★ and Rio de Janeiro ★★.

THE CARIBBEAN

The CARIBBEAN is a transit area, both for the transport of the drug and for the translation of the profits into more acceptable forms. The traveller is unlikely to catch sight of one of the small planes landing to be refuelled at secret staging posts on the islands or in Central America. But there are many small boats plying between South America and the United States, as carriers in the trade, and the perceptive traveller is certain to sight-see in similar manner.

Stops should be made at the Netherlands Antilles ★, the Cayman Islands ★★, and the Bahamas ★★, where the local custom of laundering drug money is a major tourist attraction.

The prime attraction, however, is Panama ★★★, where the Colombian drug barons have invested heavily in real estate - they reputedly own half of the 200 or so high-rises along Panama City's ocean front - and control various financial institutions, such as currency exchange houses, through which they launder their profits. 'They do not rob banks', it has been said of them, 'they buy them'.

The Sicilian connection

The Sicilian Mafia is now believed to control much of the heroin traffic in Europe and, with its US cousins, well over half the heroin trade in the north-east United States, the world's richest heroin market.

Estimates of the value of this big illegal business vary widely. One estimate being quoted during the long trial of alleged Mafia members, that started early in 1986 at Palermo, is that the trade is worth around $10 billion a year to the Mafia alone.

Foreign financiers visiting Rome in 1984 were astonished to be told by a senior banker: 'You don't want to believe Italy's GDP (national production) figures - they don't include our drug industry.'

BUSINESS CRIME

Many major legitimate business companies have been accused of illegal activities, including fraud and corruption, either at home or abroad.

Fraud

Fraud is the most common and the most characteristic crime in the business system. According to a British government-sponsored survey, whose findings were published in March 1986, some 40 per cent of large British companies had suffered at least one fraud involving more than £50,000 in the previous 10 years. Some companies admitted that they had never reported such frauds because of the embarrassing publicity involved. Of the cases reported, almost 30 per cent involved, as offenders, managers and directors or partners. With the increasingly sophisticated operations of the business system, fraud is also increasingly difficult to prove in a court of law. Defendants often succeed in justifying their actions on the basis of accepted commercial motives, the custom and practice of the market place. Even so, in Britain for instance, convictions have been growing in number.

Offenders found guilty of fraud, Britain, 1974-84

Year	Number
1974	13,829
1975	15,287
1976	16,683
1977	16,438
1978	15,756
1979	17,193
1980	20,274
1981	20,952
1982	22,454
1983	22,734
1984	22,456

Fraud in the City

The City of London is one of the world's great financial centres and the capital of the international trading system in foreign exchange.

'The City of London stands at a lower point in the public's esteem than it has for many years. Fraud allegations dominate the national newspapers and are an increasing preoccupation in Parliament. Standards of behaviour in the financial markets have slipped to the point where transactions which used to be undertaken on trust now have to be scrutinized by teams of lawyers.'

Financial Times editorial, 1985

Rising company fraud

Cases investigated by the Metropolitan and City Police (London), Company Fraud Department

Metropolitan Branch	1981	1982	1983	1984
arrests for a major crime	217	257	262	350
cases under active consideration	376	393	443	594
money at risk (£ million)	279	294	264	617

City of London Branch	1981	1982	1983	1984
arrests	35	40	65	77
cases under active consideration	90	96	103	117
money at risk (£ million)	na	100	115	159

Such figures are misleadingly low. For so difficult has conviction proved to be in company fraud cases that proceedings are often avoided where the chance of successful prosecution seems slight.

Representatives of the securities industry told the government that those committing an elaborate fraud know that they will probably not be prosecuted; while if they are prosecuted, it takes years to formulate charges and they will probably escape the main ones. The Attorney-General declared, in 1984, that the extent of fraud in the City was 'quite unacceptable, as well as being very damaging to the many honest firms'.

Particularly embarrassing have been the scandals in the Lloyd's insurance market. In one case, the authorities of Lloyd's itself took action, fining one of its members £1 million and expelling him from the market. The malefactor had diverted, to his personal benefit, millions of pounds that belonged to 1,525 underwriting members. He had used the money to buy a villa in the south of France; to invest in Florida real estate, a Spanish orange juice company, film and musical production, and to give key members of his staff regular cash payments 'in envelopes'.

To deal with the problem, a special Fraud Trials inquiry, the Roskill Committee, was appointed, and reported in January 1986. Its most fundamental and controversial recommendation was that trial by jury should be abandoned for complex cases of fraud, which would be tried instead by a special Fraud Trials Tribunal, composed of a judge and two lay members with experience of complex business transactions.

The government had already moved towards a much stricter regulation of the City. In December 1985, it had instituted a Board of Banking Supervision to assist the Bank of England in closer surveillance and control of the banking sector; and announced legislation to tighten the law on the investment business.

A special board for the supervision of the City would also be created with powers to regulate the securities industry, commodity futures trading and life insurance marketing.

The fall-out from scandals affecting Lloyd's insurance business led to the announcement, in January 1986, of an inquiry into the adequacy of Lloyd's arrangements for self-regulation.

The unfortunate survey

'In many instances where people are not lining their own pockets, you can only explain corporate crime in terms of produce or perish.'
Stanley Sporkin, SEC's enforcement chief

Of 1,043 major US companies covered in a survey, by Fortune magazine, no less than 117 had been involved in at least one serious delinquency since 1970. Some companies had been multiple delinquents.

The survey confined itself to such cases as resulted either in conviction on federal criminal charges or in 'nolo contendere' pleas, tantamount to admissions of guilt, and similar administrative settlements. 'It is axiomatic', commented Fortune, 'that there was more crime than was exposed in public proceedings.'

Ironically, among the guilty companies, was Time Inc., the publisher of Fortune. In 1976, its Eastex packaging subsidiary was charged with fixing prices of folding cartons and had offered a 'nolo contendere' plea.

Fortune's delinquents

anti-trust violations	98
bribery, kickbacks or illegal rebates	28
illegal political contributions	21
fraud	11
tax evasion	5
total companies delinquent	117

Excluded from the survey were:

■ Monopolistic practices which were the subject of civil anti-trust suits.

■ Federal Trade Commission complaints against companies that 'signalled' price changes to competitors.

■ Any foreign instances of delinquency, such as bribes and kickbacks abroad.

■ Instances of delinquency by businesses of modest size. 'The bribing of purchasing agents by small manufacturers and the skimming of receipts by cash-laden small retail businesses are a commonplace of commercial life.'

■ Minor cases of corruption far down the chain of command.

The standard throughout was corporate responsibility at a high level.

IMF's blind eye

In the aftermath of a money broker crash in Turkey, the Turkish Finance Minister asked the International Monetary Fund (IMF) to allow an expansion of the Turkish currency in circulation. The IMF, concerned not to create a precedent for the breaking of commitments by member states to which it had extended credit, refused.

Caught between openly flouting the IMF and risking massive corporate bankruptcies, the Turkish Finance Minister hit upon a solution.

Each Friday, the Ministry transferred the cash deposits of the country's largest bank, the Ziraat (Agriculture) Bank, to the central bank; held them while figures for the currency in circulation were recorded; and returned them in time for normal banking business on Monday morning. The figures grew steadily and unalarmingly in line with inflation.

Then, in the first week of November 1982, the Finance Minister decided to stop the practice, and the currency in circulation leapt by 36 per cent, the sharpest weekly increase in Turkish history. An official was dispatched to inform the IMF. But IMF officials, the Finance Minister later related, 'merely said that they knew all about it already and were fully aware of the situation.'

Cooking the books

In 1982, it was reported that fraudulent claims from Italian olive oil producers might be costing the EEC more than £160 million a year.

Embarrassed officials were unclear as to whether the Community had 10 million olive trees, or 100 million, or even 1,000 million.

Bid-rigging

Indicating the extent of corruption at the lower level of US business was the rash of prosecutions for bid-rigging in the roadbuilding industry.

In the first two or three years of the 1980s, federal prosecutors in 20 states obtained 400 criminal convictions resulting in total fines of some $50 million and 141 prison sentences. Hundreds of contractors were convicted of rigging arrangements that had apparently cost taxpayers at least several hundred million dollars a year.

Most state or county highway officials had been dealing with the bid-riggers for a long time and regarded them as respected members of the community who had never been involved in anything illegal. Some conspirators were heads of charities or of their local contractors' associations. One convicted contractor had headed the law enforcement committee of his contractors' association.

The pattern was much the same throughout. Bids for new projects were taken at regularly scheduled meetings called lettings. Dishonest contractors would get together the night before such a letting and split the jobs among themselves at prices that suited them. Most conspiracies were conducted at smart hotels. A group of electrical contractors used the Duquesne Club, the bastion of the Pittsburgh establishment.

One contractor from North Carolina let his business dwindle to virtually nothing because he was able to thrive entirely on the pay-offs he demanded in return for not bidding on projects.

When, on occasion, a contractor proposed to submit a legitimate bid, he was usually cowed into collaboration by threats of concerted underbidding to ruin him. In one instance, a corporate chief executive sent his assistant to participate in bid-rigging on two construction projects. By some miscalculation, the assistant won both jobs and, when he got back to his office, was summarily demoted.

Holding up the state

Number of companies blacklisted by the Pentagon for alleged malpractice

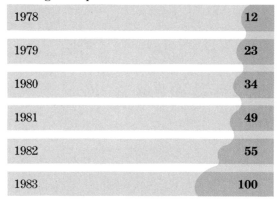

1978	12
1979	23
1980	34
1981	49
1982	55
1983	100

Some of the largest US companies have been in trouble.

■ General Dynamics, facing various allegations of overcharging on a number of defence contracts, offered to pay $23 million.

■ Lockheed suddenly dropped the price of a special line in toilet seats for the US Navy from $640.09 per item to around $100.

■ General Electric pleaded guilty to defrauding the US Air Force by filing 108 fake invoices.

■ National Semiconductor paid $1.7 million in fines and costs after pleading guilty to charges that it lied about reliability tests it had failed to perform on thousands of integrated circuits for use in military and aerospace systems.

Corruption and conscience

A study of more than 900 executives in 16 industrialized countries outside North America and the Eastern bloc, published in 1983, showed that many of the managers surveyed had been pressed or had chosen to behave corruptly:

■ Some 27 per cent of senior managers surveyed had got involved in questionable business practices such as bribery, falsifying information, and even blatant law-breaking.

■ 53 per cent of managers surveyed had recently faced at least one conflict between the demands of their company and what they personally believed to be right.

■ 10 per cent had been confronted with having to take unethical decisions at least six times in the preceding five years.

■ 38 per cent stated that they had recently either made or been offered an 'irregular payment'.

■ Just over 20 per cent of European executives, almost a third of managers in the Middle East and 44 per cent in Latin America, had been asked to make irregular payments.

■ Some 10 per cent in Europe and Latin America (though only 2 per cent in the Middle East) admitted to having received gifts or bribes.

■ Around 50 per cent in Europe and 40 per cent in Latin America declared that in the course of their work they had been asked to conceal or falsify information.

■ Some 20 per cent of businessmen in Belgium said that they had frequently been asked to be unethical.

■ More than two thirds of the managers who acted according to their consciences rather than to company dictates claimed to have suffered no disadvantage in consequence. Of the remaining third that did suffer, most endured the traditional penalties of job loss or reduced promotion prospects.

Corrupt practices abroad

In 1973, the Lockheed Corporation distributed almost $10 million in a campaign to push sales of its TriStar airliner to Nippon Airlines of Japan. Some $2 million went to bribe the then Japanese Prime Minister, Kakuei Tanaka, who was subsequently forced to resign and, in October 1983, found guilty by a Japanese court.

Moved by this and similar scandals, the US government passed the Foreign Corrupt Practices Act in 1977, to deter, with the threat of severe penalties, the bribery of foreign officials for the purpose of gaining orders. (The Act expressly permits 'grease' payments to minor officials for such purposes as the avoidance of red tape.)

At public hearings in mid-1981, representatives of US companies informed senators that the Act was crippling the US export drive.

According to a study published by the General Accounting Office, a Federal agency, 30 per cent of the companies polled claimed to have lost business as a result of the Foreign Corrupt Practices Act, and 60 per cent believed that, other things being equal, they could not successfully compete with foreign companies still engaged in bribery.

In 1982, Boeing Aircraft was fined $400,000 after pleading guilty to concealing the payment of 'irregular commissions' to help sell aircraft in Spain, Lebanon, Honduras and the Dominican Republic. A US Justice Department document, released in August 1983, reported unproven allegations that US companies had given or planned to give bribes to three prime ministers, two presidents, and several government ministry heads abroad, in the form of cash, guns, automobiles and, in one instance, 'sexual favours'.

Corporate larceny

Corporate larceny is intrinsic to a business system in which innovation and discovery are so commercially valuable. Business counterfeits and corrupts; it snoops and steals.

Costly counterfeits

Counterfeiting - turning out goods that are sold by passing them off as others - is big business, in which many specialist companies are now involved.

West African cocoa farmers lost $20 million worth of harvest because the company providing the fungicide provided a useless substitute.

The British motor industry is losing some $200 million worth of business a year to makers of counterfeit car parts.

Taiwan has been turning out 3,000 look-alike computers a month, amongst a large array of other fakes that have included Cabbage Patch dolls. This illicit trade is estimated to be costing US manufacturers $6 billion to $8 billion a year in lost sales.

DONNE, RILEY & LEVINE

Memorandum

To: President, Clytemnestra Electronics

We tender the following on the legal position with regard to eliciting information on the activity of corporate competitors.

Send your engineers to conferences and trade shows to question the technical representatives of your competitors. Without misrepresentation or bribery, you may gain valuable information.

Advertise and hold interviews for jobs so that applicants, wishing to impress you, provide valuable information. You do not need to appoint any of the applicants.

You may hire key executives from the competition, to benefit from their knowledge. It is legal to make 'unintentional but inevitable' rather than 'intentional' use of the information the employee brings.

Use the same design consultants (for a project strategically unimportant to you) as your competitors. While conferring with a consultant, you may find out something important that a competitor is developing.

Ask your key customers who have dealings with a competitor, for information on any new product being offered to them.

Ask your loyal customers to solicit bids from the industry's competitors for products not yet in stock. This may elicit information on technical capabilities.

Question suppliers about their capacity and production figures to find out what the competition is getting or may be requiring.

Provide engineers to customers free of charge, in the hope that they may cultivate the customer's design staff and learn what new products the competition is offering.

Examine help-wanted ads to see where your competition is heading.

It is trespassing to photograph a competitor's plant from the air. But such photographs may be legally obtained from the Geological Survey or the Environmental Agency. Examine these public documents for plant expansions and even inventory build-ups.

Spying is an ugly word, but you are entitled to observe the numbers and sizes of cartons on tractor-trailers leaving your competitor's bays.

Once it has left a competitor's premises, refuse is abandoned property in terms of the law. Much can be discovered from examining the 'unstrategic' and so unshredded paper of marketing and public relations departments.

John Donne Jr.

John Donne Jr

THE OTHER SIDE OF BUSINESS

Industrial espionage

Soviet corporate technology has failed to keep up with Western innovations in such areas as plastics, artificial fibres, float glass and, above all, micro-processing and computers. Access to Western, especially American, high technology has come to be increasingly restricted by US government embargoes, on security grounds. The CIA claims that only 20-30 per cent of militarily-valuable technology imports reach the USSR by legal means: bought on the open market or gleaned from technical publications. Much Western technology is illegally acquired by the USSR, through espionage or other illegal practices.

For alleged involvement in espionage mainly concerned with acquiring high technology, during 1983 some 100 Soviet diplomats were expelled from Australia, Belgium, Britain, France, Japan, the US, and even neutral Switzerland.

During 1982-83, Operation Exodus, a US-government crackdown on technology-smuggling, resulted in more than 350 cases of export control violation being referred to the Department of Justice for criminal prosecution. Out of 276 arrests, there were 211 convictions.

In one of the most publicized cases, a powerful Vax 11/782 computer was exported to a dummy South African company controlled by a West German citizen, who had been wanted in the US since 1979 for allegedly having sold US semiconductor equipment illegally to the USSR. The dummy company then re-exported the computer to West Germany, where it was seized by customs, en route to the USSR, and returned to the US.

Within the US, companies have been stealing secrets from one another as long as there were profits to be made from doing so. Industrial espionage has been especially rife in Silicon Valley and other centres of high-tech manufacturing. Bribery, blackmail and infiltrating spies supplement the most common forms of obtaining trade secrets: hiring employees from rival firms, for the technological information that they may, more or less illegally, bring along with them.

In Japan, a huge industrial espionage case hit the headlines during 1983, after three pharmaceutical companies were charged with various acts involving the theft of confidential data on new drugs.

The Hitachi sting

No act of industrial larceny has attracted anything like the publicity accorded to Hitachi of Japan's attempt to buy IBM secret technology. The motivation was undeniably strong. Hitachi makes IBM-compatible computers and must keep pace with IBM innovations or perish. The earlier it could discover the design of a new IBM product, the earlier it would be able to produce a similar machine, and one that might well sell for less than the IBM original.

In November 1980, Raymond Cadet, a computer scientist, left IBM's computer labs in Poughkeepsie, New York, and took along with him ten of the 27 confidential workbooks on the programme for a new generation of computers, the 308X.

In June 1981, he was recruited by National Advanced Systems, a subsidiary of National Semiconductor, which marketed Hitachi products in the US. In August, copies of the ten workbooks found their way to Hitachi computer specialists.

Maxwell O Paley, president of a small consulting firm, had Hitachi among his clients. Paley offered a study he had prepared of the 3081, the first model of the 308X generation, to Kenji Hayashi, of Hitachi. Hayashi revealed that his company already had various IBM workbooks and wanted to know whether Paley had any others. Paley, former head of the Advanced Computer Systems Laboratory at IBM, informed his former employers, who sent in their chief security troubleshooter, Richard A Callahan.

In October, Callahan and a colleague, Robert Domenico, flew with Paley to Tokyo. Paley and Domenico met Hayashi at the Imperial Hotel where they produced a hand-written index of the 27 workbooks as bait and asked to see those already in Hayashi's possession, so as to be able to identify the genuine article.

Four days later, Hayashi brought in copies of three workbooks and asked for four others listed on the index, which were wanted 'very badly'. He also asked Paley to get him an early look at IBM's most advanced disk-drive system. Callahan confirmed to IBM that the workbooks in Hitachi's hands were genuine. IBM then decided to institute a criminal case through the US Department of Justice.

Under instruction from Callahan, Paley then arranged to meet with Hayashi at the Las Vegas Hilton early in November. In a room bugged by the FBI, he introduced Callahan to him as a retired lawyer, and Alan Garretson, an FBI agent, as a possible source of IBM information. Hayashi gave details of Hitachi's requirements, and made arrangements for futher contacts.

The trap was baited. Garretson took Jun Naruse, of Hitachi, into a high-security zone at the Pratt & Whitney plant in Hartford, Connecticut, to see one of the new memory systems in operation. Naruse photographed the machine, had Garretson photograph him hugging the machine, and then paid Garretson $3,000. Subsequently, he paid a further $7,000 in cash for the relevant maintenance manuals.

Hitachi's appetite grew with the feeding. More and more requests for secret IBM data and equipment reached Garretson at his cover firm in Silicon Valley. Complex arrangements were made to transfer funds. Hitachi was offered a package deal that would give it virtually everything it wanted, for a sum eventually set at well over half-a-million dollars. A first payment of $31,500 was made on 19 May 1982 and a second sum of $514,000 on 18 June, through an intermediary company.

The trap was sprung on 22 June. Hayashi and Isao Ohnishi, a Hitachi software expert, arrived at Garretson's offices to find the IBM material piled high on a desk. As Hayashi, in a moment of jubilation, pocketed an IBM sticker as a souvenir, two FBI agents stepped into the room and placed the two Japanese under arrest.

In February 1983, Hitachi pleaded guilty in San Francisco's US District Court to charges of having conspired to steal IBM secrets. In terms of an agreed plea bargain, the company was fined $10,000 and faced no further criminal charges. Kenji Hayashi was fined $10,000 and placed on five years' probation; Isao Ohnishi, fined $4,000 and placed on probation for two years.

In an out-of-court civil suit settlement of October 1983 Hitachi agreed not to use the stolen computer secrets; to return the relevant IBM documents; and to disclose the names, addresses and business affiliations of all those who had offered to sell IBM secrets to Hitachi. IBM was given the right to inspect all Hitachi's new products for five years, to ensure that Hitachi did not make use of IBM secrets. Hitachi agreed to pay all IBM's legal and other costs, estimated at several million dollars.

A GLOSSARY OF COMMERCIAL CRIME

'We are talking about fraud on a scale which can undermine governments. The sums that are being earned can buy up countries, or at least a lot of protection in the judicial system.'

'We have been looking for organized crime in the wrong places. Today the criminal is likely to be in a financial, rather than a street, setting. He adopts corporate structures, controlling the money but never getting near the drugs or the frauds.'

Dr Barry Rider, head of the Commonwealth Commercial Crime Unit

Advance fee fraud

Governments in the developing world, and companies in the main trading countries, are offered large loans in return for an advance fee. Once the fee has been paid, the fraudster disappears, and the loan never materializes. One fraud officer in Britain has stated that such frauds involve 'telephone number amounts' running into billions of dollars.

Banking frauds

Fraudsters may gain control of a bank and then obtain money from investors which goes into their own pockets.

Bankruptcy frauds

Businesses continue to trade and obtain money or goods with no prospect of paying their debts. They then go into liquidation and are rapidly reconstituted under other names.

Charity frauds

Money is collected from the public, often with innocent members of the public as collectors, ostensibly for charitable purposes but actually for misappropriation.

Commodity frauds

Large and rapid swings in the futures commodity markets provide considerable scope for the dishonest to take advantage of the uninformed and the unwary. International commodity frauds perpetrated from London were running at some £100 million a year in the mid-1980s, and involved some 50 firms, according to police estimates.

Computer fraud

The increasing use of electronic transfer to move funds from one bank to another is creating new opportunities for fraud which has hit a number of banks. A computer consultant for Security Pacific, in Los Angeles, visited the bank's wire transfer room and obtained the electronic funds transfer code. Later, posing as a bank manager, he called from a public telephone and used the code to send money to a Swiss account. The take was $10.3 million. He was caught only because he took to boasting of his feat.

Container fraud

Criminals have become increasingly adept at breaking container seals. The loss is usually discovered when the container reaches its final destination. Investigators cannot easily find out where the contents were removed.

Counterfeiting currencies or negotiable bonds
Fraudsters arrange an extra print run of legitimate securities for their own benefit.

Cube-cutting
Shipping agents overestimate the size of a cargo to a customer and underestimate it to the shipping line, to pocket the difference.

Discounting or factoring frauds
Fraudsters borrow money from a merchant bank on the evidence of falsely documented orders.

Forged bills of lading
Blank bills of lading can be bought for a few pence, and entries on them forged, to demonstrate that goods have been loaded onto a vessel. Fraudsters can then claim funds from the buyer's bank.

Franchise frauds
Investors are allured to buy franchises which offer big returns on the money invested. Once payment has been made, the franchise turns out to be worthless.

Government subsidy frauds
False claims are submitted, often with much planning and skill, to government departments.

Insurance frauds
Fraudulent insurance brokers swindle clients or insurance companies by overcharging for premium payments or falsifying applications for payouts.

Investment frauds
Generous rewards are promised to investors and paid out of the money received for subsequent investment, until the money runs out.

Laundering funds
Criminals need to legalize suspiciously large sums made from drug-trafficking, the arms trade or fraud. Such money may be lent to governments, with the added advantage of acquiring influence with the borrowers. In 1985, US Federal investigators were looking into the books of 41 US banks and planning to scrutinize the books of 250 more in order to trace the routes taken by an estimated $100 billion a year of laundered money, a third of it from drugs. At least 40 large banks asked the American Bankers' Association to help them negotiate an immunity pact with the US Treasury.

Long-term fraud
Fraudsters set up as wholesalers, place orders with suppliers and pay promptly to establish a reputation for credit-worthiness. Then large orders are placed; and when the goods have been sold, the fraudsters disappear.

Maritime fraud
Of the 48 ships which sank in the South China Sea during a two-year period, 28 went down in suspicious circumstances, according to an insurance investigation. Owners allegedly scuttled vessels to hide the theft of the cargo or to claim the insurance on ships valued at much more than their market worth. So easy are the pickings, the head of the International Maritime Bureau (IMB) reported in 1982, that a Greek captain seemed quite unconcerned when a $300,000 deal to sell information to the bureau fell through. He admitted that he already had a contract to sink three more ships.

In 1984, the IMB investigated 109 cases, involving losses of $262 million. This was reckoned to be only 2 per cent of all losses from maritime fraud, making a figure worldwide of about $13 billion.

Overseas land frauds
Investors are persuaded to buy plots abroad for development as holiday or retirement homes. If a small plot exists for exhibition purposes, it is the only one owned by the fraudsters.

Piracy: audio and video tapes, books, computer software
In countries such as Nigeria and India, pirated tapes account for more than 80 per cent of all pre-recorded tapes sold. The total value of world book piracy is estimated at $1.5 billion a year. A leading manufacturer of computer software in San Rafael, California, with some $26 million in sales a year, estimates its loss from illegal reproduction at $20-60 million a year.

Product counterfeiting
A Bulgarian tobacco factory, which had been producing cigarettes under licence for two US companies, resumed production shortly after the licence deal had ended. Cigarettes in packs similar to the originals were exported to Italy.

Stock exchange fraud
Investors are induced to buy stocks and lose their money through manipulation of the market and insider trading (dealing in shares on the basis of inside information). In Britain, since 1980, when insider trading was made a criminal offence, 284 full-scale investigations have been conducted, and some 50 of these have been frustrated because the suspected offenders, institutions and individuals, had made use of offshore companies with local secrecy safeguards.

A Guide for the Innocent

1. Be especially cautious of a fast talking unknown voice on the telephone that promises easy enrichment. Commit yourself to nothing.

2. Investment circulars that reach you unasked should be treated with considerable scepticism.

3. If you are attracted by an investment offer find out as much as you can about the company and examine the published accounts.

4. Ascertain the full extent of your commitment before signing anything. The more impatient that the sales representative seems to get your signature the more suspicious you should be.

5. Examine with particular care and expert advice investment offers in off-shore places.

6. Be especially wary of trading in futures. Even the most experienced can get their fingers burnt. If you are determined to get involved make sure that the level of commission is not in excess of the usual market rate.

7. Beware of offers that promise unusual rewards and that accordingly may carry unusual risks. The quickest way to instant impoverishment is often the lure of instant enrichment.

8. Speculate only with what you can comfortably afford to lose.

The Chinese experience

The Chinese leadership has sought faster economic growth by promoting material incentives, relaxing central financial controls and giving more decision-making power to local officials. But Deng Xiaoping's advice to 'get rich through labour' has been followed in ways that he never intended.

Those managing the businesses of the state have been quick to find opportunities for profit in corruption. The China Auditing Administration has claimed to have discovered waste, fraud and tax evasion involving some $2.9 billion in the two years 1984-85. Published cases of crime include bribery; the illegal sale of industrial materials; sending unnecessary delegations on business trips; visiting tourist attractions at public expense; demanding rewards for routine services; giving relatives illegal help in business ventures: currency speculation; smuggling; and fraud.

Most spectacular has been the Hainan island import racket. The island was given special power in April 1983 to use foreign currency and sign contracts to the value of $5 million, in a government effort to create a major tourist attraction. Island officials illegally borrowed $570 million in hard currency to profit from the duty concessions on certain import items, by purchasing them for resale on the mainland.

According to the Communist Party's central discipline inspection committee: 'From 1 January 1984 to 5 March 1985, leading cadres of Hainan approved the import of 89,000 automobiles, 2.86 million television sets, 252,000 video recorders and 122,000 motorcycles.'

The Communist Party head of Hainan was stripped of all his posts; other senior officials were demoted; some, who had used the racket for blatant personal gain, received long prison sentences; and one, the purchasing agent for a public health institute, was given life imprisonment.

QUESTIONABLE PRACTICES AND PRODUCTS

'I regret to inform you that my bomb-proof, reinforced nuclear survival shelter has been totally wrecked by vandals.'
Extract from a client's letter to international insurance brokers, Stewart Wrightson

Outside of business crime, legitimate business often operates beyond the bounds of good practice and sets questionable standards.

Most disturbingly, some products that are sold as useful and harmless may be damaging, downright dangerous or even deadly.

A question of packaging

In 1981, a jury at Croydon Crown Court in Britain decided that a 54-gram pot of Astral cream, with 'double shell construction' (or, in lay language, a false bottom), contravened the Trades Descriptions Act.

The company, an associate of the giant Unilever group, argued that its packaging was simply in line with cosmetic industry practice.

In a sample of 22 similar cosmetic products, no fewer than 16 used the 'double shell' technique to look bigger. Other articles used in evidence were a box of Black Magic chocolates (with an empty space equivalent of around 42.5 per cent); a 500 gram box of Kellogg's cornflakes (32 per cent); a jar of Prince's Salmon and Shrimp Spread with a thick glass bottom (35 per cent of empty space equivalent); a 25-unit plastic phial of Paracetamol tablets (with some 24 per cent of the volume taken up by cotton wool).

Such packaging practices, the company submitted, had been so widespread for so many years that the consumer 'must be aware that the size of containers is not necessarily representative of their contents.'

A question of product

Lloyd's monthly publication Product Liability International carries reports on unsafe products. The items cited at different times included:

■ a US company's home computer with a potential defect in an electrical transformer that could electrocute the user;

■ a brand of Spanish gas heater sold in the UK that released dangerous asbestos fibres;

■ defects in some industrial robots that caused injuries and deaths in Japan;

■ packs of artificial sweeteners in North Carolina that contained a near fatal dose of a chemical used in water treatment;

■ packs of herbal tea imported to Britain that were contaminated with deadly nightshade;

■ an intra-uterine contraceptive device in the US that could seriously infect the user.

Defects in road vehicles have been particularly numerous. The issue of February 1983 alone carried reports of potential faults in nearly 500,000 General Motors cars, 100,000 Renaults and 600 Suzuki motorcycles, all withdrawn from the market.

Attempts at recall may have a low rate of success: In 1979 and 1980, Sears Roebuck set out to recall 60,000 electric fans which could overheat and burst into flames. They were able to reach little more that 2 per cent, or 1,300 customers.

Product liability

US courts have been awarding much larger sums in damages to victims of faulty products. And insurance premiums for product liability have accordingly been raised from three to ten-fold for a whole range of products: textiles, office automation equipment, machine tools, bicycles, motorcycles, automobiles, pharmaceuticals.

Bitter harvest

In 1981, the wine growers of the Mosel Valley in West Germany were beset by the worst scandal in their history.

More than six million tonnes of liquid sugar, or about a 1/4oz per bottle, had been added to white wines in the vintage years 1977, 1978 and 1979, to make the wines stronger and supposedly of higher quality.

Some 2,400 trials of grape growers, co-operative owners, wholesalers and sugar merchants were set in motion, with three-year jail terms, or fines for smaller fry, handed down by courts in the initial cases.

More dangerous was the use, by some Austrian vintners, of diethylene glycol, a chemical used as an anti-freeze in motor vehicles, for the same effect as sugaring. The chemical may be fatal if swallowed in large quantities, while smaller amounts may cause nausea and vomiting.

By the time the affair was made public in mid-1985, bottles of wine carrying one or other of the 350 brand names on a West German blacklist were available in France, Greece, Japan, Poland and the US, as well as West Germany.

In Austria, eight wine dealers and two chemists were arrested for their part in the affair.

Terrible consequences

The worst wine scandal so far broke in Italy early in 1986 when at least 23 people died after drinking wine laced with methyl alcohol. Many more were blinded or otherwise injured.

During May 1981, hospitals in Spain experienced a sudden intake of people suffering respiratory complaints. The number of deaths from this 'atypical pneumonia' mounted, and doctors connected the mysterious illness with consumption of a toxic cooking oil.

In a country where the adulteration of olive oil is a time-honoured practice, certain entrepreneurs had been adding to it imported French rape-seed oil stained with a poisonous dye that made it unsafe for any but industrial use.

Seven companies were found to have dealt in the adulterated oil under 10 brand names, and the authorities impounded 3,000 tonnes of it.

By early 1983, the official death toll stood at 339, with an estimated total of 20,000 victims, many of whom may be crippled for life.

THE PHARMACEUTICAL BUSINESS

'We are not trading in magic, and the public is not entitled to expect it.'

Sir James Black, British scientist who developed two of the world's best-selling drugs: H2-antagonists for ulcers and beta blockers for heart disease

The pharmaceutical business is big business, with a world market estimated to be worth some $80 billion a year. Traditionally, profits have been high: the 'losers' earning 10 per cent on sales; and the more successful pharmaceutical companies, 20 per cent or more.

It is a business that has a proud record, having contributed to an increase in life expectancy of 25 years since 1900. But it is increasingly coming under fire, from both governments and private bodies, for the soaring costs of health care. In 1983, General Motors spent more on workers' health insurance than it did on steel for its cars.

Such costs, coupled with an alarming number of drug withdrawals, following the discovery of serious side-effects, is raising the question of whether the pursuit of profit in a highly competitive business may not be taking precedence over the very criteria of health care to which the companies claim to subscribe.

Pharmaceutical sales, 1982, $ billion

USA	16.6
Japan	11.5
West Germany	5.7
France	4.4
Italy	2.7
Britain	2.7
Other	36.4

Sales of leading pharmaceutical companies, 1983, sales, $ billion

American Home Products (US)	2.7
Hoechst (West Germany)	2.6
Bayer (West Germany)	2.4
Merck (US)	2.4
Bristol-Myers (US)	2.3
Warner Lambert (US)	2.1
Pfizer (US)	2.1
Ciba-Geigy (Switzerland)	2.0
Eli Lilly (US)	1.9
Smith Kline (US)	1.8

What's in a name?

The World Health Organization (WHO) has drawn up a list of just 200 drugs it recommends as essential to prevent death and disease. Most of them are generic or unbranded and require no promotion. According to the Oxfam publication 'Bitter Pills', drug companies promote costly and unnecessary preparations to boost their profits and drive cheap generic substitutes from the market.

A question of priorities

■ In 1978, Japanese courts ruled that clioquinol, a drug introduced by the Swiss company Ciba-Geigy and sold under the name of Entero-Vioform in the treatment of diarrhoea, had caused a disease of the spinal and optic nerves known as subacute myelo-optico-neuropathy (SMON). Before the government banned the drug in 1970, some 11,000 Japanese had fallen ill of whom 200 died and more were permanently paralysed or blinded. Some 7,400 victims sued Ciba-Geigy's Japanese subsidiary, its selling agent (Takeda Chemical Industries), or another clioquinol manufacturer (Tanaba Seiyaku). Ciba-Geigy claimed that clioquinol could not be the sole cause of SMON but was unable, during the eight-year legal proceedings, to prove that there was any other.

After the drug was banned in Japan, consumer groups, doctors and medical journals insisted that the company should stop marketing Entero-Vioform elsewhere or at least provide a warning on the label that prolonged usage could be harmful. The company, arguing that SMON occurred in Japan only because the drug had been taken in excessive doses, refused to withdraw the product and did not satisfy its critics with the changes in labelling that it agreed to make. Cases of SMON occurred in Australia, Britain and in Switzerland. There were also 42 cases reported in Sweden, and Swedish doctors began boycotting Ciba-Geigy products. Finally, in 1982, or some 12 years after the Japanese government ban, the company agreed to withdraw the drug. Settlements in Japan alone had cost Ciba-Geigy $200 million by mid-1983. It was estimated that when all cases in Japan against the three defendants were settled, total damages would exceed $600 million.

■ The potential danger of Opren (benaoxaprofen) the anti-arthritis drug that is claimed to have killed 74 people in Britain and to have caused misery to many more, was made known to the manufacturers, Eli Lilly, by two British geriatricians in scientific articles published 15 months before the drug was withdrawn in August 1982.

In May 1982, Lilly marketed the drug in the US under the name of Oraflex, two years after it had introduced the product in Europe. In August 1982, Lilly withdrew the drug. In November 1983, a fed-eral jury in the US awarded $6 million to a man who claimed that his mother had died because she took Oraflex, and that Lilly had failed to report the deaths overseas before Oraflex was approved by the US Food and Drug Administration for use in the US. Lilly 'strongly disagreed' with the verdict; declared that it had acted 'properly and responsibly in the development and marketing of Oraflex'; and drew attention to the judge's instructions to the jury that FDA regulations were not clear as to whether Lilly was required to submit to the FDA reports of adverse side-effects.

■ Lomotil is sold only by prescription in the West, and its US manufacturer, G D Searle, was required by the US authorities to warn American doctors that it should not be given to children under two years old.

Lomotil is an anti-diarrhoea drug which acts as a powerful chemical plug. In cases of pernicious tropical diarrhoea induced by severe infection, a drug which does not kill the infection but merely binds can be less effective and more dangerous than drinking plenty of fluids.

Yet Lomotil was sold over the counter in poor countries and without an infant age warning. Under some public pressure, the company subsequently agreed to include the warning; though it is far from certain that the small print is always read, understood, or applied.

■ In February 1984, the United Nations Commission on Narcotic Drugs voted to tighten restrictions on the sale of benzodiazepines, used in such best-selling tranquillizers and sedatives as Valium and Librium. The scheduling of the ingredients under international drug control treaties, along with other addictive drugs, meant that, worldwide, such drugs would subsequently be available only by prescription. The decision was fiercely contested by the large pharmaceutical companies concerned: despite the report of the International Narcotics Control Board which stated that the menace of drug abuse had reached 'unprecedented proportions', and that the illicit drug trade was moving into synthetic and psychotropic drugs such as tranquillizers.

Fatal counterfeiting

In the aftermath of the Israeli war, pirate operators flooded Lebanon with bogus and useless drugs cleverly disguised in the counterfeit packaging of such life-saving drugs as antibiotics. Despite their knowledge that this was happening, Western companies whose genuine products were the subject of the counterfeiting exercise made no clear declaration to warn people of the pirate problem. Asked to explain this strange silence, a spokesman for the Association of the British Pharmaceutical Industry stated: 'There is a great deal of concern but it is difficult to declare a problem without damaging legitimate business.'

Pesticidal business

The Swiss pharmaceutical giant Ciba-Geigy, which also manufactures pesticides, sprayed unprotected Egyptian children in 1976 with Galecron, a pesticide subsequently linked with cancer, to test their urine for toxic levels of the pesticide. In 1982, after a Swiss pressure group had publicized the experiments, Ciba-Geigy declared: 'It was not correct for us to have done this. Children should never have been used in the experiment.'

Between 1981 and 1983, at least 50 people are believed to have died in the interior of northern Brazil, as a result of poisoning from a herbicide containing dioxin, one of the most potent poisons ever created.

Used over a 300-yard wide, 125-mile long strip of jungle, to prepare the route of a new electricity transmission trunk line, the poison was carried by water and air well beyond the planned strip, to affect people in the small town of Tailandia.

Dioxin was a constituent of 'agent orange', the defoliant used by US forces in the Vietnam War. Suits by the Vietnam veterans, who blamed agent orange for a variety of cancers in themselves and birth defects in their children, were settled out of court in 1984, for a total $180 million.

Dioxin continues to be used in the manufacture of widely- sold pesticides. Agricultural workers in particular suffer a disproportionate incidence of cancers, as well as birth defects in their children. Employees of companies involved in manufacturing products with dioxin have also been found to be more likely to contract cancer.

OCCUPATIONAL HAZARDS

Some businesses engage in production which is dangerous, even deadly, to workers. The long-standing asbestos industry has now been under fire for some time. But newer industries, such as microelectronics, may also turn out to be hazardous to workers.

The fatal fibre: asbestos

British factory inspectors first publicly warned of some connection between asbestos and lung diseases as long ago as **1898**. Since then, the evidence has relentlessly accumulated, to be suppressed, belittled or ignored.

In **1943,** Dr Leroy Gardner, director of the Saranac Laboratory in New York, completed a study commissioned by the US industry's Asbestos Association. Referring to lung cancer deaths among asbestos workers, he declared: 'There are now on record 10 cases of lung cancer. Compared to the total number of autopsies on asbestosis, this number is excessive.'

His report was sent to Johns-Manville, the leading US manufacturer, and to Keasby and Mattison, US subsidiary of the British manufacturer Turner and Newell, who also received a copy. A Keasby and Mattison executive advised the parent company that reference to the question of cancer susceptibility should be omitted from the report because the evidence was inconclusive.

Later studies by Dr Gardner showed that mice inhaling long-fibre asbestos had more than 16 times the incidence of lung cancer, while mice exposed to short-fibre asbestos had more than seven times the incidence in mice inhaling other dusts. These findings were communicated to Johns-Manville.

In February 1983, when Gardner's 1943 report finally saw the light of day, the managing director of Turner and Newell declared that he could find no earlier trace of it and that the key date for the association of asbestos with lung cancer was **1955**, after Sir Richard Doll's findings at Oxford.

In May 1982, Johns-Manville made an out-of-court settlement with Dr Kent Wise, who had sued the company for withholding information about tests on asbestos workers during **1963-72** when he was working at one of their plants. Part of the settlement was provision for legal costs that Dr Wise might incur in 100 law suits filed against him by former workers at the plant.

In September 1982, Manville denied any concealment or cover-up. 'Before **1964**, we knew dust was not healthy, but not that it was as hazardous as it turned out.'

In **1976,** the British Ombudsman criticized conditions at Acre Mill, an asbestos factory owned by Cape Industries in Hebden Bridge, where at least 200 people had contracted asbestosis and mesothelioma (asbestos cancer of the lung lining). In consequence, an Advisory Committee on Asbestos was set up.

Not one of the committee's 41 recommendations, themselves later found to be inadequate, had become law, by the time the asbestos scandal broke in Britain during 1982.

An Oxford researcher found that deaths from lung cancer in 1977, among Rochdale factory personnel of Turner and Newell, were twice the expected rate for the general population. In **1978,** the company declared, in an internally issued Guide to Asbestos and Health, that the number did not differ significantly from the national average.

In **1982** the company informed the General and Municipal Workers' Union that its 1978 statement 'was incorrect, and should have been qualified to refer to our experience to date in respect of low dust levels in the weaving department since 1951.' It confirmed that paper masks worn by workers in the factory were of cosmetic value only.

Casualty toll

Between 1930 and 1976 asbestos production doubled worldwide, according to the World Health Organization. It was then expected to double again by the end of the century.

According to court testimony from a leading US authority, Dr William Nicholson, some 13 million workers were significantly exposed to asbestos between 1940 and 1979.

In the US, the death rate from asbestos-related cancer alone was 8,500 a year by 1982; and the figure was expected to rise to an annual 10,000 by 1990. He estimated asbestos-related deaths, excluding deaths from other causes brought about by asbestos disabilities, at 400,000 for the 1980s and described the situation as a 'first magnitude occupational health disaster'.

Legal costs

The ultimate cost of asbestos-related diseases to the companies concerned could run to many billions of dollars. By the end of 1984, there were more than 30,000 individual claims at various stages of processing and some 500 claims being entered every month. So far most of the money seems to have gone in fees to lawyers and doctors, with only a minor part to victims as compensation.

A study by the Rand Corporation research unit found that an average personal liability case related to asbestosis produced payments of $95,000. Of this figure, $60,000 went in legal fees and the remainder in awards for damages.

In June 1985, to reduce the litigation costs and to meet mounting criticism of the time taken for plaintiffs to settle their cases satisfactorily, asbestos producers (excluding Manville) and insurance companies reached an agreement to speed up personal liability claims in the US.

In 1982, Manville had filed for protection from its creditors - victims of asbestosis or their families - under Chapter 11 of the US bankruptcy law. In 1985, the Manville board proposed to set up an independent trust to handle the multitude of claims. The company would fund the trust with $815 million of cash and insurance proceeds and with 50-80 per cent of its stock (depending on the extent of future claims). This would clear the way for the company to emerge from bankruptcy proceedings and to operate as an entity protected from claims. Manville not only faced a sharp growth in health-related claims, but was confronted by asbestos-related property claims that might exceed $69 billion.

How safe is tomorrow?

The tidy smoke-free 'science parks' that symbolize the electronics revolution seemed to promise a remarkably clean and safe way of doing business. Paradoxically, however, because the new fac-tories need to be so clean, they contain much potential for harm. Manufacturing the silicon chip involves the use of powerful acids to etch the circuit, and powerful solvents to clean away the residue. Many chemicals used, some in considerable quantity, during the process are deadly.

Hundreds of workers in Silicon Valley, California, claim to have been affected by exposure at work to a cocktail of chemicals. Thousands more have been affected by contaminated water supplies.

According to the acting chief of occupational medicine at the University of California, in nearby San Francisco, 'there is a strong statistical case that something is wrong', with miscarriages 24 times and birth defects three times the normal figures.

The chip manufacturers themselves reveal a growing sense of unease.

'A key question is that there still may be chemicals in use we don't know enough about, and that may be more harmful than we know. We're still learning. Even consultants in the field aren't sure how these things react.'

Ron Deutsch, a spokesman for the Signetics Corporation

A public danger

Some businesses engage in production which is dangerous not only to their own workers but to people who live in the vicinity. The dangers are virtually universal, but conspicuously greater in poorer countries.

In Britain alone, some 1,500 plants handle dangerous chemicals in quantities large enough to have off-site effects in the event of some accident. A chemical plant explosion at Flixborough, near Scunthorpe, in 1974, killed 28 people.

The valley of the shadow

In February 1984, a liquified petroleum gas (LPG) pipeline, owned by Petrobras, Brazil's state oil company, exploded outside a refinery in the Cubatoan industrial area near São Paulo. At least 80 people were killed, but the exact number of casualties was never determined, because the explosion and subsequent fire swept through a populous slum in the vicinity.

In November 1984, an LPG explosion at a plant owned by Pemex, Mexico's state oil company, killed at least 452 people, injured more than 4,200, and drove some 31,000 residents away from their homes in the surrounding area.

Two weeks later, a leak of the highly poisonous methal-isocyanate (MIC) gas, at the chemical plant of the US company Union Carbide in Bhopal, India, killed more than 2,000 people and injured some 200,000, many of whom were permanently blinded and many more of whom may suffer various other consequences, from fibrosis of the lungs to the uncontrolled division of blood cells, a condition closely associated with cancer. Most frightening of all, perhaps, is the fact that nobody knows. A spokesman for Union Carbide explained that MIC is simply too dangerous to have allowed any studies of long-term effects.

Safety standards

In rich countries, there is greater observed provision for minimizing risk. Under West Germany's industrial safety laws, for instance, nobody is allowed to live within a mile of an MIC plant.

And public opinion is generally a far more potent factor. Days after the Seveso incident in 1976, when a quantity of lethal dioxin was released in northern Italy, the Coalite Group, sole British manufacturer of the chemical, closed its Bolsover plant for checks and, though nothing was found to be wrong, never reopened it.

Industrial safety standards in poor countries, hungry for industrial plant and employment opportunities, are lower, or honoured far more in the breach than in the observance. Foreign companies, operating in the poor countries, are less concerned with the need to reassure local opinion and authority.

Nuclear disaster

In April 1986, the reactor at a nuclear power station in Chernobyl, 62 miles north of Kiev, USSR, caught fire with an explosion that shot a plume of radioactive gas into the atmosphere. The poisonous cloud drifted over Europe, with radioactivity deposited in its wake.

The immediate casualties were announced as two dead and 204 injured. But this did little to conceal the extent of the disaster.

In the ensuing weeks, the death toll rose; and months afterwards, contaminated lambs as far away as Wales were banned from sale for consumption.

The horror of the event lies precisely in the fact that nobody knows, or ever will, how many people, how far away, may die from cancers produced by the radioactivity released.

Ethical equities

In 1984 the Stewardship Unit Trust was launched to invest in 'socially responsible' British equities. The fund refuses to profit from human weaknesses and so avoids tobacco companies, breweries, distilleries and other liquor producers, as well as companies involved in gambling. It wants nothing to do with armaments or South African investments.

The Trust turned for help to the Ethical Investment Research and Information Service (EIRIS),

which came up with 200 public companies that conformed to the guide-lines. There were no banks, merchant banks, insurance companies or insurance brokers. Of the 30 leading British industrial firms that comprise the Financial Times Index, only Associated Dairies qualified.

KLEPTOCRACY

RULES

Kleptocracy is played with two dice, counters, money and cards, by any number of players.

Each player starts with a stake of 100,000 roubles. One player acts as banker.

Players move their counters around the board according to the numbers on the squares (instructions overleaf). A player who throws a double moves accordingly and throws again.

Cards may be bought by a player only before the dice are thrown; except Black Cards, which a player acquires through landing on one of the Black Card squares.

Cards, excluding Black Cards, may be sold back to the bank, but only at half their face value.

A White Card may at any time be surrendered to the bank to cancel a Black Card. A player who collects two Black Cards and has no White Cards to use in exchange is shot.

A player who lands on a square imposing a fine that cannot be paid is out of the game.

The winner is the player who first gets 10,000,000 roubles or is the only one to survive.

A **Yellow Card** costs 30,000 roubles and represents appointment as a People's Judge.

A **Green Card** costs 50,000 roubles and represents appointment as Head of the District Militia.

A **Blue Card** costs 70,000 roubles and provides high-level contact with a foreign firm.

A **Red Card** costs 100,000 roubles and represents the protection of the party secretary.

A **White Card** costs 1,000,000 roubles and represents immunity from prosecution.

GAMES

START ▶
1

2

39

40

BLACK
38
CARD

37

35

36

34

33

PRISON
31

32

30

29

28

27

CARDS

YELLOW ⭐ People's Judge 30,000 roubles	**GREEN** ⭐ Head of District Militia 50,000 roubles	**BLUE** ⭐ Contact with foreign firm 70,000 roubles
RED ⭐ Protection of Party Secretary 100,000 roubles	**WHITE** ⭐ Immunity from prosecution 1,000,000 roubles	**BLACK**
YELLOW ⭐ People's Judge 30,000 roubles	**GREEN** ⭐ Head of District Militia 50,000 roubles	**BLUE** ⭐ Contact with foreign firm 70,000 roubles
RED ⭐ Protection of Party Secretary 100,000 roubles	**WHITE** ⭐ Immunity from prosecution 1,000,000 roubles	**BLACK**
YELLOW ⭐ People's Judge 30,000 roubles	**GREEN** ⭐ Head of District Militia 50,000 roubles	**BLUE** ⭐ Contact with foreign firm 70,000 roubles
RED ⭐ Protection of Party Secretary 100,000 roubles	**WHITE** ⭐ Immunity from prosecution 1,000,000 roubles	**BLACK**

SQUARES

Game within a game. All but two of the following are actual cases. See if you can identify the exceptions. Answers at the bottom of page 191.

1 Start. Collect 30,000 roubles each time you reach this square.

2 You are appointed head of the engineering department at a provincial university. Collect 30,000 roubles and a year's supply of sausages in bribes for giving good marks.

3 You are put in charge of state-owned restaurants in the select Black Sea resort of Gelendzhik. The suitable entertainment of party bosses, with a few years of embezzlement, nets you 560,000 roubles.

4 Successful black market trading in tea. Collect 150,000 roubles, but pay 10,000 roubles to every other player for collusion.

5 You are a customs official at Moscow's Sheremetevo airport and are arrested for accepting bribes at 400 roubles a time. Pay a fine of 50,000 roubles.

6 If you have a Yellow Card, surrender it in return for your freedom; otherwise go to prison and miss one turn, in punishment for minor corruption.

7 Association with an Arab diplomat in Moscow gives you access to foreign currency for black market trading. Collect 50,000 roubles.

8 Appointment as Deputy Minister of Fisheries. Provided that you have both a Blue Card and a Red Card, export caviar in cans marked smoked herring and collect 1,000,000 roubles.

9 Appointment as Deputy Minister of Aviation enables you to misappropriate hard currency. Collect 50,000 roubles.

10 You are caught selling misappropriated petrol. Pay a fine of 50,000 roubles.

11 Black market sale of 10 residence permits in Odessa at 500 roubles each. Collect 5,000 roubles.

12 If you have a Green Card, surrender it in return for your freedom; otherwise go to prison and miss two turns, in punishment for middling corruption.

13 Black market sale of 10 plots in the select burial ground of Moscow's Novodevichy Monastery. Collect 25,000 roubles.

14 Appointment as head of Moscow's Nutrition Research Institute. Transform it into a health farm for overweight members of the elite. Collect 100,000 roubles.

15 You are a Ukrainian tolkach, or broker, in charge of ensuring fresh vegetable supplies for the Kremlin kitchens, and are found to be passing off second-grade tomatoes as the best available. Too valuable for liquidation, you are fined 50,000 roubles as an object lesson.

16 You are appointed director of a chain of 20 stores selling gastronomic delicacies, whose managers each pay you 2,000 to 3,000 roubles a month in personal gratuities. Collect 600,000 roubles for your first year of full operations and the Order of the October Revolution.

17 Collect 80,000 roubles for motor repairs in non-existent tractor repair factory.

18 Appointment as General Director of All-Union Association for Supplying Complete Sets of Furniture. If you have a Blue Card, collect 500,000 roubles.

19 You are found guilty of corruption as Director of a cotton cleaning plant in the Central Asian republic of Kirghizia. Receive a Black Card.

20 You are a KGB agent and organize a ring for trading in foreign currency. Provided that you have a Blue Card, collect 200,000 roubles.

21 Appointment as Deputy Minister for the Petrochemical Industry in the Soviet Republic of Azerbaijan. If you have a Red Card, collect 2,000,000 roubles.

22 You are Finance Minister in Georgia and are investigated for large-scale embezzlement. Pay half of all you have in bribes and surrender all cards.

23 Black market sale of 50 residence permits in Moscow at 3,000 roubles each. Collect 150,000 roubles.

24 You lay hands on a consignment of 200 pairs of Western jeans, saleable on the black market at 250 roubles each. Collect 50,000 roubles.

25 If you have a Yellow Card, surrender it in return for your freedom; otherwise go to prison and miss one turn, in punishment for minor corruption.

26 You are a Director of Soviet State Circuses and a friend of the First Secretary's daughter. Sell permits for travel to the West and collect 1,000,000 roubles.

27 You run an underground business network, based on a fabric plant in the Nazranov region of Chechen-Ingush, that produces and markets linen and knitted goods. After bribing the Minister of Local Industry, collect 500,000 roubles.

28 You have access to information on minimum bids acceptable for new factory equipment. If you have a Blue Card, collect 200,000 roubles.

29 You are a party official in Uzbekistan and found guilty of involvement in falsifying production figures. Pay 100,000 roubles in bribes and fines.

30 You are a railway worker involved in a ring that smuggles gold and diamonds to Vienna in the heels of women's shoes. Collect 20,000 roubles in bribes.

31 Appointment as Soviet Deputy Minister of Light Engineering. Under threat of trial for more serious offences, pay 100,000 roubles in bribes and accept dismissal for gross corruption and incompetence.

32 If you have a Green Card, surrender it in return for your freedom; otherwise go to prison and miss two turns, in punishment for middling corruption.

33 You are the brother-in-law of the First Secretary and are appointed head of the MVD security services. Collect 1,000,000 roubles in bribes.

34 You are reported buying a diamond for 20,000 roubles at a Moscow jewellery store and can only show a monthly salary of 175 roubles. Pay a fine of 40,000 roubles.

35 You are the key figure in a ring smuggling icons and ancient artefacts to Paris. Collect 200,000 roubles.

36 Your boss is suspected of selling priority places in the petition queues at the Justice Ministry. Take the rap, pay a fine of 20,000 roubles, and wait for promotion.

37 Provided that you have a Red Card, achieve appointment as head of the Medical Training Institute in Azerbaijan and sell 10 entry places at 30,000 roubles each, to collect 300,000 roubles.

38 You are a public prosecutor in the Soviet republic of Azerbaijan and found guilty of involvement in a 1,500,000 rouble swindle. Receive a Black Card.

39 You are director of a clothing factory. Divert half of your production to the underground market and collect 150,000 roubles.

40 You are appointed Minister of Culture and use state labour and materials to build a 120,000 rouble dacha for your daughter. In the ensuing scandal, you lose your black limousine, access to the special Politburo food store and other privileges, amounting in all to a fine of 150,000 roubles.

8

THE BOTTOM LINE

The business system is the power and the glory of the modern world. It is the context of vast social organizations, whose very conflicts are no more than variations on its single theme of material accumulation.

Business is fascinatingly ambiguous. It nourishes the most adventurous flights of the mind, and it confronts imagination with the lowest impulses of fear, distrust and greed. It is infinitely creative and infinitely destructive. It is insatiable, intolerant and cruel. It has triumphed as no other system before it. Where it has not swept aside other ways of organizing and thinking, it has subverted and appropriated them.

It has subjected or reduced all considerations - moral, aesthetic, intellectual, spiritual - to the material imperative.

'Between the idea
And the reality
Between the motion
And the act
Falls the shadow,'

T S Eliot, 'The Hollow Men'

In the business system, money separates acts from their consequences in time and space. There are, in general, no visible individual victims; only some distant, impersonal targets on the map.

People become workers, and workers become labour; people become managers, and managers become management; people become investors, and investors become investment; people become citizens, and citizens become the state.

Outside of what little is left to them as their private lives, people do not have personal relations. They are related as implements in processes of power which deal equally in abstractions: in supply and demand; profit and loss; riches and poverty; patriotism and treachery or subversion. But since everything is merchandized - creativity, compassion, love, identity itself - few private lives are proof against the invasions of the system. And the bottom line, of success or failure as a human being, is seen - in a tragic paradox - by the numerals themselves as a mere book-keeping entry.

A coastguard was answering a distress signal
from a yacht.
'What is your position?' he asked.
Silence was the only reply.
'What is your position?' he repeated.
'Well', came the reply at last, 'I am the marketing
director of a middle-sized computer software firm
in Birmingham. But I'm in line for managing
director.

Health itself, the normal manifestation of a harmonious life, the natural outcome of a balance between the physical and the mental, the material and the moral, the personal and the public, is increasingly seen as the business of profit-driven medical businesses. Recognition of the universal right to necessary medical care, which informs the British National Health Service Act of 1947 along with its imitations and adaptations elsewhere, is in retreat everywhere.

The health business worldwide is currently worth some $420 billion a year, but is growing rapidly with the explosion of new technology.

The big four

In the US, total spending on the health care business has soared from 4.4 per cent of gross national product in 1955, to around 11 per cent in the mid-1980s. Companies play god with money. Some 69 per cent of the US population is covered by employer-provided health insurance, 80 per cent of which is paid for by the employer. It is the employer who decides what treatment, if any, to sanction.

An increasingly assertive beneficiary of the rich West's health business system is the so-called 'medical-industrial complex', which runs hospitals for profit. Four major companies in the US dominate the business: American Medical International (AMI), Hospital Corporation of America (HCA), Humana, and National Medical Enterprises. Together they account for 90 per cent of the investor-owned beds in the country. Most profitable of the four is Humana, run by former accountant David Jones, with sales of $2.6 billion and profits of $193 million in 1984. Humana reached the big league in 1977, by taking over a much larger company, American Medicorp, for a mere $57,000 a bed or a fraction of the cost involved in building a new hospital.

All four companies, each of which has expanded abroad, earn only a third of their profits from basic nursing fees. The bulk comes from ancillary services, tests, and intensive care facilities. In the words of Paul Starr, in the Social Transformation of American Medicine, 'The rise of the for-profit chains has, for the first time, introduced managerial capitalism into American medicine on a large scale.'

'Competition and marketing - relatively new factors in the hospital field - increasingly differentiate the successful from the unsuccessful health care provider.'
HCA Annual Report, 1984

But there is mounting evidence that, however high the cost, the health care business may not always be purveying health. While claims to compassion are pegged for the record, activity is directed at mining every identified deposit of profit. Significantly, up to 30 per cent of all medical expenditure in the US is incurred during the last four weeks of the patient's life. And the treatment received by other patients is not all safe.

'One out of three patients develops complications from the treatment received. One out of 11 of those instances results in a disabling or life-threatening complication. One out of 50 of those complications contribute to the patient's death.'
Dr Gertman of the Health Data Institute

Dr Marvin J Shapiro, vice president of medical affairs at US Administrators, is scarcely more reassuring. He has estimated that 20 per cent of medical care is useless and that a proportion of it is potentially dangerous.

Marketing health

An instrument developed to recover an egg in a human uterus may become the subject of a landmark patent 'that will allow a corporate structure to build a whole health care system surrounding infertility.'

'Health care has always been a commodity. The money flows into the hands of doctors - who avoid treating patients who cannot afford to pay - but now it would flow to investors, too.'
Dr John E Buster, professor of obstetrics and gynaecology at UCLA Harbor Medical Center

'We carry on a very aggressive marketing program, and we tend to feature one thing at a time' (cataract operations in September, surgery for ailing feet in October)
James E Buncher, chief executive of Republic Health Corporation

'You can create a demand for mental health. It is one of the only health care areas you can actually market.'
Michael Pinkert, founder, Mental Health Management

Wealth care in China

United Medical Enterprises of London has been discussing the provision of a 6000-bed $110 million hospital between Daya Bay, site of a proposed Anglo-French built nuclear power station, and the Shenzhen Special Economic Zone adjoining Hong Kong. The main purpose of the hospital would be to provide care for senior government officials, nuclear power station workers, offshore oil personnel, wealthy overseas Chinese, and 'compatriots' from Hong Kong and Macao.

Addressing itself to the needs of the remaining one billion Chinese, China's Health Ministry has called on doctors, active or in retirement, to open private practices, in a reform designed to mobilize the 'enthusiasm of medical workers'.

THE SPORTS BUSINESS

Sport, ideally a spring of personal exhilaration and well-being, social bonding and public pleasure, is increasingly dominated and distorted by the operations of business. Sponsorship, advertising and commercialism on a massive scale have subverted the traditional ideals of the Olympic movement, while professionalism and the lure of big prize money have corrupted and hardened many top sports performers.

Sponsorship

Sport's principal sponsor is Horst Dassler, who runs one of the world's largest privately owned multinationals in Adidas, a West German-based manufacturing concern with annual sales of some $1.4 billion.

Adidas supplies 80 per cent of sponsored sportswear equipment throughout the world and invests in sport some 5 per cent of its total budget (or around $70 million annually), through advertising, promotion and public relations.

Together with Dentsu, the giant Japanese advertising agency, Dassler owns the Swiss-based marketing company ISL, which handles stadium advertising and merchandizing concessions worldwide for FIFA (the international football federation), IOC (the International Olympic Committee), the Athletes' Federation and others. In 1984, ISL guaranteed athletics $50 million in a three-year package and will greatly increase IOC income in 1988 by handling global rights to the Olympic five-ring logo.

At the 1981 congress of the IOC in Baden-Baden, the Japanese city of Nagoya was considered the clear favourite to host the 1988 Olympics. It was Dassler who was reportedly influential in swinging the decision towards Seoul, South Korea. If Nagoya had been selected, Japanese commercial interests would have dominated the show.

In 1982, at an international athletics conference in Rome, the Soviet Union protested about 'opening the doors to commercialism'. In 1984, the Soviet Union hosted the Coca Cola sponsored FIFA Youth Championship in Moscow. (The Soviet Union had opened its home market to the bottled delights of Coke some time before.) Dassler's influence was widely credited with having secured this harmony between FIFA and the Soviet sports administrator.

No less powerful - and equally criticized (for example, by Britain's Central Council of Physical Recreation) for the financial involvement of big business with the governing bodies of sport - is the International Management Group (IMG) of Mark McCormack. It is not only negotiating agent for television deals worth billions of dollars, on behalf of various sports bodies and involving such major events as Wimbledon, the Suntory World Match Play Golf Championships, the Calgary Winter Olympics, the Seoul Olympics. It is also representative agent for a host of international sports stars.

IMG has more than 750 clients. McCormack started it in 1960 with a friend, champion golfer Arnold Palmer. McCormack's advice is 'make friends . . . All things being equal, people will buy from a friend'. In due course, IMG searched out early promise and signed up the 15-year old Swedish tennis player Bjorn Borg. It missed 14-year old Argentinian tennis player Gabriela Sabatini, in a rare lapse. McCormack commented, 'That's a case of not checking out Argentinian 12-year-olds well enough.'

The TV Olympics

Nowhere has commercialism had a more dramatic effect than on the Olympic movement, once the most hallowed ground of idealism. One development, more than any other, has promoted the process. 'The combination of the Olympic movement and television', declared Willi Daume, president of the West German Olympic Committee, 'spells out big business'.

The Berlin Olympics of 1936 were transmitted to a few large screens, in an early experiment. The following Games, in London in 1948, were recorded by nine cameras and seen on 80,000 screens within a radius of 50 miles from the transmitter at Alexandra Palace. By 1980, in Moscow, there were 250 cameras relaying the Games to more than two billion viewers. And the 1984 Olympics, in Los Angeles, reached an estimated viewing public of two-and-a-half billion.

As the number of viewers soared, so did the commercial potential, along with the bids submitted by television companies. In 1948, the BBC, having been offered the rights for nothing at one stage, ended a year's haggle by paying a fee of £1,500. By 1968, ABC was buying the US television rights from the Mexico Organizing Committee for $4 million. In 1976, for the Montreal Games, ABC paid $25 million to buy US rights. Four years later, NBC paid $87 million to cover the Moscow Games.

The Los Angeles Games cost ABC $225 million for the US rights alone, and the company forked out a further $100 million for staffing. Two months before the Games began, it had already booked $428 million worth of advertising, at prices as high as $260,000 for a 30-second commercial. It had insured itself - for a premium of $8 million - against boycott, disruption, outright cancellation, and, in a first for the industry, low television ratings (which could have triggered rebates of $75 million to advertisers).

With all this money, as well as much more, in sponsorship, licensing and management deals, the Games proclaim less the values of the founders than those of the marketplace at its most predatory and meretricious.

Glittering prizes

With so much money and acclaim as the rewards of success, sports stars are becoming increasingly rich and increasingly the victims of their riches.

Prize money - with, at the top, the enormous sums to be earned by endorsing products in advertising campaigns - rises year by year. Sponsorship deals become more lavish with every new championship played.

Special arrangements allow stars in Eastern Europe to live well at home and abroad, so as to reduce any temptations to defect. Special arrangements are made elsewhere too, to ease naturalization for defectors and other budding stars.

For love or money: Tennis:

Grand Slam men's singles first prize

	French '000FF	Wimbledon '000£	US Open '000$	Australian '000US$
1968	15	2	15	5
1969	35	3	16	4
1970	56	3	20	10
1971	48	4	15	2
1972	48	5	25	9
1973	70	5	25	10
1974	120	10	23	12
1975	120	10	25	32
1976	130	13	30	32
1977	190	15	33	28
1978	210	19	38	41
1979	208	20	39	50
1980	221	20	46	65
1981	250	22	60	65
1982	400	42	90	70
1983	500	66	120	78
1984	1,059	100	160	100
1985	na	130	187	⊘128

⊘ estimate

Team spirit?

Baseball stars are among the highest paid sportsmen in the US. In 1985, as no more than a promising young pitcher, Dwight Gooden earned a mere $265,000. In 1986, he signed a contract which guaranteed him $1.32 million for the year - the first $1 million plus salary for a player under the age of 22. Moreover, advertising and special promotions were expected to bring his annual earnings well above $2 million. But he would still not be the highest paid pitcher. Fernando Valenzuela had just signed a contract worth $5.5 million, in salary alone, over three years. Hitters were doing even better. Two of them each made more than $2 million in 1985. And in all, 40 players each made at least $1 million during the year.

Clubbing them towards the slots

One hundred miles from Johannesburg, in the Bophuthatswana 'tribal homeland', there is a £50 million resort and casino complex, Sun City, financed principally by Southern Sun Hotels, the biggest hotel chain in South Africa and itself 70 per cent owned by South African Breweries. There, on 31 December 1981, five top golfers - Jack Nicklaus, Sevvy Ballesteros, Lee Trevino, Johnny Miller and Gary Player - teed off, together with ten showbiz personalities, including Sean Connery and Telly Savalas. The five golfers were to share $1 million: with $500,000 going to the winner and $100,000 to the last. No less than $340,000 might have hung on a single stroke, and $100,000 was assured even for total ineptitude. The last five holes were sponsored by South African companies at $40,000-50,000 each. A hole in one at the 16th would win a $150,000 Lamborghini with the compliments of John Player cigarettes.

The purpose of this extravaganza was to attract white South Africans to the Casino or, as a Southern Sun spokesman put it, 'to get the bodies to the slots'. At that time, the average income per head in the area was less than $200 a year.

The performers

With success measured in money, and money so plentiful for success, the pressure to succeed becomes all but irresistible. Promising teenage players are tested to destruction, physically and emotionally, on the professional circuits at an ever earlier age.

'If I am going to be a professional and make my living out of this game, it will be like committing myself to religion. It's no use saying you can afford to grow up naturally. There is not time.'

Andrea Jaeger, born in 1965 and a tennis professional by 1980

The players, solitary, utterly dedicated to a single goal, are thrown together in long plane journeys, isolated hotels, tense locker rooms. Whatever moral standards they may bring into their enclosed, rootless way of life, are too often abandoned. There are those who fall easy prey to dubious practices, from fiddling exhibition matches and splitting prize money to gambling. In their isolation and terror of finding themselves suddenly in a losing streak, many turn to religion, superstition, or despair. None of this encourages social ease, public grace or a sporting attitude. Commenting on the increasingly ill-tempered outbursts that have come to disfigure tennis championships, Lee Jackson, tennis referee for the Women's Tennis Association, declared, 'Let's face it - in this day and age obscenity is a way of life.'

In their own words

'Millions, we're talking millions'.

Bill Johnson, US Olympic downhill skiing champion, in the course of describing what his gold medal meant to him

'It's OK if someone makes $20 million in business; he's a wizard or something. But it's not OK if he makes it in sports. I'm just playing tennis. Every match is another day at the office...and I didn't put the money there.'

John McEnroe, responding to criticism of his product endorsements

'We want the promoters to pay what the market will stand. We put a lot into the sport and we take our share in return. It's good honest capitalism'.

Geoff Capes, champion shot putter

Sport and politics

Although sport has long been suborned for purposes of national propaganda, it has increasingly become the business of the state, with whole educational systems distorted to secure the prestige and international acceptance that success in sport promises.

Sport über alles

'In the German Democratic Republic, the programme of socialism corresponds to the interests of the workers and the youth. This makes it possible to satisfy their desire to practise physical education and sport in a new, socialist way, for the benefit of the people as a whole.'

Declaration of Principle, GDR State Council, 1968

Seventy to eighty per cent of the 18 million people in East Germany belong to sports clubs, most of which are workplace-based, and 20 per cent of all adults regularly practise a competitive sport with regular training and periodic competitions. Thirty per cent of 14 to 18-year-olds are members of the Deutscher Turn und Sport Bund, the confederation of the national bodies for each individual sport.

At school, 'it is essential to start selection very early, in the first or second year', according to a report to school sports inspectors; 'otherwise there is a danger that children will become interested in subjects or get into circles that have nothing to do with sport.'

Three million school students take part in the qualifying competition for the biennial Spartaciad, and 10,000 winners are brought to the final rounds in Berlin. There are special 10-year sports schools, to which 10-year-olds are sent on the joint decision of parents, school head and the physical education teacher.

And before school? A confidential document from the Leipzig Sports Research Institute recommends: 'Preparations for the Olympic Games must start before school age. If we can convince crèche and nursery school teachers of this, it should be possible to analyse the development of the children over at least the three years before they go to school and thereby obtain the information needed to improve their sports education.'

Nothing is left to chance. Everyone has a national sports card which records body measurements, results of medical examinations and successive performances in the field.

GOD'S BUSINESS

'If I were going to be blunt, I would say I was in the God business.'

Dr Peter Baelz, Dean of Durham Cathedral

Not even religion, supposedly concerned above all else with the spiritual, has escaped the approaches and attitudes of the business system.

Indeed, in many of its organized manifestations, religion is itself big business. The Mormon Church is the dominant economic force in the state of Utah, USA, and has considerable investments beyond. The Church of England has vast holdings in property, stocks and bonds. At the beginning of 1985, it had a portfolio worth some £1.8 billion; some £707 million of it in stock exchange investments.

Richest of all is the Roman Catholic Church.

The Vatican connection

'Money is necessary to build churches and other works for our apostolate. Unfortunately, however, in our activity we must use the operating means and methods of a bank.'

Archbishop Paul Casimir Marcinkus, head of the Vatican's Institute for Religious Works (IOR), in a rare interview

Where those 'means and methods' were to lead, Marcinkus himself could scarcely have suspected.

In June 1942, the IOR was founded as a Vatican bank, to accept deposits and invest moneys for 'the purposes of religious works and works of Christian piety'. In the mid-1960s, Michele Sindona, an Italian financier, became an increasingly influential adviser. He helped the Vatican to diversify its investment portfolio (after a scandal about investment in a chemical firm mainly producing contraceptives and explosives) and to move assets abroad (especially after the 1968 Italian government's decision to abolish tax exemption on Church assets in Italy). The Vatican in turn helped establish, and became a minority shareholder in, Sindona's Swiss bank, Finabank.

In 1971, Paul Marcinkus was promoted from secretary to president of the IOR. At about this time, Roberto Calvi, a protégé of Sindona's, became managing director of Banco Ambrosiano, a small bank in Milan that included in its statutes an acceptance clause, limiting share purchases to 'good Roman Catholics', and that closed its annual balance sheet with the words, 'Thanks be to God'. Sindona secured Calvi's introduction to Marcinkus and was subsequently to claim that the IOR regularly moved funds out of Italy (Italian exchange controls did not apply to the Vatican) for Ambrosiano and other Italian banks. Both Sindona and Calvi, though it was not known at the time, were members of the secret masonic lodge Propaganda Due or P-2, which was later accused of attempting to subvert the Italian state by taking control of its institutions.

In 1974, Sindona's Banca Privata Italiana and his Franklin National Bank in New York both collapsed, followed by the closure of Finabank in 1975, on the orders of the Swiss government. This left the Vatican with estimated losses of over $50 million. But Marcinkus claimed that the profits which had been made permitted the Church comfortably to write off the shortfall. Calvi became president of Banco Ambrosiano, took over as the Vatican's lay financial partner, and was soon dubbed 'God's banker' by the Italian press. In 1976, Sindona was tried in absentia in Italy, on charges of having violated the banking laws. He was sentenced to three-and-a-half years' imprisonment.

Later, in 1980, he was sentenced in New York to 25 years' imprisonment for fraud connected with the operations of the Franklin National Bank and, in 1984, was extradited to face trial in Italy. There, he was sentenced to 15 years' imprisonment for fraudulent bankruptcy in the 1974 collapse of his Italian banking empire. In June 1985, he went on trial again in Milan on a charge of having arranged the killing in 1979 of Giorgio Ambrosoli, a lawyer appointed by the Bank of Italy to investigate his finances and liquidate his Italian interests.

Meanwhile, from 1975 onwards, Calvi channelled an estimated $1.3 billion to various 'shell' companies, mainly in Panama, to finance undisclosed Latin American operations but mainly to buy stock in Banco Ambrosiano, Milan, and its subsidiary companies. The IOR holding of Ambrosiano shares was, officially, 1.6 per cent, but it was unofficially estimated to be up to 10 per cent. In 1978, Bank of Italy inspectors expressed concern about the overseas operations of Banco Ambrosiano. In 1981, Calvi was prosecuted for the illegal export of capital from Italy and was given a four year suspended prison sentence, with a fine of $11.7 million, for the offence.

'We put our money where it does best, and from our point of view our investment in the Ambrosiano has been excellent. Calvi has our trust.'
Archbishop Marcinkus

Less trustful than Marcinkus, international bankers became wary of continuing to provide the Ambrosiano group with money. In response to an appeal from Calvi for help in reassuring the directors of Ambrosiano's Peruvian bank, which had lent around a billion dollars to the 'shell' companies, IOR supplied so-called 'letters of comfort', declaring that the companies involved were controlled, directly or indirectly, by itself. This, in effect, vouched for the credit-worthiness of the companies; and though not legally binding the IOR to pay their debts, clearly implied a moral obligation to do so.

In May 1982, the Bank of Italy demanded information on the Ambrosiano group's foreign subsidiaries and on some $1.3 billion in loans from these to a number of Panamanian companies. In June, Calvi disappeared; the shares of Banco Ambrosiano were suspended on the Milan exchange, after falling 20 per cent in one day; and the Bank of Italy took control of the bank. Calvi was found hanged under Blackfriars Bridge in London.

In July 1982, Italy's Treasury Minister asked the IOR to accept its responsibilities and provide the funds for the Panamanian companies to repay their borrowings. Marcinkus refused. The Vatican, acting in its identity as a sovereign state, declined to receive an Italian magistrate's notices of possible legal action against Marcinkus and two top lay officials of the IOR. The three officials moved into Vatican City. The new management of the Banco Ambrosiano in Milan declared that the parent could accept no legal responsibility for the debts of its subsidiaries - to much gnashing of teeth in the Euromarket, where Banco Ambrosiano Holdings (Luxembourg) had raised some $450 million.

In August 1982, the Italian government ordered the liquidation of Banco Ambrosiano in Milan, with its domestic operations taken over by a new bank, Nuovo Banco Ambrosiano. The Vatican's Secretary of State, referring to the celebrated 'letters of comfort', declared that 'the tone of these letters, which are part of standard banking practice, is such as not necessarily to imply a full obligation. I think there are limits to the commitment many people think the letters involve.' In 1984, the IOR agreed to pay $241 million, 'in recognition of moral involvement', to creditors of the collapsed Banco Ambrosiano. Apparently, moral involvement had a price of some 20 cents in the dollar.

In March 1986, Michele Sindona was sentenced to life imprisonment for having arranged the murder of Giorgio Ambrosoli. Taken to Vorhera prison near Milan, he was, within a few days, found in a coma after drinking coffee in his cell, and died of cyanide poisoning soon afterwards. Whether he had committed suicide or had been murdered became the subject of urgent investigation and dispute. He had often threatened to reveal embarrassing associations. Now there remained undisclosed the exact nature of his links with the Mafia, the Vatican, and leading Italian political figures; the part played by the masonic lodge P-2 in the whole complex series of events; and the truth about the death of Roberto Calvi.

THE PRICE WE PAY

Health, education, art, sport, public service, religion - all have been appropriated by the business system. No alternative set of values, implicit or explicit, has survived unscathed its contact with the system's supremely powerful and exclusive ethos.

Intensely competitive, rational only in terms of measurable efficiency, essentially authoritarian and ruthless, the values of business are now the common, virtually the sole, currency of behaviour in the world. Everything is invested in the success of one approach to nature, society and personality.

The business ethos muscles aside all alternatives, impeding the development of the balanced personalities and communities which are essential to the continued existence of every system, including that of business itself. It makes impossible the harmonious integration of human society with nature on which any sustained social arrangement, perhaps human survival, ultimately depends.

In the so-called centrally planned states, lakes shrink, rivers run sluggishly with industrial waste, forests sicken, acid rain falls indifferently on the heads of the innocent and the guilty alike. In the West, environmental damage is already far advanced. In the poorer states, conventional - or imitative - economic progress is the impulse to environmental mayhem.

Planning catastrophe

Life expectancy at birth is declining in many parts of Eastern Europe. It is two years shorter in Poland's industrial heartland than in the rest of the country.

The centre of industrial development has been the Katowice district. The streams there are so full of chemicals that they no longer freeze in winter; the summer sun often appears as only a blur in the thick air; and local government posters warn that the vegetables in private allotments may have a dangerously high lead content. Even local officials, previously involved in planning intensive

industrial development, have begun to recognize that the area is not far from ecological catastrophe and are resisting further industrial growth.

And, however the system may promote and exploit the divisions of the world into contending states and alliances, nature itself is a unity without frontiers. The acid rain produced in Britain falls on Scandinavia. The pollution from US factories falls on Canada as well. The rain forests being cut down in Brazil or tropical Africa, to make room for ranching or to supply wood processing plants, impoverishes the very air we breathe, as well as killing multitudes of species whose potential benefits to us may now never be known.

The business system, in its very triumph, seems increasingly directed at its own destruction.

Costing it out

In 1981, the Legal and General Insurance Company in Britain valued a wife (or house husband) at £204 for a 98-hour working week (up by £33 since 1975). This was equal in salary to a sergeant major, some bishops, a fire chief, head teacher or second division footballer.

Also in Britain, the Department of Transport has valued a human life at £140,000: £100,000 for lost production, and £40,000 for 'pain, grief and suffering'.

In the US, the Occupational Safety and Health Administration assesses the value of a life at between $2 million and $5 million; the Environmental Protection Agency, at between $1 million and $7.5 million; and the Federal Aviation Administration, at some $650,000.

US companies apparently rate life less highly, at least in foreign parts. Union Carbide, in late March 1986, offered $350 million in settlement of damage claims on behalf of the more than 2,000 dead and more than 200,000 injured in the Bhopal gas disaster of late 1984. This would be equivalent to $17,500 per death, or $175 per injured, or varying figures between the two for the victims in both categories. The New York based Citizens' Commission on Bhopal, a broad coalition of US environmental, consumer, labour, religious and medical organizations, called this proposal outrageous and declared that its own investigations suggested a sum of 'no less than $4 billion' would be needed. Meanwhile, claims totalling $100 billion had been filed in the US on behalf of 103,000 Indian plaintiffs.

In the USSR, where the cost of living is a lot lower, the families of travel accident victims get 1,000 roubles (around $1400) for death or total disablement.

Rich and poor

Even within its own narrow and exclusive terms, the business system is showing signs of distress and incipient failure. Within this decline, wealth is increasingly being concentrated among a small minority of people in virtually every state.

In rich, intermediate and poor countries alike, the gulf between the relatively few who live in ostentatious affluence and the many millions who suffer the various afflictions of want is a cruel social reality.

Debts to the people

Perhaps nowhere has this tendency been more evident and socially destructive than in Latin America. There, perilous amassing of foreign debt was supposedly directed at rapid development of the relevant economies. The reality was rather different.

In the single year of 1980, Argentina's foreign debt grew by $9 billion, as Argentinian residents increased their foreign holdings by $6.7 billion. Mexico's foreign debt leapt by $16.4 billion, while Mexicans sent $7.1 billion abroad. Brazil's foreign debt rose by $11.2 billion, while very tight foreign exchange controls did not prevent Brazilians from increasing their foreign holdings by $1.8 billion. Venezuela's foreign debt grew by $3.2 billion, while Venezuelans increased their holdings abroad by the even more massive sum of $4.7 billion. Altogether, since the Latin American debt explosion began in the mid-1970s, private citizens in these four countries acquired almost $100 billion in foreign assets. Were it not for this flight of private capital over the ten years 1976-85, Argentina would have had just $1 billion in foreign debt, instead of $50 billion; and Mexico a manageable $12 billion instead of $97 billion.

'Those Latin American countries whose residents have been exporting capital on a massive scale would be well advised to put their house in order so as to end this capital outflow and even, hopefully, to draw some of the flight capital back. It is too much to expect the rest of the world - whether multilateral institutions, governments, banks, or corporations - to perform the development functions that these countries' own nationals refuse to assume.'
Bank for International Settlements (the bank of central banks) in its Annual Report, 1984

Inequalities worldwide

In Britain, while the press periodically lists the number of millionaires created by new company flotations, more than one quarter of the population is estimated to be living on or below the official poverty line.

In France , while the rich protested at proposals to increase the wealth tax from 1.5 per cent to 2 per cent on those with capital of over FF20 million (more than $2 million), some 600,000 long-term unemployed were having to live on an allowance of FF40 a day.

In the US, the richest country in the world, some 66.5 million people, or 30 per cent of the population, live in households that receive some form of welfare payment. Between 1980 and 1984, the average spending power of the bottom 20 per cent of the population fell by 7.6 per cent, while that of the top 20 per cent increased by 8.7 per cent. Nor is need a feature only of the poor as traditionally defined.

'There are tens of thousands of malnourished children who are middle class. We've gone out at 5 or 6 a.m. and shown people who are living in $100,000 homes how to trash pick and how to get food out of garbage bins behind supermarkets. Their kids are hungry but they can't get food stamps if they live in their own homes.'
Mitch Snyder, Community for Creative Non-Violence

In Brazil, 41 per cent of the 'economically active' population earned less than the official minimum wage in late 1982. And only 60 per cent of the employable population were fully employed.

In Chile, where imported luxury items, such as television sets, continued flowing into the country, the minimum monthly wage in late 1984 was 6,000 pesos, and from 2,000 to 4,000 pesos for the unemployed on government schemes. A survey in Santiago found that a family of five needed at least 11,000 pesos a month to cover the cost of food and transport, excluding rent payments and power bills.

In Black Africa, 60 per cent of the population live below the poverty line recognized by the World Bank, and 20 per cent suffer from malnutrition.

In the world as a whole, some 500 million people were estimated to be undernourished in the early 1980s: in ten years, a rise of 22 million.

The jobless toll

Multitudes are declared 'redundant', to join the far greater numbers who are denied all hope of ever being other than surplus to requirements.

Unemployment statistics are often fudged, by such expedients as government job training schemes that reduce the figures but seldom lead onward to jobs. But even official figures and estimates are alarming.

Official unemployment, March 1986, percentages

Italy	14.0
UK	13.7
Netherlands	13.2
Belgium	12.2
France	10.5
West Germany	9.1
US	7.2
Japan	2.6

They exclude the millions, mainly women, who would look for work if they thought that there was any prospect of finding any. And they conceal the even higher rates of unemployment among the young, who see their lives wasting away at their economically productive beginning.

Youth unemployment, percentages

Italy	mid-1986	34.0
France	mid-1986	25.0
UK	mid-1986	22.0
USA	mid-1985	16.4
West Germany	mid-1985	10.8
Japan	mid-1985	4.3

In poor countries, there is scarce point in fudging unemployment figures which, where they are produced at all, are meaningless. But out of a poor world population (excluding China) of 2,267 million in 1982, the wholly unemployed made up about 20 per cent, while 51 per cent, or 1,166 million, were estimated to be in 'basic needs poverty'.

Social pressures

'We are at a loss to know what to put in the cooking pot, our children are malnourished and so are our husbands. No one can study or work properly in this situation. Yet all we hear from the bosses and the government are demands for more output.'
Blanca Guzman Castro de Arancibia, president of the Catavi Housewives' Committee, Bolivia, 1984

'Imagine your salary being cut by 25 per cent and your mortgage going up by 30 per cent. Then you comprehend the nature of the situation.'
Rodrigo Capeda Yzaga, head of Peru's External Debt Committee, 1984

'Who can say when we will reach the point when the flames start?'
Michel Hansenne, Belgium's Minister of Labour, on the social consequences of high unemployment among young people in Europe

One indication of increasing stress is the growing rate of suicide in many industrial countries. Japan has long been the world's major business success story - but at a considerable and dramatically rising cost.

A Japanese government report of 1984 put the number of officially recognized suicides, in 1983, at a record of nearly 25,000, or 20 per cent up on the figure for 1982. The increases for men in their forties and fifties had risen even more steeply: by 35 per cent and 47 per cent respectively. Sociologists linked this increase to pressures of earlier retirement and greater financial burdens, and to a grow-

ing perception that Japan is somehow less secure and predictable than it was.

Other relatively new phenomena of stress include sudden outbreaks of teenage violence, a higher incidence of alcoholism among housewives, and a dramatic rise in sex offences.

A dead end society

Rises in suicide rate, 1970/71 - 1980/81, percentages

Norway	47.6
Luxembourg	42.9
Switzerland	33.2
Hungary	30.2
New Zealand	30.1
France	26.0
Iceland	24.1
Netherlands	20.5
Austria	19.4
Bulgaria	10.6
England and Wales	9.9
Japan	9.6
Greece	3.1
Hong Kong	3.1
West Germany	2.4

Only Australia, Czechoslovakia and Sweden, of the countries for which figures were available, showed a fall in the incidence of suicide.

POSTSCRIPT

Ultimately, perhaps, there can be no more crushing indictment of the business system's triumph than four small shreds of comment and information.

'When their parents lose their jobs, they are simply told they are not wanted.'
Margie Berger, head of a Hollywood centre for runaway children

'We live in a society where we use things and just throw them away. I swear a lot of people have this attitude towards kids.'
Sister Dolores Gartanutti, of Noah's Ark Shelter in New York

'Couples in the most industrialized Eastern European countries weigh having children against possessing a car and supplying it with petrol.'
Financial Times, 1984

In Britain, the number of reported incidents involving the physical abuse of children under 15 years old is increasing each year. The figures rose from 4,699 in 1977, to 7,038 in 1984: a rise of 50 per cent in just eight years.

INDEX

This index lists all individuals and public companies, some public institutions and selected subjects.

ACKNOWLEDGEMENTS

We owe much to many people, only some of whom may be acknowledged.

Among those in the world of business and finance: Annette Allen, MacDonald's, London; Penny Frynn, Press Office, Shell International, London; Peter Janke, Control Risks, London; executive officers at Arthur Andersen, London; Bank for International Settlements, Basle; Dun & Bradstreet, Imperial Chemical Industries, Jeremy Oates, all of London; Morgan Guaranty, London; Moscow Narodny Bank, London; Peat Marwick, London; Saatchi & Saatchi Compton, London; Volkswagenwerke, Wolfsburg; and especially, Joe Smith, Laurence Keen & Co., London; and Kurt Noll, Union Bank of Switzerland, Vevey.

Among officials of industry and trade associations: Dave Dyster, Society of Motor Manufacturers and Traders, London; Bill Geddes, Uranium Institute, London; the late David Gray, International Tennis Federation, Wimbledon, Surrey; John Presland, London Chamber of Commerce; Brian W Rooks, British Robot Association; Tony St Aubyn, Tobacco Advisory Council, London; and officials of the Italian Chamber of Commerce, the Canada-UK Chamber of Commerce, the German Chamber of Commerce and Industry, all of London.

Among trade union officials: Dan Gallin and Bob Ramsay, International Union of Food Workers, Geneva.

Among officials of government and international organizations: M F Collins, Sheila Handley and colleagues; the Sports Council, London; John Brotherton and Betty Powell, Information Division, and E J Wright, International Trade Statistics, Department of Trade and Industry, London; Wendy Simpson, OECD, Paris; Commercial Counsellors at the embassies of Belgium, France and Sweden, in London; and officials at the UK Atomic Energy Commission, London, and at the International Labour Office, Geneva.

Among academics and experts: Bob Benewick, Steve Burman and Vivien Hart, University of Sussex; Linda Hesselman; Jonathan Luxmore; Ron Smith, Birkbeck College, London; Doron Swade, Science Museum, London; Richard Thakrah, Police Staff College, Camberley, Surrey; Alison Trapmore, Walton-on-Thames, Surrey.

Among journalists and commentators: Susan Adams, World Tennis, New York; Bobby Campbell and Nick Pitt, Sunday Times, London; Philip Mattera, Fortune, New York; Stephen Hugh-Jones, The Economist, London; John Plender, London; the editor, Tennis Business; staff on Advertising Age, Chicago.

Among librarians: Ian Bushnell of the Business Statistics Office, Department of Trade and Industry, London; Stephen Gregory, Institute of Criminology, Cambridge; Helena Beck, Nicola Gallimore, Denis Jones, Margaret Julian, John Montgomery and Leslie Pitman, Royal Institute for International Affairs; Arthur Danagh, Jenny Green, Tobacco Advisory Council; Tony Hay, Barbara Heciak, Uranium Institute; and library staff at the British Library, the British Library of Political and Economic Science, the City Business Library, the Home Office, the London Library, the International Institute for Strategic Studies, the Metals Society – all of London.

Among those who have helped to create and produce this book: Michael Howell, Martin Humphries, Martin Joyce, Nick Lewis, Mike March, Loretta Olusanya.

Among many friends and colleagues: Pat Douglas, Jane Gregory, Christopher Hird, Robin Jenkins, Nina Kidron, Richard Kuper, Peter Lion, Jan Maulden, Chris Sadler, Dan Smith.

Kleptocracy answers (from page 177): Squares 15 and 36.

Servopoly M10 **BMP MONEY** *Kleptocracy* 10,000r	*Servopoly* M10 **BMP MONEY** *Kleptocracy* 10,000r	*Servopoly* M10 **BMP MONEY** *Kleptocracy* 10,000r
Servopoly M20 **BMP MONEY** *Kleptocracy* 20,000r	*Servopoly* M20 **BMP MONEY** *Kleptocracy* 20,000r	*Servopoly* M20 **BMP MONEY** *Kleptocracy* 20,000r
Servopoly M50 **BMP MONEY** *Kleptocracy* 50,000r	*Servopoly* M50 **BMP MONEY** *Kleptocracy* 50,000r	*Servopoly* M50 **BMP MONEY** *Kleptocracy* 50,000r
Servopoly M100 **BMP MONEY** *Kleptocracy* 70,000r	*Servopoly* M100 **BMP MONEY** *Kleptocracy* 70,000r	*Servopoly* M100 **BMP MONEY** *Kleptocracy* 70,000r
Servopoly M500 **BMP MONEY** *Kleptocracy* 100,000r	*Servopoly* M500 **BMP MONEY** *Kleptocracy* 100,000r	*Servopoly* M500 **BMP MONEY** *Kleptocracy* 100,000r
Servopoly M1,000 **BMP MONEY** *Kleptocracy* 500,000r	*Servopoly* M1,000 **BMP MONEY** *Kleptocracy* 500,000r	*Servopoly* M1,000 **BMP MONEY** *Kleptocracy* 500,000r
Servopoly M5,000 **BMP MONEY** *Kleptocracy* 1,000,000r	*Servopoly* M5,000 **BMP MONEY** *Kleptocracy* 1,000,000r	*Servopoly* M5,000 **BMP MONEY** *Kleptocracy* 1,000,000r